Western Psychological and Educational Theory in Diverse Contexts

Education departments in universities throughout the Western world are increasingly recruiting international students who are subsequently exposed to educational and psychological theories and practices that, it is assumed, will inform best practice on their return home. Such ethnocentric (and sometimes ideological) understandings may also be reinforced by powerful international agencies which, by means of financial incentives and inducements, can exert a significant influence upon practice.

While academic proponents of such theories and practices are unlikely to deny the observation that these are culturally situated, and simplistic notions of 'transfer' to other cultures may be inappropriate and potentially undermining of existing practice, such caution may be less in evidence in professional contexts where there is a desire for change and new ideas, together with a desire for the status and influence that such knowledge may bring.

This book examines aspects of Western psychological and educational theory in relation to educational practice around the world, and considers the extent to which current understandings are truly applicable to a range of diverse settings. In so doing, it also seeks to question, where appropriate, existing orthodoxies within Western educational systems. This book was previously published as a special issue of *Comparative Education*.

Julian Elliott is Professor of Education at Durham University, England. His research interests include achievement motivation, cognitive education and special education.

Elena Grigorenko is Associate Professor of Child Studies and Psychology at Yale University and an Associate Professor of Psychology at Moscow State University. Her research interests span a broad range of fields in child development, in particular, genetics and environmental aspects of learning difficulties.

Western Psychological and Educational Theory in Diverse Contexts

Edited by Julian Elliott and Elena Grigorenko

Routledge
Taylor & Francis Group

LONDON AND NEW YORK

First published 2008 by Routledge
2 Park Square, Milton Park, Abingdon, Oxon, OX14 4RN

Simultaneously published in the USA and Canada
by Routledge
270 Madison Avenue, New York, NY 10016

Routledge is an imprint of the Taylor & Francis Group, an informa business

Transferred to Digital Printing 2009

© 2008 Julian Elliott and Elena Grigorenko

Typeset in Plantin by Genesis Typesetting Ltd, Rochester, Kent

British Library Cataloguing in Publication Data
A catalogue record for this book is available from the British Library

Library of Congress Cataloging in Publication Data

ISBN10: 0-415-41852-6 (hbk)
ISBN10: 0-415-49136-3 (pbk)

ISBN13: 978-0-415-41852-2 (hbk)
ISBN13: 978-0-415-49136-5 (pbk)

CONTENTS

1. Are western educational theories and practices truly universal?
   Julian Elliott and Elena Grigorenko   1

2. Culture, instruction, and assessment
   Robert J. Sternberg   5

3. Bridging between orthodox western higher educational practices
   and an African sociocultural context
   Robert Serpell   23

4. Orthodoxy, cultural compatibility, and universals in education
   Roland G. Tharp and Stephanie Stoll Dalton   53

5. Western influences on Chinese educational testing
   Weihua Niu   71

6. The impact of the west on post-Soviet Russian education:
   change and resistance to change
   Julian Elliott and Jonathan Tudge   93

7. Teachers' ethnotheories of the 'ideal student' in five western cultures
   Sara Harkness, Marjolijn Blom, Alfredo Oliva, Ughetta Moscardino,
   Piotr Olaf Zylicz, Moises Rios Bermudez, Xin Feng,
   Agnieszka Carrasco-Zylicz, Giovanna Axia, and Charles M. Super   113

8. Schooling's contribution to social capital: study from a native Amazonian
   society in Bolivia
   Ricardo Godoy, Craig Seyfried, Victoria Reyes-García, Tomás Huanca,
   William R. Leonard, Thomas McDade, Susan Tanner and Vincent Vadez   137

9. Hitting, missing, and in between: a typology of the impact
   of western education on the non-western world
   Elena L. Grigorenko   165

   Index   187

Are western educational theories and practices truly universal?

Education departments in universities throughout the western world are increasingly recruiting international students, who are subsequently exposed to educational and psychological theories and approaches to teaching and learning that, it is assumed, will inform educational policy and classroom practice on their return home.

Academic proponents of western theories and practices would most likely accept the observation that these are culturally situated, and argue forcefully that simplistic notions of 'transfer' to other contexts may be inappropriate and potentially undermine existing practice. However such cautions may be less evident in those professional contexts where policy-makers and consultants are seeking educational reform and the introduction of new ideas and techniques. In addition, ethnocentric (and sometimes ideological) understandings may also be reinforced by powerful international agencies which, by means of financial incentives and inducements, can exert a significant influence on practice. Tabulawa (2003), for example, contends that democratic learning (also known as learner-centred pedagogy), an orientation that has been widely promoted by bilateral aid agencies, is not purely technical and value-free. Indeed, he suggests that such approaches to learning are underpinned by a particular ideological outlook suited to the fostering of those liberal democratic perspectives deemed important for the operation of free market economies.

This volume is concerned with aspects of western psychological and educational theory relating to educational practice around the world, and considers the extent to which western understandings are really applicable to a range of diverse settings. It also seeks to question, where appropriate, existing orthodoxies within western educational systems. The volume begins with a general introduction to the issue of culture and education, discusses possible applications of western approaches to education in diverse settings, and exemplifies issues raised by offering readers a journey across four continents (Africa, the Americas, Asia, and Europe).

That western modes of formal schooling, and understandings of intelligence and ability, may not necessarily be applicable to all cultures is the central component of Robert Sternberg's article. He argues that in some contexts, schooling may be seen as a distraction from the development of skills perceived to be necessary to thrive, or even to survive. In framing his article in the form of ten lessons, Sternberg draws on his extensive theoretical and empirical work in the domains of intelligence, assessment, and instruction to underpin his message of the importance of rooting these domains in specific cultures. He shows how skilled performance may often be inadequately recognized because of western preconceptions of intelligent behaviour and respondents' unfamiliarity with standardized psychometric testing procedures. In his review of the relevant literature, Sternberg concludes that children's performance will be heightened when they are taught and assessed in meaningful ways appropriate to their culture.

In his role as Vice-Chancellor of a major African university, Robert Serpell has an academic (in every sense of this term) interest in the promotion of meaningful learning. He notes that western higher education 'tends to decontextualize the learning process by extracting learners from everyday life into a detached mode of full-time reflection, with an emphasis on structured exercises and analytical review of authoritative texts' (p.24). While noting some evolution in western universities (often for vocational rather than pedagogical reasons), Serpell contends that the traditional approach, with its remoteness from the cultural practices of everyday life, is particularly inappropriate for university education in Africa. In describing in some detail the operation of one educational approach, the project assignment, and in giving voice to his students, he illustrates how academic knowledge can be related to, and tested by, students' own life experiences.

Roland Tharp and Stephanie Dalton touch on a conceptual challenge that confronted several of the contributors to this volume, including the editors: what exactly are the parameters of the 'western' educational model? Tharp and Dalton note that studies of educational practices across the world show remarkable similarity, and suggest that, rather than being considered western, these might best be described as transnational. Tharp and Dalton espouse an alternative, universalist (rather than universal) approach that originally grew out of the first author's seminal work in Hawaii, and subsequent work with the Navajo. More recently this has been implemented within a diverse range of cultures and socio-economic groupings. Reflecting a Vygotskian perspective, their Five Standards for Effective Pedagogy emphasize joint teacher–student productive activity; an emphasis on language in the context of student linguistic competence; the centrality of the role of dialogue in the learning process; the importance of contextualizing learning by making it relevant to students' lives; and the need to teach higher-order, complex thinking. Tharp and Dalton's paper provides a model of educational practices and principles that may be applicable for most, if not all cultures, yet which permits the essential processes of application and contextualization, the absence of which are often seen as a weakness of the direct cross-cultural transfer of traditional approaches.

The next two papers are each concerned with western educational and psychological influences in countries where Communism underpinned the modern system of schooling. Weihua Niu remarks on the current heavy emphasis on testing in China. Noting the Chinese saying, 'Chinese learning for essential principles and western learning for practical application', she illustrates how western testing practices have been gradually absorbed over the past century. Niu describes a shift in emphasis from the testing of factual knowledge to the development of standardized aptitude measures, although the residual eminence of the former is seen as deleterious to the development of creativity and independent thought. Although she concludes that western influences on testing have largely proven helpful in guiding reforms in Chinese educational policy and pedagogy, she recognizes the less benign consequences that can result from an excessive belief in the power of testing. These include unduly heavy demands on students and the danger that estimates of an individual's abilities and potential may be reduced to those aspects that can be most easily tested.

Continuing with the theme of absorption and adaptation, Julian Elliott and Jonathan Tudge examine western influences on Russian education since the collapse of the Soviet Union. Rejecting any simplistic notions of straightforward transfer of educational practices or beliefs, they draw on Bronfenbrenner's ecosystemic theory of human development to help illuminate the ways in which students, parents, and teachers have responded in varying degrees to the modernizing agenda of increased individualism and autonomy.

As many of the contributions illustrate, the parameters of the physical or intellectual space that may be conceived as western frequently vary—often as a consequence of the particular domain under consideration. In psychology, as in mass culture, the United States is almost wholly the central point of reference. In education, however, western European countries, with their strong colonial past, have equal, if not greater, salience. However, as new alliances form, the boundaries of economic communities shift, and political reframing (for example, recent references to Old Europe and New Europe) all subtly alter our perceptions, so will our understandings of what we mean by the term *western* change. Thus, it is interesting that Sara Harkness and colleagues include Poland in their study of teachers' ethnotheories in five western countries. Arguing that the notion of the western mind may hinder understandings of differing ideas and practices across the US and Europe, their article considers teachers' perceptions of the ideal student. A key finding is that, despite their differences, teachers in all the countries surveyed placed significant emphasis on social competence. This may not surprise those who work closely with teachers on a regular basis. However it is more akin to some of the non-western notions of intelligence and competence that are discussed in other papers in this volume than it is to the heavily cognitive orientation of most western formal educational theories.

Utilizing the notion of 'western' in its broadest sense, Ricardo Godoy and his team examine the potentially negative effects of that noted western invention, formal schooling, on traditional cultures. Noting that schooling may have a deleterious effect on aspects of traditional culture, such as knowledge of the local environment, social organization, ethos, and local language, these researchers focus on schooling's effect on social capital. Examining studies of industrialized nations, they suggest that existing estimates of the effect of schooling on social capital may be inflated by the various methodological procedures employed. Subsequently noting the paucity of related work in pre-industrial societies, they seek to address both this gap and prior methodological weaknesses by means of an examination of the effects of schooling on social capital in the native Amazonian society of the Tsimane'. In discussing the weak relationships obtained, the authors suggest that both methods and circumstances play a part. In their concluding remarks, the authors suggest that the future for the Tsimane' may be marked by disparity of educational provision and, potentially, a degree of social dislocation.

In the concluding article of this volume, Elena Grigorenko discusses a number of ways in which non-western cultures have adopted and used western educational approaches. She provides illustrations of each category in her typology, briefly presenting the history of the category, detailing its modern state, and discussing selected aspects of the effectiveness of a particular educational system.

Thus, issues concerning the general and specific applicability and value of western educational approaches in non-western countries and societies are central to this volume. We are thankful to the contributors for their willingness to share with us and other readers their thoughts and observations on this topic. Finally, we hope that lessons learned from these accounts will prove valuable not only for the particular contexts under examination but also for educational theorizing and practice more generally.

Reference

Tabulawa, R. (2003) International aid agencies, learner-centred pedagogy and political democratization: a critique, *Comparative Education*, 39, 7–26.

Julian Elliott
Durham University
Elena L. Grigorenko
Yale University

Culture, instruction, and assessment

Robert J. Sternberg

There are many lessons to be learned about optimal instruction and assessment by studying how they interact with cognition, in general, and intelligence, in particular, in diverse cultures. In this article, I describe some of what we have learned in our own cultural studies.

What is culture?

Because the topic of this article is culture, instruction, and assessment, it is important to define at the outset what is meant by culture.

There have been many definitions of culture (e.g., Kroeber & Kluckhohn, 1952; Brislin *et al.*, 1973). I define culture here as 'the set of attitudes, values, beliefs and behaviors shared by a group of people, communicated from one generation to the next via language or some other means of communication (Barnouw, 1985)' (Matsumoto, 1994, p. 4). The term *culture* can be used in many ways and has a long history (Boas, 1911; Mead, 1928; Benedict, 1946; see Matsumoto, 1996). Berry *et al.* (1992) described six uses of the term: descriptively to characterize a culture, historically to describe the traditions of a group, normatively to express rules and norms of a group, psychologically to emphasize how a group learns and solves problems, structurally to emphasize the organizational elements of a culture, and genetically to describe cultural origins.

The theory motivating much of my colleagues' and my culturally-based work is the theory of successful intelligence (see Sternberg, 1985, 1997, 1999, for more details), which proposes its own definition of intelligence. I use the term *successful* intelligence to refer to the skills and knowledge needed for success in life, according to one's own definition of success, within one's sociocultural context. One acquires and utilizes these skills and this knowledge by capitalizing on strengths and by correcting or compensating for weaknesses; by adapting to, shaping, or selecting environments; through a balance of analytical, creative, and practical abilities.

Of course, there are many alternative theories of intelligence as well (e.g., Spearman, 1927; Thurstone, 1938; Cattell, 1971; Gardner, 1983; Carroll, 1993; Ceci, 1996), many of which are reviewed in Sternberg (1990, 2000). Some of these, such as Ceci's and Gardner's, are like the theory of successful intelligence in arguing for a broader conception of intelligence than typically has emerged from psychometric research. I do not claim that these theories are incapable of accounting for any or even many of my colleagues' and my results. I find the theory of successful intelligence particularly useful, however, because of its specification of a universal set of information-processing components complemented by culturally defined contexts in which these components are enacted.

Now, here are the lessons learned.

Lesson 1. The very act of assessing cognitive and educational performance affects that performance differentially across cultures

We tend to assume that an assessment is an assessment is an assessment. Not quite. The cultural meaning of an act of assessment can vary from one place to another. For example, Greenfield (1997) found that it means a different thing to take a test among Mayan children than it does among most children in the United States. The Mayan expectation is that collaboration is permissible, and that it is rather unnatural *not* to collaborate. Such a finding is consistent with the work of Markus and Kitayama (1991), suggesting different cultural constructions of the self in individualistic versus collectivistic cultures.

A study done in Tanzania (see Sternberg & Grigorenko, 1997, 2002; Sternberg *et al.*, 2002) points out the risks of giving tests, scoring them, and interpreting the results as measures of some latent intellectual ability or abilities. We administered to 358 school children between the ages of 11 and 13 years near Bagamoyo, Tanzania, tests including a form-board classification test (a sorting task), a linear syllogisms test, and a Twenty Questions Test ('Find a Figure'), which measure the kinds of skills required on conventional tests of intelligence. Of course, we obtained scores that we could analyse and evaluate, ranking the children in terms of their supposed general or other abilities. However, we administered the tests dynamically rather than statically (Vygotsky, 1978; Feuerstein, 1979; Brown & Ferrara, 1985; Lidz, 1991; Haywood &

Tzuriel, 1992; Guthke, 1993; Tzuriel, 1995;Grigorenko & Sternberg, 1998; Lidz & Elliott, 2000; Sternberg & Grigorenko, 2002).

Dynamic testing is like conventional static testing in that individuals are tested and inferences about their abilities made. But dynamic tests differ in that children are given some kind of feedback in order to help them improve their performance. Vygotsky (1978) suggested that the children's ability to profit from the guided instruction they received during the testing session could serve as a measure of children's zone of proximal development (ZPD), or the difference between their developed abilities and their latent capacities. In other words, testing and instruction are treated as being of one piece rather than as being distinct processes. This integration makes sense in terms of traditional definitions of intelligence as the ability to learn ('Intelligence and its measurement', 1921; Sternberg & Detterman, 1986). What a dynamic test does is directly measure processes of learning in the context of testing rather than measuring these processes indirectly as the product of past learning. Such measurement is especially important when not all children have had equal opportunities to learn in the past.

In the assessments, children were first given the ability tests. Experimental-group children were then given an intervention. Control-group children were not. The intervention consisted of a brief period of instruction in which children were able to learn skills that would potentially enable them to improve their scores. For example, in the twenty-questions tasks, children would be taught how a single true–false question could cut the space of possible correct solutions by half. Then all children— experimental and control—were tested again. Because the total time for instruction was less than an hour, one would not expect dramatic gains. Yet, on average, the gains from pre-test to post-test in the experimental group were statistically significant and significantly greater than those in the control group.

In the control group, the correlations between pre-test and post-test scores were generally at the .8 level. One would expect a high correlation because there was no intervention and hence the retesting was largely a measure of alternate-forms reliability. More importantly, scores on the pre-test in the experimental group showed only weak although significant correlations with scores on the post-test. These correlations, at about the .3 level (which were significantly less than those in the control group), suggested that when tests are administered statically to children in developing countries, they may be rather unstable and easily subject to influences of training. The reason could be that the children are not accustomed to taking western-style tests, and so profit quickly even from small amounts of instruction as to what is expected from them.

Of course, the more important question is not whether the scores changed or even correlated with each other, but rather, how they correlated with other cognitive measures. In other words, which test was a better predictor of transfer to other cognitive performances on tests of working memory, the pre-test score or the post-test score? We found the post-test score to be the better predictor of working memory in the experimental group. Children in the dynamic-testing group improved significantly more than those in the control group (who did not receive intervening dynamic instruction between pre- and post-tests).

In work in Jamaica (Sternberg *et al.*, 1997), we had failed to find effects of an anti-parasitic medication, albendazole, on cognitive functioning. Might this have been because the testing was static rather than dynamic? Static testing tends to emphasize skills developed in the past. Children who suffer from parasitic illnesses often do not have the same opportunities to profit from instruction and acquire skills that well children do. Dynamic testing emphasizes skills developed at the time of test. Indeed, the skills or knowledge are specifically taught at the time of test. Would dynamic testing show effects of medication (in this case, albendazole for hookworm and praziquantel for schistosomiasis) not shown by static testing?

The answer was yes. Over time, treated children showed an advantage over children who did not receive treatment, and were closer after time had passed to the control (uninfected) group than were the untreated children. In other words, conventional static tests of intelligence may fail fully to reveal children's intellectual potentials. Thus, when tests are modified in different environments, one may wish to modify not only their content, but the form in which they are administered, as we did in our dynamic testing.

Lesson 2. Individuals in different cultures may think about concepts and problems in different ways. The result is that teachers of one culture teaching students of another culture may not understand how their students think about concepts and problems

Nisbett (2003) has found that some cultures, especially Asian ones, tend to be more dialectical in their thinking, whereas other cultures, such as European and North American ones, tend to be more linear. And individuals in different cultures may construct concepts in quite different ways, rendering results of concept-formation or identification studies in a single culture suspect (Atran, 1999; Coley *et al.*, 1999; Medin & Atran, 1999). Thus, groups may think about what appears superficially to be the same phenomenon—whether a concept or the taking of a test—differently. What appear to be differences in general intelligence may in fact be differences in cultural properties (Helms-Lorenz *et al.*, 2003). Helms-Lorenz *et al.* (2003) have argued that measured differences in intellectual performance may result from differences in cultural complexity; but complexity of a culture is extremely hard to define, and what appears to be simple or complex from the point of view of one culture may appear differently from the point of view of another.

Lesson 3. Behaviour that is viewed as smart in one culture may be viewed as not so smart or even stupid in another

People in different cultures may have quite different ideas of what it means to be smart. One of the more interesting cross-cultural studies of intelligence was performed by Michael Cole and his colleagues (Cole *et al.*, 1971). They asked adult members of the Kpelle tribe in Africa to sort terms. In western culture, when adults are given a sorting task on an intelligence test, intelligent people will typically sort hierarchically. For example, they may place names of different kinds of fish together, and then the word 'fish' over that, with the name 'animal' over 'fish' as well as 'birds', and so on. Less intelligent westerners will typically sort functionally. They might sort 'fish' with 'eat', for example, because we eat fish, or 'clothes' with 'wear', because we wear clothes. Members of the Kpelle tribe generally sorted functionally even after investigators tried indirectly to encourage them to sort hierarchically.

Finally, in desperation, one of the experimenters directly asked one of the Kpelle to show how a foolish person would do the task. When asked to sort in this way, the Kpelle had no trouble at all sorting hierarchically. He and the others had been able to sort this way all along. They just had not done so because they viewed it as foolish. Moreover, they probably considered the questioners rather unintelligent for asking such foolish questions. Why would they view functional sorting as intelligent? In ordinary life, we normally think functionally. When we think of a fish, we think of catching or eating it. When we think of clothes, we think of wearing them. However, in western schooling, we learn what is expected of us on tests. The Kpelle did not have western schooling. They had not been exposed to intelligence testing. As a result, they solved the problems the way western adults might do in their everyday lives but not on an intelligence test.

Thus, what North Americans might think of as sophisticated thinking—for example, sorting taxonomically (as in a robin being a kind of bird)—might be viewed as unsophisticated by the Kpelle, whose functional performance on sorting tasks corresponded to the demands of their everyday life (as in a robin flying). In a related fashion, Bruner *et al.* (1966) found that among members of the Wolof tribe of Senegal, increasingly greater western-style schooling was associated with greater use of taxonomic classification.

Lesson 4. Students do better on assessments when the material on which they are assessed is familiar and meaningful to them. But items on cognitive test batteries are differentially meaningful to individuals from different cultures

Cole's work built, in turn, upon earlier work, such as that of Luria (1931, 1976), which showed that Asian peasants in the Soviet Union might not perform well on cognitive tasks because of their refusal to accept the tasks as they were presented. Indeed, people in diverse cultures are presented with very diverse tasks in their lives. Gladwin (1970), studying the Puluwat who inhabit the Caroline Islands in the South Pacific, found that these individuals were able to master knowledge domains including wind and weather, ocean currents, and movements of the stars. They integrate this knowledge with mental maps of the islands to become navigators who are highly respected in their world.

In related work, Serpell (1979) designed a study to distinguish between a generalized perceptual-deficit hypothesis and a more context-specific hypothesis for why children in certain cultures may show inferior perceptual abilities. He found that English children did better on a drawing task, but that Zambian children did better on a wire-shaping task. Thus, children performed better on materials that were more familiar to them from their own environments.

Wagner (1978) had Moroccan and North American individuals remember patterns of oriental rugs and others remember pictures of everyday objects, such as a rooster and a fish. There was no evidence of a difference in memory structure, but the evidence of a lack of difference depended precisely upon using tests that were appropriate to the cultural content of the individuals being studied. Moroccans, who have long experience in the rug trade, seemed to remember things in a different way from participants who did not have their skill in remembering rug patterns. In a related study, Kearins (1981) found that when asked to remember visuospatial displays, Anglo-Australians used verbal (school-appropriate) strategies whereas aboriginals used visual (desert nomad-appropriate) strategies.

Goodnow (1962) found that for tasks using combinations and permutations, Chinese children with English schooling performed as well as or better than Europeans, where children with Chinese schooling or of very low income families did somewhat worse than did the European children. These results suggested that form of schooling primes children to excel in certain ways and not others (see also Goodnow, 1969).

Children from non-European or non-North American cultures do not always do worse on tests. Super (1976) found evidence that African infants sit and walk earlier than do their counterparts in the United States and Europe. But Super also found that mothers in the African cultures he studied made a self-conscious effort to teach their babies to sit and walk as early as possible. At more advanced levels of development, Stigler *et al.* (1982; see also Stevenson & Stigler, 1994) found that Japanese and Chinese children do better in developed mathematical skills than do North American children.

Carraher *et al.* (1985) studied a group of children that is especially relevant for assessing intelligence as adaptation to the environment. The group was of Brazilian street children. Brazilian street children are under great contextual pressure to form a successful street business. If they do not, they risk death at the hands of so-called 'death squads', which may murder children who, unable to earn money, resort to robbing stores (or who are suspected of resorting to robbing stores). Hence, if they are not intelligent in the sense of adapting to their environment, they risk death. The investigators found that the same children who are able to do the mathematics needed to run their street businesses are often little able or unable to do school mathematics. In fact, the more abstracted and removed from real-world contexts the problems are in their form of presentation, the worse the children typically do on the problems. For children in school, the street context would be more removed from their lives. These results suggest that differences in context can have a powerful effect on performance. (See also Saxe, 1990; Ceci & Roazzi, 1994; Nuñes, 1994, for related work.)

Such differences are not limited to Brazilian street children. Lave (1988) showed that Berkeley housewives who successfully could do the mathematics needed for comparison-shopping in the supermarket were unable to do the same mathematics when they were placed in a classroom and given isomorphic problems presented in an abstract form. In other words, their problem was not at the level of mental processes but at the level of applying the processes in specific environmental contexts.

In sum, a variety of researchers have done studies that suggest that how one tests abilities, competences, and expertise can have a major effect on how 'intelligent' students appear to be. Street children in Brazil, for example, need the same mathematical skills to solve problems involving discounts as do children in the United States about to take a high-stakes paper-and-pencil test of mathematical achievement. But the contexts in which they express these skills, and hence the contexts in which they can best display their knowledge on tests, are different. My colleagues and I have also done research suggesting that cultural context needs to be taken into account in testing for intelligence and its outcomes.

Lesson 5. Children may develop contextually important skills at the expense of academic ones. So they may have developed adaptive skills that matter in their environment, but that teachers do not view as part of 'intelligence'

Many times, investigations of intelligence conducted in settings outside the developed world can yield a picture of intelligence that is quite at variance with the picture one would obtain from studies conducted only in the developed world. In a study in Usenge, Kenya, near the town of Kisumu, we were interested in school-age children's ability to adapt to their indigenous environment. We devised a test of practical intelligence for adaptation to the environment (see Sternberg & Grigorenko, 1997; Sternberg *et al.*, 2001). The test of practical intelligence measured children's informal tacit knowledge for natural herbal medicines that the villagers believe can be used to fight various types of infections. Tacit knowledge is, roughly speaking, what one needs to know to succeed in an environment, that is usually not explicitly taught, and that often is not even verbalized (Sternberg *et al.*, 2000). Children in the villages use their tacit knowledge of these medicines an average of once a week, in medicating themselves and others. More than 95% of the children suffer from parasitic illnesses. Thus, tests of how to use these medicines constitute effective measures of one aspect of practical intelligence as defined by the villagers as well as their life circumstances in their environmental contexts. Note that the processes of intelligence are not different in Kenya. Children must still recognize the existence of an illness, define what it is, devise a strategy to combat it, and so forth. But the content to which the processes are applied, and hence appropriate ways of testing these processes, may be quite different.

Middle-class westerners might find it quite a challenge to thrive or even survive in these contexts, or, for that matter, in the contexts of urban ghettos often not distant from their comfortable homes. For example, they would know how to use none of the natural herbal medicines to combat the diverse and abundant parasitic illnesses they might acquire in rural Kenya.

We measured the Kenyan children's ability to identify the medicines, where they come from, what they are used for, and how they are dosed. Based on work we had done elsewhere, we expected that scores on this test would not correlate with scores on conventional tests of intelligence. In order to test this hypothesis, we also administered to the 85 children of the study the Raven Coloured Progressive Matrices Test (Raven *et al.*, 1992), which is a measure of fluid or abstract-reasoning-based abilities, as well as the Mill Hill Vocabulary Scale (Raven *et al.*, 1992), which is a measure of crystallized or formal-knowledge-based abilities. In addition, we gave the children a comparable test of vocabulary in their own Dholuo language. The Dholuo language is spoken in the home; English in the schools.

To our surprise, all correlations between the test of indigenous tacit knowledge and scores on fluid-ability and crystallized ability tests were *negative*. The correlations with the tests of crystallized abilities were significantly so. For example, the correlation of tacit knowledge with vocabulary (English and Dholuo combined) was $-.31$ ($p < .01$). In other words, the higher the children scored on the test of tacit knowledge, the lower they scored, on average, on the tests of crystallized abilities (vocabulary).

This surprising result can be interpreted in various ways, but based on the ethnographic observations of the anthropologists on the team, Prince and Geissler (see Prince & Geissler, 2001), we concluded that a plausible scenario takes into account the expectations of families for their children. Many children drop out of school before graduation, for financial or other reasons, and many families in the village do not particularly see the advantages of formal western schooling. There is no reason they should, as the children of many families will for the most part spend their lives farming or engaged in other occupations that make little or no use of western schooling. These families emphasize teaching their children the indigenous informal knowledge that will lead to successful adaptation in the environments in which they will really live. Children who spend their time learning the indigenous practical knowledge of the community may not always invest themselves heavily in doing well in school, whereas children who do well in school generally may invest themselves less heavily in learning the indigenous knowledge—hence the negative correlations.

The Kenya study suggests that the identification of a general factor of human intelligence may tell us more about how abilities interact with cultural patterns of schooling and society and especially western patterns of schooling and society than it does about the structure of human abilities. In western schooling, children typically study a variety of subject-matters from an early age and thus develop skills in a variety of skill areas. This kind of schooling prepares the children to take a test of intelligence, which typically measures skills in a variety of areas. Often intelligence tests measure skills that children were expected to acquire a few years before taking the intelligence test. But as Rogoff (1990, 2003) and others have noted, this pattern of schooling is not universal and has not even been common for much of the history of humankind. Throughout history and in many places still, schooling, especially for boys, takes the form of apprenticeships in which children learn a craft from an early age. They learn what they will need to know in order to succeed in a trade, but not a lot more. They are not simultaneously engaged in tasks that require the development of the particular blend of skills measured by conventional intelligence tests. Hence it is less likely that one would observe a general factor in their scores, much as we discovered in Kenya.

From the standpoint of an academic test, the rural Kenyan children would not look very bright. But, in fact, they had learned knowledge that was important in their own cultural context. A teacher might be inclined to 'write off' such children because of their underdeveloped academic skills, without appreciating that the children had developed other skills that were, arguably, more important for adaptation in their own cultural milieux. Ideally, the teacher would attempt to capitalize on what the children do know, using it as a starting point or scaffolding upon which other knowledge could be built. But certainly, the children could not be faulted for lacking learning skills. They merely had applied these skills to content other than that sanctioned by the schools.

Lesson 6. Children may have substantial practical skills that go unrecognized in academic tests

We have found related although certainly not identical results in a study we have done among Yup'ik Eskimo children in south-western Alaska (Grigorenko *et al.*, 2004). We assessed the importance of academic and practical intelligence in rural and semi-urban Alaskan communities.

This research was motivated by an observation we made while working both with the Eskimo children and with their teachers. The teachers made it clear that they considered the children not to be particularly bright. And indeed, in terms of the knowledge and skills emphasized in traditional schooling, the children did not fare well. But at the same time, the children had developed superior skills of other kinds. They possessed knowledge about hunting, fishing, gathering, herbal treatments of illnesses, and other topics that their teachers did not possess. For example, they could take a dog sled from their village to another village in the dead of winter and find their way. Their teachers, in contrast, if they tried to do the same in the dead of winter, would end up dead. They would not be able to discern the landmarks the children can use to find their way. They quickly would get lost. So the children had adaptive skills relevant to their own environments that the teachers did not have. But of course, it is the teachers whom society sanctions to do the evaluations, not the students.

A total of 261 children were rated for practical skills by adults or peers in the study: 69 in grade 9, 69 in grade 10, 45 in grade 11, and 37 in grade 12. Of these children, 145 were females (74 from the rural and 71 from the semi-urban communities) and 116 were males (62 were from the rural and 54 were from the semi-urban communities). We measured academic intelligence with conventional measures of fluid (the Cattell Culture Fair Test of *g*, Cattell & Cattell, 1973) and crystallized intelligence (the Mill-Hill Vocabulary Scale, Raven *et al.*, 1992). We measured practical intelligence with a test of tacit knowledge of skills (hunting, fishing, dealing with weather conditions, picking and preserving plants, and so on) as acquired in rural Alaskan Yup'ik communities (the Yup'ik Scale of Practical Intelligence, YSPI). The semi-urban children statistically significantly outperformed the rural children on the measure of crystallized intelligence, but the rural children statistically significantly outperformed the semi-urban children on the measure of the YSPI . The test of tacit knowledge skills was superior to the tests of academic intelligence in predicting practical skills as evaluated by adults and peers of the rural children (for whom the test was created), but not of the semi-urban ones.

This study, like the Kenya study, suggests the importance of practical intellectual skills for predicting adaptation to everyday environments. Here, as in Kenya, the processes of intelligence do not differ from those in the environments in which most readers of this article live. The Eskimo children need, for example, to plan trips, just as you or I do. But the constraints of planning these trips, often by dog sled in environments with no landmarks you or I would recognize, are very different, and hence different tests are needed.

Lesson 7. Failure of children to thrive in school may reflect ill health, not lack of ability. Teachers need to know children's health status before assuming their performance reflects a lack of cognitive or educational skills

In interpreting educational outcomes, whether from developed or developing cultures, it is always important to take into account the physical health of the participants one is testing. In a study we did in Jamaica (Sternberg *et al.*, 1997), we found that Jamaican school children who suffered from parasitic illnesses (for the most part, whipworm or Ascaris) did more poorly on higher level cognitive tests (such as of working memory and reasoning) than did children who did not suffer from these illnesses, even after controlling for socio-economic status. The children with parasitic illnesses did better on fine-motor tasks, for reasons unknown to us.

Thus, many children were poor achievers not because they innately lacked abilities, but rather, because they lacked the good health necessary to develop and display such abilities. If you are moderately to seriously ill, you probably find it more difficult to concentrate on what you read or what you hear than if you are well. Children in developing countries are ill much, and even most, of the time. They simply cannot devote the same attentional and learning resources to schoolwork that well children have to devote. Here, as in Kenya, their health knowledge would be crucial for their adaptation to the environment. Testing that does not take into account health status is likely to give false impressions.

Lesson 8. Children may fail to do well in school not because they do not understand the material, but because they do not understand the instructions regarding what to do with the material

In our work in Zambia (Grigorenko *et al.*, 2003), we investigated following of instructions. Children in school and outside it continually need to be able to follow instructions. Often they are not successful in their endeavours because they do not follow instructions as to how to realize these endeavours. Following complex instructions is thus important for the children's success. A test of following instructions has dynamic elements, in that one learns the instructions at the time of test.

Yet, it is not a complex instructional intervention. Indeed, *all* tests require test-takers to follow instructions.

The Z-CAI (Zambia Cognitive Assessment Instrument) was designed to measure children's ability to follow oral, written, and pictorial instructions that become increasingly complex. It is also designed to be simple to implement, so that teachers can easily be trained to administer the instrument. We further created a test that would be sensitive specifically to any improvement in cognitive functioning that was a result of improved health status. And finally, we needed the test to be psychometrically sound (valid and reliable) in Zambia.

The Z-CAI measures working memory, reasoning, and comprehension skills in the oral, written, and pictorial domains. We found that among children tested on the Z-CAI, those who were treated for parasitic illnesses ($N = 1000$) outperformed children who were not treated ($N = 1000$) relative to baseline performance.

Lesson 9. When children are taught in culturally appropriate ways, their achievement increases

We have shown that when children are taught in a way that better matches their culturally acquired knowledge, their school performance improves (Sternberg *et al.*, in press). Grade 6 students from seven communities in three school districts in Alaska participated in a mathematics curriculum project. Eight classes of students containing a total of 196 students were taught the concepts of area and perimeter using an Alaskan culturally-based, triarchic curriculum and 5 classes containing 55 students were taught the same subject-matter using a conventional textbook-based curriculum. Both groups contained students from rural regions with a population that was almost 100% Alaskan Native (predominantly Yup'ik) and urban regions with a population that was approximately 71% ethnically white and 12% Alaskan Native. (The urban settings were 'urban' in the context of remote regions of Alaska, where cities tend to be relatively small and isolated.)

Due to absenteeism a total of 17 students did not complete the pre-test and 30 students did not complete the post-test. This resulted in a total of 158 students (35 rural and 123 urban) in the culturally-based triarchic curriculum group and 46 students (29 rural and 17 urban) in the conventional curriculum group being included in the analysis.

Pre- and post-test measures of the 'area and perimeter curriculum' were collected for all the students. Only students who completed both the pre- and post-test measures were included in the study sample.

Teachers in the culturally-based curriculum group received a maths unit entitled 'Fish Racks' as part of the NSF sponsored curriculum 'Adapting Yup'ik Elders' Knowledge' (Lipka, 2000). The unit addressed the National Council of Teachers of Mathematics (NCTM) standards for the topics of area and perimeter using both native content (building of fish racks) and native teaching strategies (demonstrations by Yup'ik elders). The building of fish racks is a native tradition and requires everyday, practical mathematics to build racks that will be stable, strong, and have sufficient area for placing salmon on them. The maths unit comprised two complex problems, each involving a number of different activities revolving around the building of fish racks and the concepts of area and perimeter.

Teachers in the control group used their mathematics textbooks to teach the concepts of perimeter and area. The approach used in these textbooks is a procedurally based approach for teaching perimeter and a formula based approach for teaching area. The perimeter and area unit covered approximately the same material and began and ended at approximately the same time as the treatment group.

Prior to and following the intervention, students completed a test designed to capture their knowledge of area and perimeter concepts. The tests were each composed of 15 questions involving a combination of multiple-choice, short-answer, and open-ended items.

The intervention for students lasted between three and four weeks; approximate time for instruction was an hour a day. The training session for teachers lasted two days.

The results were simple. There were no pre-test differences. At the post-test, the treatment group outperformed the control group on all indicators. In other words, teaching in ways that capitalized on cultural knowledge enhanced student performance.

Lesson 10. What it means to be smart may vary from one culture to the next. In trying to act intelligent in their school performance, therefore, students may think differently as to what intelligent performance means

Intelligence may be conceived in different ways in different cultures (see reviews in Berry, 1984; Sternberg & Kaufman, 1998; and Serpell, 2000). Such differences are important, because cultures evaluate their members, as well as members of others' cultures, in terms of their own conceptions of intelligence.

Yang and Sternberg (1997a) reviewed Chinese philosophical conceptions of intelligence. The Confucian perspective emphasizes the characteristic of benevolence and of doing what is right. As in the western notion, the intelligent person spends a great deal of effort in learning, enjoys learning, and persists in lifelong learning with a great deal of enthusiasm. The Taoist tradition, in contrast, emphasizes the importance of humility, freedom from conventional standards of judgement, and full knowledge of oneself as well as of external conditions.

The difference between eastern and western conceptions of intelligence may persist even in the present day. Yang and Sternberg (1997b) studied contemporary Taiwanese Chinese conceptions of intelligence, and found five factors underlying these conceptions: (a) a general cognitive factor, much like the g factor in conventional western tests; (b) interpersonal intelligence (i.e., social competence); (c) intrapersonal intelligence; (d) intellectual self-assertion; and (d) intellectual self-effacement. In a related study but with different results, Chen (1994) found three factors underlying Chinese conceptualizations of intelligence: nonverbal reasoning ability, verbal reasoning ability, and rote memory. The difference may be due to different subpopulations of Chinese, to differences in methodology, or to differences in when the studies were done.

The factors uncovered in Taiwan differ substantially from those identified in US people's conceptions of intelligence by Sternberg, *et al.* (1981)—(a) practical problem solving, (b) verbal ability, and (c) social competence—although in both cases, people's implicit theories of intelligence seem to go quite far beyond what conventional psychometric intelligence tests measure. Of course, comparing the Chen (1994) to the Sternberg *et al.* (1981) study simultaneously varies both language and culture.

Studies in Africa in fact provide yet another window on the substantial differences in conceptions of intelligence across cultures. Ruzgis and Grigorenko (1994) argued that, in Africa, conceptions of intelligence revolve largely around skills that help to facilitate and maintain harmonious and stable inter-group relations; intra-group relations are probably equally important and at times more important. For example, Serpell (1974, 1996) found that Chewa adults in Zambia emphasize social responsibilities, cooperativeness, and obedience as important to intelligence; intelligent children are expected to be respectful of adults. Kenyan parents also emphasize responsible participation in family and social life as important aspects of intelligence (Super & Harkness, 1982, 1986, 1993). In Zimbabwe, the word for intelligence, *ngware*, actually means to be prudent and cautious, particularly in social relationships. Among the Baoule, service to the family and community and politeness toward and respect for elders are seen as key to intelligence (Dasen, 1984).

It is difficult to separate linguistic differences from conceptual differences in cross-cultural notions of intelligence. In our own research, we use converging operations in order to achieve some separation. That is, we use different and diverse empirical operations in order to ascertain notions of intelligence. So we may ask in one study that people identify aspects of competence; in another study, that they identify competent people; in a third study, that they characterize the meaning of 'intelligence', and so forth.

The emphasis on the social aspects of intelligence is not limited to African cultures. Notions of intelligence in many Asian cultures also emphasize the social aspect of intelligence more than does the conventional western or IQ-based notion (Lutz, 1985; Poole, 1985; White, 1985; Azuma & Kashiwagi, 1987).

It should be noted that neither African nor Asian notions emphasize exclusively social notions of intelligence. These conceptions of intelligence emphasize social skills much more than do conventional US conceptions of intelligence, at the same time that they recognize the importance of cognitive aspects of intelligence. In a study of Kenyan conceptions of intelligence (Grigorenko *et al.*, 2001), it was found that there are four distinct terms constituting conceptions of intelligence among rural Kenyans—*rieko* (knowledge and skills), *luoro* (respect), *winjo* (comprehension of how to handle real-life problems), *paro* (initiative)—with only the first directly referring to knowledge-based skills (including but not limited to the academic).

It is important to realize, again, that there is no one overall US conception of intelligence. Indeed, Okagaki and Sternberg (1993) found that different ethnic groups in San Jose, California, had rather different conceptions of what it means to be intelligent. For example, Latino parents of schoolchildren tended to emphasize the importance of social-competence skills in their conceptions of intelligence, whereas Asian parents tended rather heavily to emphasize the importance of cognitive skills. Anglo parents also emphasized cognitive skills more than Latinos. Teachers, representing the dominant culture, also placed greater emphasis upon cognitive than social-competence skills. The rank order of children of various groups' performance (including subgroups within the Latino and Asian groups) could be perfectly predicted by the extent to which their parents shared the teachers' conception of intelligence. In other words, teachers tended to reward those children who were socialized into a view of intelligence that happened to correspond to the teachers' own.

In sum, people have different conceptions, or implicit theories, of intelligence across cultures. From a practical point of view, one may still try to draw restricted comparisons of scores on given tests across cultures. For example, western tests may still be predictive in other cultures (Vernon, 1969), even if their appropriateness varies according to the culture and the use to which they are put. Comparisons need, however, to be conditional ones that take into account the context of the individuals' development (Laboratory of Comparative Human Cognition, 1982; Sternberg, 1990). The scores may not mean the same thing across the cultures.

Conclusion

When cultural context is taken into account, (a) individuals are better recognized for and are better able to make use of their talents, (b) schools teach and assess children better, and (c) society utilizes rather than wastes the talents of its members. Instruction and assessment can only be improved by taking cultural context into account.

Curiously, many educators tend to assume that whatever kind of education they had, or that they are accustomed to provide, is the best kind. They are like carpenters who have a tool—a hammer—and then look for ways to use it. The message of this article is that one hammer just won't do it. Neither will multiple hammers of different sizes (corresponding to different levels of pounding material into children's heads). We need a whole range of tools, and the tools must be made appropriate for the cultural context of the children we are teaching. This means first understanding that cultural context, and then tailoring instruction and assessment so that they are appropriate for the context. Students may be cognitively and emotionally in very different places from where we expect them to be, just as they are physically in very different environments. We can adapt ourselves, or we can dismiss students who do not fit our prototype of a 'bright' student. Such dismissal of students hurts their futures, and impugns our own teaching skills. We need to teach to who the students are, not some idealization of who we might want them to be. In that way, we make instruction culturally relevant rather than culturally blind, deaf, and dumb.

Acknowledgements

I am grateful to my many collaborators at and affiliates of the Psychology of Abilities, Competencies and Expertise (PACE) Centre for their collaborations. My principal collaborator in this work has been Elena L. Grigorenko, who has made invaluable contributions to our research for this article. The work in Kenya and Jamaica was supported primarily by the Partnership for Child Development, centred at Imperial College, University of London. The work in Tanzania was supported by the James S. McDonnell Foundation. The work in Alaska was supported by the Institute of Educational Sciences (formerly the Office of Educational Research and Improvement), US Department of Education. The work in Zambia was supported by USAID. The work in Taiwan was supported by the US Office of Educational Research and Improvement. The work in San Jose, CA, was supported by the Spencer Foundation.

Notes on contributor

Robert J. Sternberg is Dean of the School of Arts and Sciences and Professor of Psychology at Tufts University, Massachusets, USA.

References

Atran, S. (1999) Itzaj Maya folkbiological taxonomy: cognitive universals and cultural particulars, in: D. L. Medin & S. Atran (Eds) *Folkbiology* (Cambridge, MA, MIT Press), 119–213

Azuma, H. & Kashiwagi, K. (1987) Descriptions for an intelligent person: a Japanese study, *Japanese Psychological Research*, 29, 17–26.

Barnouw, V. (1985) *Culture and personality* (Chicago, Dorsey Press).

Benedict, R. (1946) *The chrysanthemum and the sword* (Boston, Houghton Mifflin).

Berry, J. W. (1984) Towards a universal psychology of cognitive competence, in: P. S. Fry (Ed.) *Changing conceptions of intelligence and intellectual functioning* (Amsterdam, North-Holland), 35–61

Berry, J. W., Poortinga, Y. H., Segall, M., H. & Dasen, P. R. (1992) *Cross-cultural psychology: research and applications* (New York, Cambridge University Press).

Boas, F. (1911) *The mind of primitive man* (New York, Macmillan).

Brislin, R. W., Lonner, W. J. & Thorndike, R. M. (Eds) (1973) *Cross-cultural research methods* (New York, Wiley).

Brown, A. L. & Ferrara, R. A. (1985) Diagnosing zones of proximal development, in: J. V. Wertsch (Ed.) *Culture, communication, and cognition: Vygotskian perspectives* (New York, NY, Cambridge University Press), 273–305.

Bruner, J. S., Olver, R. R. & Greenfield, P. M. (1966) *Studies in cognitive growth* (New York, Wiley).

Carraher, T. N., Carraher, D. & Schliemann, A. D. (1985) Mathematics in the streets and in schools, *British Journal of Developmental Psychology*, 3, 21–29.

Carroll, J. B. (1993) *Human cognitive abilities: a survey of factor-analytic studies* (New York, Cambridge University Press).

Cattell, R. B. (1971) *Abilities: their structure, growth, and action* (Boston, Houghton Mifflin).

Cattell, R. B. & Cattell, (1973) *Measuring intelligence with the Culture Fair Tests* (Champaign, IL, Institute for Personality and Ability Testing).

Ceci, S. J. (1996) *On intelligence* (expanded edn.) (Cambridge, MA, Harvard University Press).

Ceci, S. J. & Roazzi, A. (1994) The effects of context on cognition: postcards from Brazil, in: R. J. Sternberg & R. K. Wagner (Eds) *Mind in context: interactionist perspectives on human intelligence* (New York, Cambridge University Press), 74–101.

Chen, M. J. (1994) Chinese and Australian concepts of intelligence, *Psychology and Developing Societies*, 6, 101–117.

Cole, M., Gay, J., Glick, J. & Sharp, D. W. (1971) *The cultural context of learning and thinking* (New York, Basic Books).

Coley, J. D., Medin, D. L., Proffitt, J. B., Lynch, E. & Atran, S. (1999) Inductive reasoning in folkbiological thought, in: D. L. Medin & S. Atran (Eds) *Folkbiology* (Cambridge, MA, MIT Press), 205–232.

Dasen, P. (1984) The cross-cultural study of intelligence: Piaget and the Baoule, *International Journal of Psychology*, 19, 407–434.

Feuerstein, R. (1979) *The dynamic assessment of retarded performers: the Learning Potential Assessment Device theory, instruments, and techniques* (Baltimore, MD, University Park Press).

Gardner, H. (1983) *Frames of mind: the theory of multiple intelligences* (New York, Basic Books).

Gladwin, T. (1970) *East is a big bird* (Cambridge, MA, Harvard University Press).

Goodnow, J. J. (1962) A test of milieu effects with some of Piaget's tasks, *Psychological Monographs*, 76, Whole No. 555.

Goodnow, J. J. (1969) Cultural variations in cognition skills, in: D. R. Price-Williams (Ed.) *Cross-cultural studies* (Hardmondsworth, England, Penguin), 246–264.

Greenfield, P. M. (1997) You can't take it with you: why abilities assessments don't cross cultures, *American Psychologists*, 52, 1115–1124.

Grigorenko, E. L., Geissler, P. W., Prince, R., Okatcha, F., Nokes, C., Kenny, D. A., Bundy, D. A. & Sternberg, R. J. (2001) The organization of Luo conceptions of intelligence: a study of implicit theories in a Kenyan village, *International Journal of Behavior Development*, 25, 367–378.

Grigorenko, E. L., Jarvin, L., Kaani, B., Kapungulya, P. P., Kwiatkowski, J. & Sternberg, R. J. (2003) *Effects of interventions against parasitic illnesses on a test of cognitive skills administered in Zambia.* Unpublished manuscript.

Grigorenko, E. L, Meier, E., Lipka, J., Mohatt, G., Yanez, E. & Sternberg, R. J. (2004) The relationship between academic and practical intelligence: a case study of the tacit knowledge of Native American Yup'ik people in Alaska, *Learning and Individual Differences*, 14, 183–207.

Grigorenko, E. L. & Sternberg, R. J. (1998) Dynamic testing, *Psychological Bulletin*, 124, 75–111.

Guthke, J. (1993) Current trends in theories and assessment of intelligence, in: J. H. M. Hamers, K. Sijtsma & A. J. J. M. Ruijssenaars (Eds) *Learning potential assessment* (Amsterdam, Swets & Zeitlinger), 13–20

Haywood, H. C. & Tzuriel, D. (Eds) (1992) *Interactive assessment* (New York, Springer-Verlag).

Helms-Lorenz, M., Van de Vijver, F. J. R. & Poortinga, Y. H. (2003) Cross-cultural differences in cognitive performance and Spearman's hypothesis: g or c? *Intelligence*, 31, 9–29.

'Intelligence and its measurement': a symposium (1921) *Journal of Educational Psychology*, 12, 123–147, 195–216, 271–275.

Kearins, J. M. (1981) Visual spatial memory in Australian Aboriginal children of desert regions, *Cognitive Psychology*, 13, 434–460.

Kroeber, A. L. & Kluckhohn, C. (1952) *Culture: a critical review of concepts and definitions* (Cambridge, MA, Peabody Museum).

Laboratory of Comparative Human Cognition (1982) Culture and intelligence, in: R. J. Sternberg (Ed.) *Handbook of human intelligence* (New York, Cambridge University Press), 642–719.

Lave, J. (1988) *Cognition in practice* (New York, NY, Cambridge University Press).

Lidz, C. S. (1991) *Practitioner's guide to dynamic assessment*, (New York, Guilford Press).

Lidz, C. S. & Elliott, J. G. (Eds) (2000) *Dynamic assessment: prevailing models and applications* (Greenwich, CT, Elsevier-JAI).

Lipka, J. (2000) *Fish Racks. Unpublished curriculum* (Fairbanks, AL, University of Alaska, Fairbanks).

Luria, A. R. (1931) Psychological expedition to central Asia, *Science*, 74, 383–384.

Luria, A. R. (1976) *Cognitive development: its cultural and social foundations* (Trans M. Lopez-Morillas & L. Solotaroff) (Cambridge, MA, Harvard University Press).

Lutz, C. (1985) Ethnopsychology compared to what? Explaining behaviour and consciousness among the Ifaluk, in: G. M. White & J. Kirkpatrick (Eds) *Person, self, and experience: exploring Pacific ethnopsychologies* (Berkeley, University of California Press), 35–79.

Markus, H. R. & Kitayama, S. (1991) Culture and the self: implications for cognition, emotion, and motivation, *Psychological Review*, 98, 224–253.

Matsumoto, D. (1994) *People: psychology from a cultural perspective* (Pacific Grove, CA, Brooks-Cole).

Matsumoto, D. (1996) *Culture and psychology* Pacific Grove, CA, Brooks-Cole).

Mead, M. (1928) *Coming of age in Samoa* (New York, Morrow).

Medin, D. L. & Atran, S. (Eds) (1999) *Folkbiology* (Cambridge, MA, MIT Press).

Nisbett, R. E. (2003) *The geography of thought: why we think the way we do* (New York, NY, The Free Press).

Nuñes, T. (1994) Street intelligence, in: R. J. Sternberg (Ed.) *Encyclopedia of human intelligence*, Vol. 2 (New York, Macmillan), 1045–1049.

Okagaki, L. & Sternberg, R. J. (1993) Parental beliefs and children's school performance, *Child Development*, 64, 36–56.

Poole, F. J. P. (1985) Coming into social being: cultural images of infants in Bimin-Kuskusmin folk psychology, in: G. M. White & J. Kirkpatrick (Eds) *Person, self, and experience: exploring Pacific ethnopsychologies* (Berkeley, University of California Press), 183–244.

Prince R. J. & Geissler P. W. (2001) Becoming 'one who treats': a case study of a Luo healer and her grandson in Western Kenya, *Educational Anthropology Quarterly*, 32, 447–471.

Raven, J. C., Court, J. H. & Raven, J. (1992) *Manual for Raven's Progressive Matrices and Mill Hill Vocabulary Scales* (Oxford, Oxford Psychologists Press).

Rogoff, B. (1990) *Apprenticeship in thinking: cognitive development in social context* (New York, NY, Oxford University Press).

Rogoff, B. (2003) The cultural nature of human development (London, Oxford University Press).

Ruzgis, P. M. & Grigorenko, E. L. (1994) Cultural meaning systems, intelligence and personality, in: R. J. Sternberg & P. Ruzgis (Eds) *Personality and intelligence* (New York, Cambridge) 248–270.

Saxe, G. B. (1990) *Culture and cognitive development: studies in mathematical understanding* (Mahwah, NJ, Erlbaum).

Serpell, R. (1974) Aspects of intelligence in a developing country, *African Social Research*, 17, 576–96.

Serpell, R. (1979) How specific are perceptual skills? A cross-cultural study of pattern reproduction, *British Journal of Psychology*, 70, 365–380.

Serpell, R. (1996) Cultural models of childhood in indigenous socialization and formal schooling in Zambia, in: C. P. Hwang & M. E. Lamb (Eds) *Images of childhood* (Mahwah, NJ, Lawrence Erlbaum), 129–142.

Serpell, R. (2000) Intelligence and culture, in: R. J. Sternberg (Ed.) *Handbook of intelligence* (New York, Cambridge University Press), 549–580

Spearman, C. (1927) *The abilities of man* (London, Macmillan).

Sternberg, R. J. (1985) *Beyond IQ: a triarchic theory of human intelligence* (New York, Cambridge University Press).

Sternberg, R. J. (1990) *Metaphors of mind* (New York, Cambridge University Press).

Sternberg, R. J. (1997) *Successful intelligence* (New York, Plume).

Sternberg, R. J. (1999) The theory of successful intelligence, *Review of General Psychology*, 3, 292–316.

Sternberg, R. J. (Ed.) (2000) *Handbook of intelligence* (New York, Cambridge University Press).

Sternberg, R. J., Conway, B. E., Ketron, J. L. & Bernstein, M. (1981) People's conceptions of intelligence, *Journal of Personality and Social Psychology*, 41, 37–55.

Sternberg, R. J. & Detterman, D. K. (1986) *What is intelligence?* (Norwood, NJ, Ablex Publishing Corporation).

Sternberg, R. J. & Grigorenko, E. L. (Eds) (1997) *Intelligence, heredity, and environment* (New York, Cambridge University Press).

Sternberg, R. J. & Grigorenko, E. L. (2002) Just because we 'know' it's true doesn't mean it's really true: a case study in Kenya, *Psychological Science Agenda*, 15(2), 8–10.

Sternberg, R. J., Forsythe, G. B., Hedlund, J., Horvath, J., Snook, S., Williams, W. M., Wagner, R. K. & Grigorenko, E. L. (2000) *Practical intelligence in everyday life* (New York, Cambridge University Press).

Sternberg, R. J., Grigorenko, E. L., Ngrosho, D., Tantufuye, E., Mbise, A., Nokes, C., Jukes, M. & Bundy, D. A. (2002) Assessing intellectual potential in rural Tanzanian school children, *Intelligence*, 30, 141–162.

Sternberg, R. J. & Kaufman J. C. (1998) Human abilities, *Annual Review of Psychology*, 49, 479–502.

Sternberg, R. J., Lipka, J., Newman, T., Wildfeuer, S. & Grigorenko, E. L. (in press) Triarchically-based instruction and assessment of sixth-grade mathematics in a Yup'ik cultural setting in Alaska, *International Journal of Giftedness and Creativity*.

Sternberg, R. J., Nokes, K., Geissler, P. W., Prince, R., Okatcha, F., Bundy, D. A. & Grigorenko, E. L. (2001) The relationship between academic and practical intelligence: a case study in Kenya, *Intelligence*, 29, 401–418.

Sternberg, R. J., Powell, C., McGrane, P. A. & McGregor, S. (1997) Effects of a parasitic infection on cognitive functioning, *Journal of Experimental Psychology: Applied*, 3, 67–76.

Stevenson, H. W. & Stigler, J. W. (1994) *The learning gap: why our schools are failing and what we can learn from Japanese and Chinese education* (New York, Simon & Schuster).

Stigler, J. W., Lee, S., Lucker, G. W. & Stevenson, H. W. (1982) Curriculum and achievement in mathematics: a study of elementary school children in Japan, Taiwan, and the United States, *Journal of Educational Psychology*, 74, 315–322.

Super, C. M. (1976) Environmental effects on motor development: the case of African infant precocity, *Developmental Medicine and Child Neurology*, 18, 561–567.

Super C. M. & Harkness, S. (1982) The development of affect in infancy and early childhood, in: D. Wagnet & H. Stevenson (Eds) *Cultural perspectives on child development* (San Francisco, W.H. Freeman), 1–19.

Super, C. M. & Harkness, S. (1986) The developmental niche: a conceptualization at the interface of child and culture, *International Journal of Behavioral Development*, 9, 545–569.

Super, C. M. & Harkness, S. (1993) The developmental niche: a conceptualization at the interface of child and culture, in R. A. Pierce & M. A. Black (Eds) *Life-span development: a diversity reader* (Dubuque, IA, Kendall/Hunt Publishing Co.), 61–77.

Thurstone, L. L. (1938) *Primary mental abilities*, (Chicago, University of Chicago Press).

Tzuriel, D. (1995) *Dynamic-interactive assessment: the legacy of L. S. Vygotsky and current developments.* Unpublished manuscript.

Vernon, P. E. (1969) *Intelligence and cultural environment* (London, Methuen).

Vygotsky, L. S. (1978) *Mind in society: the development of higher psychological processes* (Cambridge, MA, Harvard University Press).

Wagner, D. A. (1978) Memories of Morocco: the influence of age, schooling, and environment on memory, *Cognitive Psychology*, 10, 1–28.

White, G. M. (1985) Premises and purposes in a Solomon Islands ethnopsychology, in: G. M. White & J. Kirkpatrick (Eds) *Person, self, and experience: exploring Pacific ethnopsychologies* (Berkeley, University of California Press), 328–366.

Yang, S. & Sternberg, R. J. (1997a) Conceptions of intelligence in ancient Chinese philosophy, *Journal of Theoretical and Philosophical Psychology*, 17, 101–119.

Yang, S. & Sternberg, R. J. (1997b) Taiwanese Chinese people's conceptions of intelligence, *Intelligence*, 25, 21–36.

Bridging between orthodox western higher educational practices and an African sociocultural context

Robert Serpell

Introduction

The applicability of psychological and educational theories beyond the cultural contexts in which and for which they were originally designed has been a focus of debate in cross-cultural psychology for at least three decades. Writing from a Latin American perspective, Ardila (1982) pointed out that

> contemporary psychology shares all the characteristics of Anglo-Saxon culture: emphasis on adaptation, emphasis on function more than structure, dynamism, operationalism, evolutionism. Psychology is conceived in English, and for the most part considers problems relevant to Anglo-Saxon culture, specifically to North America. (p. 323)

But does this mean that it has no potential to illuminate behaviour and experience in other cultural contexts? In the case of Japan, Azuma (1984) identified four 'stages through which psychology apparently needed to pass', in order to establish its applicability, characterized initially by introduction by foreign experts, then translation and modelling, then indigenization, and finally integration. The third stage of 'indigenization' was an essential preliminary for psychology to 'get freed, to a certain extent, from the rigid, but otherwise unnoticed world of traditionally western concepts and logic' (Azuma, 1984, pp. 54–55). Given the international distribution of doctoral study programmes in psychology, many third world psychologists, especially in Africa, have received their advanced training abroad, and consequently face various problems in matching its orientation with the social context in which they are later expected to apply it.

In my view, the question of cultural applicability is best addressed through a dynamic perspectivist account of the relations among three different ways in which culture impacts on the form and content of theories of human behaviour and experience: the cultural context of the functioning of the subject (the person whose behaviour and experience are to be explained), the cultural background of the author of the explanation, and the cultural frame of reference of the audience to whom the explanation is addressed (Serpell, 1990). These three foci prioritize different conceptions of culture which can be evoked by the metaphors of culture as a womb, as a language or as a forum (Serpell, 1994).[1] Thus, 'in addition to its theoretical fruitfulness and its empirically predictive power, a psychological theory will always be judged by its capacity to resonate with the broader cultural preoccupations of the society of which its audience are members' (Serpell, 1990, p. 125).

Against this background, I take the view that the cultural validity of a psychological or educational theory is best conceptualized as

> a positive balance of benefits over costs for a given community at a given time engaged in a given task, where the sensitizing and heuristic power of a model outweigh the perceived narrowness of its focus and the extraneous connotations' (Serpell, 1990, p. 125).

In this publication, I advance an account of a particular curriculum construct in university education, known as the project assignment. I relate it to a body of theory that has arisen from attempts to interpret human learning and development in a variety of cultural contexts, arguing that it holds great potential as a resource for the institutional task of integrating various bodies of technical knowledge and understanding into an African society engaged in a process of planned sociocultural change.

Orthodox western higher education tends to decontextualize the learning process by extracting learners from everyday life into a detached mode of full-time reflection, with an emphasis on structured exercises and analytical review of authoritative disciplinary texts. This orthodoxy has been under critical review and progressive modification in western Europe and the USA (and in other 'western' societies such as Australia and New Zealand) for several decades. Thus it is no longer revolutionary to propose that a university curriculum should include projects that require students to engage in learning activities outside the walls of the academy, and many universities now award credit for such assignments. These changes, however, have not always been justified to the wider public on explicitly pedagogical grounds. Rather they are often presented as a way of smoothing the transition from college into industry.

The alienating hazards of a socioculturally detached, text-based curriculum are accentuated in Africa by the remoteness of the factitious exercises and formal texts of the academy from the cultural practices of everyday life. In this publication, I argue that university education in Africa should attach special importance among its methods of instruction to project assignments, for a number of complementary reasons: to afford students an opportunity to test formal theories against reality; to prepare students for the practical challenges they will face at work after graduation; and to invite students to compare and, if possible, integrate academic theories and perspectives with indigenous interpretations of experience.

The next section introduces a theoretical perspective on intellectual development, situated learning and participatory appropriation. Within that framework, I then advance a pedagogical rationale for student-based learning, together with a scoping survey of such courses at the University of Zambia (UNZA), where I am currently Vice-Chancellor. I also briefly outline a service-learning project mounted at the University of Maryland Baltimore County (UMBC), where I was previously a Professor and Director of a doctoral studies programme in Applied Developmental Psychology, in which undergraduates engaged in after-school initial literacy tutoring for second-grade children at a nearby inner-city public school. I then step back to consider more broadly the challenges of adapting the western institution of university education to the needs and aspirations of a postcolonial state in Africa. Against that background, I present a case study of a service-learning project at UNZA that engaged undergraduates in various ways with enhancing the welfare of young children in nearby, poverty-stricken neighbourhoods. The final section considers, in the light of the two case-studies, the potential benefits of such projects in terms of societal, institutional and individual student outcomes.

Theoretical background

Conceptualizing intellectual development

Two popular metaphors advanced by western theorists for the process of education are education as growth and education as a journey (Kleibard, 1975; Serpell, 1993a). According to the metaphor of education as growth, the student is a plant, the teacher is a gardener, and the curriculum is a greenhouse. The goals of education are maturity, fruition, and health. Powerful though it is, this metaphor fails to afford adequate recognition to the agency of the student. According to the metaphor of education as a journey, the student is a traveller, the teacher is a guide or companion, and the curriculum is a map or a route. The goals of education are arrival at a destination, enjoyment of the journey, and adaptation to the new world into which the journey leads.

The theoretical perspective on human development on which I will draw derives from the work of several influential theorists. I interpret their interrelationship as a progressive adaptation, incorporating and building on earlier complementary insights, rather than a parallel set of mutually incompatible, competing alternatives (Serpell, 1993b, 1999). As Piaget (1971) pointed out, from a very early age, humans reach out to grasp the world and adapt their way of grasping to the feedback they receive. Neisser (1976) noted that this idea can be melded with the perspective of James and Eleanor Gibson (1982), which emphasizes that the real world is structured in terms that afford various types of action by the human agent, and that our perception of those affordances is adaptive. Moreover, the adaptation of the developing human being to the physical environment is mediated by cultural systems of representation handed down by more experienced persons (Vygotsky, 1978; Cole, 1996). Each generation and each individual makes these systems of representation their own by adapting, expanding and transforming them, through participatory appropriation (Rogoff, 1990, 1993; Serpell, 1993c, 1998, Serpell et al., 1991, 2005).

The cultural-historical school of thought in developmental psychology traces its origins to the writings of Vygotsky (1978) in the 1930s, and has been extensively elaborated since the 1970s by Cole (1996), Scribner (1985), Wertsch (1985), Valsiner (1987) and others. According to this perspective, human development involves the internalization by each generation of children of the meaning systems that inform their elders' cultural practices. Tharp and Gallimore (1988) explained how this theoretical perspective can be applied to the design of an educational system, by specifying the various dimensions of activity settings: the participants, the nature, timing, organization and location of the tasks, and the meaning the tasks have for the participants.

Situated learning

In the late 1980s, Jean Lave began to advocate a new approach to the study of situated learning (Lave & Wenger, 1991) and development, under the rubric of legitimate peripheral participation. Reacting against some of the artificiality of the formal arrangements for learning institutionalized in the western tradition of formal schooling, these authors have advanced an account of human learning as less about the process of receiving information and more about changing forms of participation in social practices. Their elaboration of the argument is grounded in an analysis of various forms of apprenticeship, which they selected as a context in which to observe and understand human learning, that can be found in many different cultural settings around the world, and that may be less systematically biased by western culture than the institution of formal schooling.

It is not without significance that Jean Lave's formative years in academia were spent studying apprenticeship as a form of educational practice in Africa. In a much-cited paper co-authored with Patricia Greenfield, she highlighted the way in which learning can best be understood as situated in the context of a particular cultural practice (Greenfield & Lave, 1982). Scribner & Cole (1981) advanced the same argument in their book *The Psychology of Literacy*, based on a multi-faceted study of three different literacies in Liberia: in the Roman alphabet used to encode the English language taught in western-style public schools, in the Arabic alphabetic script and language of the Q'ran taught in Koranic schools, and in the indigenous Vai syllabic script taught on request by friends or neighbours in the village on an individual tutorial basis. These and other culturally situated studies have repeatedly called into question the universality of theoretical generalizations about the cognitive demands and consequences of time-honoured western cultural practices such as formal instruction and literacy.

During the second half of the twentieth century a remarkably standardized model of formal basic schooling has become institutionalized as a public service offered in countries all over the world. Serpell and Hatano (1997) contend that one of the distinctive features of this model of institutionalized public basic schooling (IPBS) is the principle of advance preparation. It is not at all clear that the rationale for this in basic education can be legitimately extended to university education, especially when we consider that increasingly the university aspires to attract into its curricula students who have already been at work for a number of years in the field for which they are now enrolling to study. Moja (2004), for instance, argues that in contemporary South Africa one of the major challenges to which higher education is expected to respond is that of addressing 'the requirements of new kinds of learners who are interested in pursuing their education in higher education', such as 'lifelong learners, mid-career training, those seeking to retool, and those acquiring skills that need to be continually updated' (p. 34). Similar changes in the learning needs of their student body have been reported by many higher education institutions in the industrialized countries of the northern hemisphere. For such students, higher education is expected to provide, not so much advance preparation for adult life as guided reflection on their prior experience, and opportunities to critique, reject or build on it for improved practices in future.

Other challenges facing the design of a socioculturally appropriate form of higher education in Africa are discussed in a later section of this publication.

Participatory appropriation

Viewing the development of learners from the perspective of their participation in cultural practices, Barbara Rogoff (1990, 1993), the present author (Serpell, 1993b) and others (Packer, 1993) have advocated for the term *appropriation* in preference to *internalization,* to capture the idea that membership of a community of practice is contingent on a sense of ownership of its cultural resources. More recently I have argued (Serpell, 2001) that this dimension of membership-ownership lies at the heart of the dilemma of enduring marginality described by Pierre Bourdieu in his influential analysis of social boundaries in the European academy (Bourdieu & Passeron, 1964). Even after mastering the technical forms and practices of the academy, according to Bourdieu, individuals whose primary socialization did not equip them with a sense of being an insider to the world of literacy remain conspicuously marginalized and alienated in the communicative nexus of the French academy.

Likewise, American city schoolchildren are more likely to master the demands of becoming literate if the intimate culture of their home endorses and promotes the theme of literacy as a source of entertainment and thus fosters children's intrinsic motivation to read, than if literacy is construed in their home culture as a difficult set of skills to be acquired through strenuous drill and practice. In the Baltimore Early Childhood Project (Serpell *et al.*, 2005) we found that the theme of literacy as a source of entertainment was relatively more prevalent in the homes of middle-class parents than in low-income, low-literacy families.

In Zambia, many university students originate from families in which literacy is relatively restricted,[2] and that rely on one or more of the indigenous languages of Zambia for expressing and sharing their practical understanding of the world. Given this background of primary socialization, I surmise that these students arrive at the University of Zambia with only a partial sense of ownership of the literate culture in which they have excelled at secondary school in the medium of instruction, which is English.[3] Their mastery of that culture is perhaps grounded less in the intrinsic motivation that arises from membership/ownership of the community of literate practices, than in a disciplined application of explicit study skills and attitudes. That explicitly studious perspective, while evidently effective for the immediate mastery they have achieved of the high school curriculum, may tend to encourage compartmentalization of the knowledge and understanding that students acquire at school, and thus insulate it from their more intuitive understanding of the world grounded in indigenous languages and beliefs. Project work has the potential to break down such isolation by engaging students' minds at both levels, the theoretical and the practical.

Student project-based learning

One strategy adopted by university curricula for bridging between social realities and the focus of the formal disciplines is the project assignment, in which a student is invited to apply aspects of his or her classroom learning to a selected topic in the real world.

As Fincher (2002) points out, one of the distinctive features of project work relative to other instructional formats of university studies is that it affords the students opportunities for situated learning: 'Students have to learn *differently* when doing project work. The (frequent) interdisciplinary nature of project work combats the artificiality of the regular educational setting. Curricula divisions often have to be abandoned. Project work is always contextualised' (p. 12).

According to Wrigley (1999), student projects as curriculum devices are distinctive in several ways. They are

- learner-centred
- inquiry-driven
- problem-focused

Moreover, they often involve learning by doing, that is, they are

- practical in character.

And in many cases they involve working in groups, and thus

- require collaboration.

Reflecting on why such projects may be of special utility to the transformational agenda of university curriculum development in Africa, I want to draw attention to their potential for

- bridging between the canons of the discipline and students' culture of origin,
- promotion of metacognitive awareness, and
- building relevance into the preparation of students for the demands of the economy in which they aspire to work after graduation.

The University of Zambia has a total of 50 departments distributed across the following 9 schools: Agricultural Sciences, Education, Humanities and Social Sciences, Law, Medicine, Mines, Natural Sciences, and Veterinary Medicine. Many of the departments offer one or more undergraduate courses that require the student to spend time in a setting outside the classroom making observations, and to report on what she or he learned in that context. The courses are typically pitched at an advanced level within the four to seven-year programme of studies leading to a Bachelor's degree, and the student must pass the course in order to graduate.

The learning opportunities that I am loosely calling student project assignments are structured in a variety of different ways across the various schools and departments, reflecting different disciplinary, professional and pedagogical traditions. In some cases, the activity in which the student is assigned to engage is called fieldwork or internship, while in other cases it is called an experiment, a survey, a moot court, action research, or service-learning.

The rationale for these courses is specified with varying degrees of explicitness in the School Handbook and/or the course syllabus. A scoping survey of a sample of these course descriptions from six of the University's nine schools[4] in 2005 revealed a mix of educational objectives including the following:

- application of theoretical concepts to the 'real world'
- integration of multi-disciplinary themes
- exposure to the demands and practices of industry

Each of these objectives can be unpackaged in a variety of different ways that have implications for assessment, and for the ultimate value the projects add to the overall curriculum.

The learning outcomes envisaged for a student engaged in application of theoretical concepts to the 'real world' include appreciation of the meaning of the theoretical concepts, of their explanatory power, of their limitations, and appreciation of the complexity of the real world. The outcomes envisaged for a student as a result of exposure to the demands of the workplace in industry include orientation towards a career in industry, detection of problematic or dysfunctional aspects of industries as currently organized, and inspiration to develop new theoretical ideas for the interpretation and/or solution of problems and challenges confronting industry.

One global dimension of the design of project courses across many different fields and disciplines is whether the relationship of the university as an institution to the host community in which the student is placed is construed as one of scientific detachment or of social engagement. In my view, at this point in the history of university education in Africa, the need to demonstrate public accountability of the institution to the wider society is of paramount importance. The systematic development of university student project placements would therefore benefit from attaching some priority to optimizing the opportunities they afford for students to participate in the advancement of human welfare.

Although a student placed in industry has important responsibilities to perform as a member of the industrial workforce, he or she is also still a student, and the design of such placements needs to acknowledge this by spelling out the learning objectives of the placement. One of these is the cultivation of a reflective attitude towards the practical tasks undertaken as a professional member of the workforce. The concept of a reflective practitioner has been influentially elaborated by Schon (1983). Engineers, doctors, lawyers and teachers all stand to benefit from the adoption of a reflective stance on their professional practices.

Many large metropolitan universities in the USA and in Europe have recognized over the past three decades a new curriculum development challenge posed by the growing cultural diversity of the society that they aspire to serve, often compounded with divisions along lines of race and social class.[5] At the University of Maryland, Baltimore County (UMBC), the service-learning project entitled 'Nurturing developmental partnerships' (NDP) was conceived among a group of graduate students under my guidance as an attempt to connect their own professional training with some of the salient social problems confronting human development in the troubled society of inner-city Baltimore. The core concept was a cascade of mentoring relationships across multiple levels of the public education system, with UMBC graduate students mentoring undergraduates, as the latter provided after-school remedial tutoring to second-graders enrolled in an adjacent inner-city public elementary school. Care Udell's (2003) evaluation of the project documented positive growth for the elementary school children on several indicators, approval by the children's class teachers, and personal growth by the college students who participated. A structured portfolio was used to link the college students' experiences to the content of a linked, taught course, to enable the students and their mentors to monitor the progress of their tutees and to record the development of their own thinking over the span of the course. Very few of these college students had grown up in the socio-economically deprived conditions of the inner city where the elementary school was located. The project evoked both compassion and a sense of transcending a cultural divide between their own more privileged family backgrounds and those of these fellow-Americans from 'across the tracks'. The intrinsic reward of delivering a service was a valuable outcome that would not have been possible with a classroom project on campus, and appeared to contribute to the growth of social responsibility in students over and above their more conventional learning experiences on campus.

Adapting the western institution of university education to the needs and aspirations of a postcolonial state in Africa

The goals of a national public university in a third world nation include not only meeting the expectations of an international community of scholarship and science, but also recognition within the national society it was established to serve. Indeed, since most of its graduates are destined to gain employment in the national economy, it is arguably even more important that its curricula and certificates be demonstrably legitimate in the eyes of the national government, business and industry than that they meet criteria established outside the national frame of reference.

Universities are not entirely new to Africa. The Islamic universities of Al-Azhar in Cairo and Sankore in Timbuktu are among the earliest institutions of formal higher education in the history of the world, and were already awarding degrees and attracting students from many different nations in the eleventh century when the University of Bologna was first established, marking the beginning of the European university tradition. Just how the scholarship of those early African universities has impacted on the intellectual fabric of African societies is currently an area of active research.[6] It is clear, however, that the influences of that tradition on most of the universities established in Africa in the twentieth century are at best remote and indirect. Just as western scholarship has only belatedly and somewhat grudgingly acknowledged the role of Arabic scholarship in mediating the preservation, continuity and reinterpretation of the classical philosophy and science generated in ancient Greece as foundations of the modern canon, so future African scholars may embark on a process of rediscovery of their debt to Islam. But I am not equipped to undertake that task and will therefore not attempt to address it in this paper.

Nurturing the spirit of inquiry[7]

The dominant intellectual tradition of universities across the world derives much of its character from the philosopher scientists of the European Enlightenment, who challenged the authority of the Christian church establishment to define truth and justice, arguing that the route to their discovery resides in systematic inquiry and egalitarian discourse. As Berlin (1956) has explained, the theme that method holds the key to certainty was first explicitly articulated by Descartes (1637) in his *Discours de la Methode*. The critical importance of egalitarian discourse has been articulated by Habermas (1984) in his analysis of the 'ideal communication situation', and his subsequent elaboration of the notion that the adequacy of an utterance depends on criteria, mutually agreed among the participants in discourse, for its acceptance as relevant, sincere, and matching with objective reality.

These fundamental principles have served humanity well, opening up new ways of conceptualizing the universe of which we are a part, and of manipulating it for the benefit of humans, as well as inspiring the foundation of governance by consent. But their embeddedness in western culture has been repeatedly challenged by intellectuals who found themselves, by virtue of accident of birth, outside the fold of the new establishment and argued that their exclusion was inherently contrary to the logic of the Enlightenment perspective.

Notable examples are Frederick Douglass (1817–1895), Elisabeth Garrett Anderson (1836–1917), and Mahatma Gandhi (1869–1948).[8] These and other landmark challenges to the contradictions and hypocrisy of cultural hegemony have informed a radical transformation of the world in which we live relative to the conditions of the mid-nineteenth century, with the almost universal abolition of slavery, the progressive emancipation of women, and the decolonization of third world nations. In Zambia, a leading exponent of the critique of western hegemony was Kenneth Kaunda, the founding President of the Republic of Zambia in 1964, who wrote, reflecting on the effectiveness of his largely peaceful, campaign for Zambia's political independence from colonial Britain: 'the inability of those in power to still the voices of their own consciences is the great force leading to change' (Obscrver, July 1965, cited in Jenkins, 1996–2002).

Public accountability

Kaunda's United National Independence Party made the establishment of the University of Zambia (UNZA) one of the cornerstones of its programmatic vision for the future of the independent nation. Belief in the importance of a national university for the fulfilment of the new nation's development agenda rests on the following premises that have been widely shared among African intellectuals over the ensuing four decades:

* governance by consent demands an informed citizenry
* increased knowledge and technology creation are the key to economic progress
* local universities are cost effective ways of generating relevant knowledge and technology and of generating an informed citizenry.

The motto of UNZA is 'service and excellence', where service refers to service of society (often equated with national development, but also sometimes more broadly as humankind), and excellence refers to standards of performance across a wide range of domains by graduating students, lecturers and researchers.

Another widespread theme in the rhetoric of higher education policies in Africa and elsewhere around the world is the goal of increasing equity of access, which can also be phrased as widening inclusion. When we talk about inclusiveness as a dimension of the public accountability of higher education institutions, it is important to recognize that inclusiveness involves more than mere accessibility: it also implies connecting the curriculum with the needs and aspirations of various constituencies of the wider society. How can the University demonstrate to those constituencies that the experience of higher education adds value to the development of the youth they commit to the institution's care for the nurturance of their personal and professional development? To do so requires two kinds of assurance: of quality, and of relevance.

We often hear that desirable outcomes of university studies are mastery of various fields of knowledge, acquisition of technical skills, and relevance of those skills and knowledge to existing employment opportunities. To that important list I would add the following: entrepreneurial motivation and know-how; the spirit of inquiry; and commitment to the public interest.[9]

An inspiring case study of 'quality assurance through curriculum design' within the framework of the strategic plan of one African university has been presented by Msolla *et al.*, (2005) of Sokoine Agricultural University in Tanzania:

> (i) The University strives to provide solutions that will improve the nation's quality of food supply and safety ...

> (ii) to train students with a view of acquiring relevant knowledge and skills and entrepreneurship but most importantly to become life-long learners, productive citizens and leaders of society,

> (iii) basic and applied research to be undertaken to develop new knowledge to meet contemporary and emerging needs of society ...

> (iv) transfer of technological innovations to meet expressed and emerging needs,

> (v)–(vii) various institutional needs in order to address goals (i)–(iv), and

> (viii) the University strives to remain dynamic in keeping with the socio-economic changes in the country, in order to alleviate/eradicate poverty for its people. (op. cit., pp. 76–77)

In order to address these goals, Sokoine's development of a responsive curriculum was guided by five important criteria:

> It must deal with pragmatic needs of mid-career agricultural extension staff (e.g., acquisition of knowledge and skills in communication, problem-solving, critical thinking and how to learn with others)

> It must be closely related to the students' work environment

> It must provide a dynamic interplay between theoretical and practical components

> It must expose participants to issues of food security, the role of women in agriculture and the relationship between population and food production

> It must enable students to develop positive attitudes and professional ethics which ensure good leadership. (op. cit., p. 79)

The claim by universities to offer a uniquely valuable contribution to the development of human knowledge rests on the claim that the knowledge they generate 'has been sustained through rigorous critical examination, according to the rules, procedures and methods of a community governed by critical and self-corrective methods'(Anderson, 1993, p. 63). Yet, to the extent that certain sociocultural groups have been systematically excluded from the academy over the course of history, the legitimacy or validity of that community's practices requires some demonstration. An especially poignant context for that agenda is that of post-apartheid South Africa, which gave rise to a set of analytical case studies of curriculum responsiveness in higher education, published by the South African Vice-Chancellors' Association

(SAUVCA)[10] in 2004. Moll (2004) distinguishes four strands of curriculum responsiveness: economic, cultural, disciplinary and learning needs. While analytically separable, he contends that these different dimensions of responsiveness must all be addressed by universities in contemporary South African Society.

Slominsky & Shalem (2004), in the same volume, articulate a set of principles that they 'hope … will seem obvious to experienced academics', (p. 99) within a 'community of practice' perspective similar to that of Lave and Wenger (1991). They identify as four 'strands of activity constitutive of academic practice': distantiation, appropriation, research and articulation, and argue that 'underprepared' students require special assistance to master these four strands. They place special emphasis on the demands of distantiation, which they construe as a process of making the familiar strange (a phrase also used by Spiro (1990) in a seminal essay on cultural psychology).

Novices to the academy, Slominsky & Shalem (2004) argue, need to 'develop a disciplinary or principled gaze' which entails 'mastering key disciplinary concepts', and recognizing that 'concepts are contested and subject to revision or supercession' (p. 91). Yet the feedback that a student requires in order to engage successfully with those demands of the discipline may be especially difficult to accept by the students who need it most. In post-apartheid South Africa, many students are entering university from high schools that offered them little or no preparation for the academy in terms of socialization into the practices of rational argument, engagement with established knowledge, in order to refute or extend it, justification of claims, proof or defence of a position, let alone principled and systematic investigation. Such underprepared students enrolling in a humanities or social science course at University

> …may be told 'we don't want you to give us back what the book says, we want you to think', or 'there is no right answer', or 'the purpose of theory is to understand the world in which we live'. This would open up apparent space for students to insert their life world, speak from their experience, address other personal subjects, play with knowledge and ideas etc. In other words, students may 'read' explicit messages being transmitted by lecturers about the 'openness' of knowledge as giving licence to personalize and break the boundaries. For these reasons, students may feel empowered by the apparent freedom within the academy to insert their own voices, interests and local realities.

> Yet … if students are not sufficiently initiated into disciplinary knowledge and text-based realities (Wertsch, 1991) they may never become full participants in academic practice—and thus their voices, experiences and knowledge may never be able to resonate or be projected beyond the 'present and particular' into other spaces and social realities… If under-prepared students are not afforded a principled gaze and ways of prising apart the form and content of their experiences, their newfound freedom to insert their own voices may ultimately prove as disempowering as their schooling'. (p. 90)

These rather sobering thoughts led Slominsky and her colleagues to design structured remedial approaches to the instruction of under-prepared university students truly to appropriate the intellectual tools of the academy. Another, complementary way of ensuring that the endogenous African experiences and knowledge that such students bring to the academy are validated within it may be to design project assignments in which that background features as an asset rather than a hindrance to performance.

'Africanization'

Moll (2004) points out that the contested question of Africanization of the higher education curriculum is both narrower and broader than the question of cultural responsiveness of the curriculum. It is narrower in the sense that African culture is both variegated and dynamic and is best understood within the context of a more general theory of culture; and it is broader in the sense that for the curriculum of a university to be responsive to the demands of its African setting attention should be paid not only to cultural parameters, but also to physical-geographical, socio-economic and political dimensions of the continent.[11]

Within the narrower conception, some theorists have argued for the inclusion of indigenous African cultural perspectives, concepts and practices among the guiding criteria for curriculum development. Among the various conceptions of education that inform the thinking and expectations of the general public in Zambia we may distinguish some that are more ingrained in the discourse and practices of the rural population than in the policies and practices of formal education promulgated by the national government. Three of these stand out for me: contextualized learning, preparation for social responsibility, and social priming.

Contextualized instruction

Fortes (1938) conducted a classic investigation of traditional modes of education in the rural community of the Tallensi of northern Ghana in the 1930s, at a time when the territory was under British colonial rule as the Gold Coast. He described how education proceeded quite seamlessly over the course of a young person's life. Most learning took place in 'real situations' which require 'organic modes of response', as contrasted with western instructional practices that often involve the learner participating in 'factitious activities' that demand 'atomic modes of response' (p. 28). As a result, traditional Tale education proceeds not so much by an accumulation of discrete elements, but rather through a holistic, evolutionary process: the desired behavioural outcomes 'are present as schemas from the beginning', and the student 'acquires a well-defined interest associated with a postural diagram of the total pattern ... as it were a contour map, extremely crude but comprehending the essential elements and relations of the full pattern ... which evolves from the embryonic form' (pp. 42–43).

Preparation for social responsibility

Between 1973 and 1987, I conducted, in collaboration with a large team of colleagues and informants, a longitudinal study of the life-journeys of a cohort of young people born into a rural Chewa community in Zambia's Eastern Province. Reflecting on our findings, I concluded that one of the salient features of the indigenous Chewa perspective on child development and socialization was a preoccupation with the cultivation of social responsibility. Moreover, this preoccupation, reflected in the vocabulary used by Chewa adults to assess the dispositions of children they know, finds 'echoes ... in the vocabulary of evaluative discourse about intellectual function-ing and development in several other African cultures' (Serpell, 1993a, p. 38). One of the terms of praise for a child in the domain of intelligence in the Chewa language is *ku-tumikila*. A person who is *wo-tumikila* is one who can be entrusted with respon-sibility. The root of the term is *–tuma*, meaning to send, and its connotations derive from the common practice of sending a young person to carry out an errand.

Social priming

The practice of assigning errands to children is very widespread across African societies and the way in which the performance of such errands is monitored by adults suggests that their primary purpose is not so much exploitative as pedagogical (Ogunnaike & Houser, 2002). An errand affords an opportunity for the person sent on it to prove herself capable of assuming responsibility. This can be construed as an instance of the more general phenomenon which the Cameroonian psychologist, Bame Nsamenang (1992) has termed 'social priming'. In his 'third world perspective' on 'Human development in cultural context', Nsamenang proposes a West African social ontogeny, positing a set of developmental stages defined in social rather than biological terms. One of the elements of his account explains the practice of placing pre-adolescent children in charge of other younger children as a kind of social priming, analogous to the priming of a pump.

These three elements of indigenous African educational orientation are all fully compatible with the theoretical account by Lave & Wenger (1991) of situated learning.

The Service Learning Project at UNZA: a curriculum innovation with liberating and empowering potential

The ideology of egalitarian discourse that informs the university tradition of scien-tific inquiry described above often suggests to university students that they should challenge all forms of authority in order to address the intellectual agenda before them. The exuberance that flows from the discovery that hypothetico-deductive reasoning opens the doors to limitless possibilities (Piaget, 1971) encourages many students, in the developmental period of late adolescence, to critique existing social practices in ways more fundamental than many adults in the world of work are willing or able to endorse. When such criticisms are expressed ostentatiously outside the walls of the institution, the university becomes at risk for a public image of irresponsibility, especially if the focus of the criticism is on their own material needs and if it is expressed in the form of violent protest (Mwanalushi, 2006). Yet the same open-ended quality of thought that leads university students to contemplate radical ideas also has the potential to inform courageous compassionate social action on behalf of others in need. African universities, like many metropolitan universities in the USA, are often situated in close proximity to economically deprived neighbourhoods where such needs are in abundant evidence. Moreover, the extremes of poverty in many African societies drive some children to live literally on the street. Confronting the challenge posed by such extremes of social deprivation was the focus of a service-learning programme initiated at the University of Zambia in 2005.

The Service-Learning programme was initiated by Professor Lewis Aptekar of San Jose State University in California, and was co-coordinated through the University of Zambia Psychology Department by two lecturers, Ms. Gertrude Kasuba Mwape and Mr. Aidan Mambwe. Aptekar and his colleagues (1997, 1999) have written extensively about street children in several African countries and he had been attached to the UNZA Psychology Department in 2001 to organize a short course on counselling. In its first iteration in July–August 2005, the project was aimed at building a partnership between the two universities, to enhance cross-cultural awareness between the two groups of students, and to carry out joint service-learning projects in three low-income communities of Zambia's capital, Lusaka-Kalingalinga, Mandebvu and Chainda. The programme involved 30 UNZA undergraduate students of psychology and 15 San Jose State University graduate students of counsellor education.

In their summary of the achievements of the project, a leadership group that emerged from the Zambian student participants wrote as follows:

> In Kalingalinga, students worked at three sites.
>
> At Kalingalinga Middle Basic School, the five students based there managed to put back in school five street children (3 girls and 2 boys) at the end of the project. Additionally, the students also gave motivational talks and education counseling to the pupils at the said school as it was time for their mock exams.
>
> At Camal Institute of Learning, the five students based there in collaboration with those at Kalingalinga Basic School, helped in teaching the pupils at this school and offering them free educational counseling. Counseling of the terminally ill was also done in the community.
>
> At Chifundo High school which is a private school, the five students who worked there taught, counseled and managed to sponsor two pupils in High School.
>
> The fifteen member group in Mandebvu tried out counseling sessions in the school for children affected by the HIV/AIDS pandemic, taught at a community school called Mandebvu Project Centre in helping to meet the education needs of the children, and gave motivational talks to the pupils. UNZA and SJSU students put their money together bought paint, brushes and painted as well as decorated the grade one classroom which was in a deplorable condition. Additionally, the students bought more than 500 exercise books, crayons, pens and pencils which were given to all the pupils while the text books were given to the teachers. The students counseled the terminally-ill patients in the community and in the nearby Marapodi compound; they worked with a home-based care life support group for people living with HIV/AIDS. The group made material contributions to the communities too.

In Chainda, the fifteen member group concentrated on teaching the children and giving them psychosocial counseling in order to fight stigmatization which appeared to be prevailing among the children leading some of the children to being isolated and lonely'. (Service-Learning Club, 2006).

Half of the UNZA students were enrolled in a fourth year course on counselling, while the other half were enrolled in a second-year course on child development. In the latter course, students were required to write joint reports in teams of two on their experience. After these reports had been assessed by their lecturer, Ms Mwape, as a basis for part of their course grade, copies were made available to me for some qualitative content analysis, which I present below.

Social problems identified

The students identified a wide range of social problems in the course of their project visits to these communities: many of them related to extreme poverty and disease. They visited a number of homes and interviewed parents living with HIV/AIDS about the challenges they face. They also conducted school surveys of the number of pupils who were either single or double orphans, revealing a very high prevalence of orphanhood among the student population of the schools to which they were assigned for the project.

Types of social intervention

Various types of social intervention were initiated or proposed by students in the context of the service-learning project:

(i) Advocacy for changes in behaviour by local community agents
- Encouraging husbands to allow their wives to enrol in the women's centre to learn productive skills as a source of additional family income (Group 2, p. 6)
- Encouraging teachers to individualize instruction (Group1, p. 12), or to avoid favouritism in distribution of food to children at school (Group 2, p. 5)
- Encouraging school administrators to waive fees for enrolment of vulnerable children, and service agency personnel to help women's centre graduates in sewing to market their produce.

(ii) Material contributions to children's welfare
- Paying for medical bills and opening schemes
- Paying for school enrolment (uniforms, shoes)
- Donating school supplies (crayons, books)
- Giving out sweets

The individual gestures made in this vein were evidently sincerely benevolent in intention, but seem to have generated considerable tensions among the project participants, throwing into relief the disparities in wealth between the two groups of students and their societies of origin. Many of the UNZA student reports advocated setting aside a component of project funds to deal with such matters.

Others suggested that a more systemic approach was preferable to acts of individual charity. For instance, one group reported that they asked a family to draw up a budget for running a small market-stall and then collectively provided an injection of capital to get the business started; while another group reported that they drew the attention of the leader of a local service centre teaching women productive skills to the constraint reported by graduates of the centre's programme that they lacked an outlet for marketing their products, and prompted her to create such an outlet for them at a city shopping centre.

Another group drew attention in their report to local strategic responses to the poverty of some families, in the form of accepting contributions in kind rather than cash towards the needs of the school as a form of payment for their child's enrolment.

(iii)Follow-up service activities. One group who had worked in Kalingalinga, a neighbourhood immediately adjacent to the University campus, proposed to monitor school attendance by children whose inclusion and exemption from fees they had advocated, by making site visits every three weeks.

Connecting the field experience with the content of the linked taught course

Despite the fact that it was acknowledged at a general rhetorical level by most of the reports, this aspect of the project did not receive much analytical attention in the reports and appears to be an aspect of the curriculum deserving further attention.

One report included a heading 'How do all these fit into the work we did in PS 241?'. But the only scientific concepts cited under that heading were: 'family social-ization, child abuse, play peer friends', and what the authors state 'helped' them was the observation that (a) there were many orphans, and (b) child care by elder siblings was widespread: 'most children are given babies to look after even when they do not have that experience, in other words we can say that babies keep their fellow babies'. This group went on to extrapolate from the testimony of one 11-year-old girl that she had been abused that 'most of these children are abused sexually by people they work for'.

Other links cited included:

- Operant conditioning/behaviour modification, in relation to techniques employed during the project
- Effects of malnutrition on children's development
- Peer-group stigmatization of children affected by HIV/AIDS, versus lack of stigma attributed to good teacher management

Many of the reports commented on what they perceived as inadequate child care and supervision. These comments were often expressed in somewhat absolutist and unreflective terms. Equally uncompromising comments were made in several reports about what the students perceived as inadequate hygiene, e.g., 'porridge ... was being served to children in dirty cups and plates and the children used their fingers when feeding which was very unhygienic'. Other critical observations focused on over-crowded service facilities, inadequately equipped service facilities (e.g., 'lack of books and pencils' at one Community School), on a dependency orientation manifested by some of the community members, and on competition rather than cooperation among different community schools in the same neighbourhood.

All of these observations could have served as productive foci for seminar discussions to open the students' reflective awareness of the culturally relative nature of normative judgements about child socialization practices (Aptekar & Ciano, 1999). For instance, the widespread Zambian traditional socialization practice of delegation by parents of the daily care and supervision of young children to their elder siblings, including pre-adolescent girls and, to a lesser extent, boys, has been discussed by Serpell and Mwape (1998/99) as informed by its own coherent and socially productive logic. Students could also have benefited from exposure to the analysis by Scheper-Hughes (1990) of child care practices that shocked her in a Brazilian poverty-stricken community as constituting adaptive responses to adversity.

Criticisms of the programme

Almost every report cited as a problem the lack of clear goals for the students to address on site, for example, '...each day in the first days we experienced as if we do not know what we are supposed to do'. Another wrote:

> While on the site, it was found that group cohesiveness was weak as different students had different expectations and were doing different courses. As such, students thus directed their services to issues where they would apply their learnt knowledge as well as where they could offer possible assistance and at the same time learn something about that community.

Several reports also focused on the lack of an UNZA supervisor, and many recommended that in future iterations of the programme, a lecturer from UNZA should be part of the supervising team.

Commitment to follow-up action

Despite these various limitations, the overall evaluation of the experience was overwhelmingly positive, as testified in a report-back session that I attended with them and their lecturers in late 2005. In fact, some of the second-year students were so inspired and determined not to lose the motivational momentum that it had generated among them, that they resolved to form a service-learning club, stating their mission as follows:

> As students, and citizens of Zambia pursuing productive careers, we have a responsibility to make our own unique contributions to programmes of productive social change. We

believe that with our knowledge and skills, we can help build a better Zambia that is pro-development. Our desire is to deliver self-sustainable programmes that empower vulnerable citizens of our country Zambia and fully utilize knowledge in constructive community programmes.

In the second iteration, a number of changes were introduced, some arising from reflection on difficulties experienced in the initial project and others from pragmatic, logistical considerations. Among the salient objectives defined by the students for the project in 2006 were the following:

To create and provide a platform for the University students to practice and gain experience in their careers. …

To disseminate information to teachers, parents and the children about children's rights based on article 12 and 29 of the United Nations Charter.

This project is aimed at ensuring that children's rights are not infringed upon so that they grow up in an environment that is conducive for full human development. Information about article 12 and 29 on children's rights will be disseminated to teachers through workshops and group discussions that will be held at the respective schools in Kalingalinga and Ng'ombe communities. Workshops will also be held for those parents with school going children. Brochures too, will be used to reach out to the community.

To reach out to the parents and non-school going children who may not have attended the workshops, specially prepared drama group performances will be used in the streets and market places. Topics on children's rights will also be the centre of discussions on community-radios and other media to reach those who could not have been reached otherwise.

The method to be used in this project will mainly consist of interactive processes. (Service-Learning Club, 2006)

Evaluating the outcomes of student project assignments

Institutional and societal outcomes

The benefits of a well-designed and executed university student project may extend well beyond those experienced by individual students, to include:

- public appraisal of universities as engaged and valuable resources for the wider society, and
- inter-institutional linkages that afford
    - mutual complementary enrichment of the institutions, and
    - economies of scale for providing students with productive learning experiences

Thus the Principal of the inner-city Elementary School in Baltimore that hosted UMBC's NDP project, and the representatives of the various community service agencies that hosted UNZA's service-learning project testified on a number of public occasions that they were impressed by the service orientation of the projects. Moreover they welcomed the focused contribution of the university students to the fulfilment of the host institution's own agenda. Consistently, they expressed the hope that these projects would continue and build on their beginnings to establish an enduring inter-institutional partnership between their institutions and the university.

Parents interviewed in the host communities in both countries expressed respect and appreciation for the commitment displayed by the students, and optimism about the contribution they were already making and would be able to make in the future to the well-being of disadvantaged sections of society. Such public recognition serves as an important counterweight to the opprobrium generated in the media by periodic outbursts of riotous behaviour and destructive violence by some students that have marked the social history of the University of Zambia and other universities on the African continent. If the public are to believe in the positive value added to society by the existence of a university, they need to see and understand examples of university student behaviour that manifests pro-social motivation and social responsibility.

In a different area of educational planning ideology, industrial placements feature as opportunities for students to gain a first-hand sense of the niche they will be expected to fill on entry into the formal labour force of the economy as graduate professionals. This may be especially valuable for graduands in new fields of specialization. Representatives of the first cohort of graduands in Food Science and Technology from UNZA's School of Agricultural Sciences testified to me in 2004 that their experience on industrial attachment provided important confirmation for them that they had something of value to add to the practices of the industry that hosted their attachment. The students gained confidence from that confirmation, and the subsequent employment of several of the graduates by those same institutions that hosted their attachments while training shows that the industries in question indeed recognized the value that university graduates could add to their operations.

Fincher *et al.* (2004) point out that industrial placements can raise significant problems for students. If there is insufficient liaison between the host institution and the university teaching staff, students may 'struggle with defining project goals and setting appropriate boundaries for their ... assignment', and the host institution may confront them with

> the necessity to adapt and to produce results quickly, regardless of their preferred learning style or the need to adjust to the organizational culture. The ... need to become familiar with the onsite processes and standards of the workplace can combine to make the experience stressful for students. (p. 8)

A good example of proactive design to minimize such problems is provided by the Auckland University of Technology (AUT) in New Zealand, where the Bachelor of Business degree programme includes a period of full immersion of the student in an off-campus business enterprise:

> Students are required to obtain their own placement in line with clearly specified criteria...At the beginning of the placement a learning contract is completed in which the student documents their work assignment, its outputs, and the learning outcomes to be achieved. This contract is signed by all three parties—student, workplace supervisor, and academic supervisor. (p. 6)

A similar arrangement was introduced at UMBC in the 1990s to regulate practicum placements for graduate students in Applied Developmental Psychology. Our experience, like that of AUT was that these contracts sometimes required renegotiation to ensure that the reciprocal interests of the university and the host organization were protected. But, overall the benefits seemed to outweigh the hazards, with students often testifying that the learning experiences afforded by these flexibly structured placements were among the most valuable elements of their programme of studies.

A certain amount of tension between the demands of the academy and those of industry is to be expected in these settings. Working to address that tension is justifiable, not only for the mutual adaptation of graduands and their potential employers, but also for operationalizing the relevance of higher education to the demands of the national economy.

Student outcomes

Evaluation of student performance in such projects faces a tension between the rigorous application of methodological principles and the generation of valid interpretations of local phenomena. One reason for this tension is that the phenomena studied in projects often lie beyond the cutting edge of the formal discipline's research endeavours, so that there is little of direct relevance to the project in the published literature. Another is that much of the student's work on a project is relatively remote from the direct observation of the academic supervisor, let alone supervision. Thus a student reporting on the experience of project work faces the challenge of communicating what he or she perceives as important lessons to be learned from the project to an audience of evaluators who are sceptical on at least two grounds:

- is the project truly relevant to the curriculum goals of the course or degree programme in which the student is enrolled ?
- has the student successfully identified the key variables requiring analysis, and applied the most relevant aspects of the academic discipline to those variables in an appropriate manner ?

Academic staff who are willing to approach these questions with an open mind stand to benefit not only by confirming the usefulness of their instructional activities to their students, but also by opening productive avenues of applied research in the wider society, and, at best, by discovering limitations in their own disciplinary training and in the theories and methods that they bring to the process of curriculum design.[12]

In many cases, peer support is built into the design of projects undertaken off campus, and this generates its own secondary challenges. On the one hand, many students welcome the opportunity to exchange ideas with their peers and engage in mutual assistance on well-defined tasks. Peer evaluation latches onto a different, and perhaps deeper dimension of personal identity than those mobilized by the conventional top-down evaluation of students by lecturers. UNZA students engaged in the ZAWECA (2005) project of peer education in respect of the challenges of HIV/ AIDS, and students enrolled in the Service Learning Club (2006) have testified to me that the opportunity afforded by those activities to work collaboratively with peers is profoundly gratifying and enriching. Indeed, informal oral testimony from many of my university-educated, adult Zambian friends and colleagues suggests that peer-group friendships formed during their years together at campus and/or in high school often generate enduring bonds of loyalty that sustain them in adult decision-making in later professional life.

On the other hand, the culture of the academy places such a heavy emphasis on individual accountability and competitive rating of performance outcomes that the suggestion that a group should collaborate in the production of a report for the evaluation of their learning in a project sometimes encounters student resistance. One way of channelling the competitive spirit into collaboration is to divide a class into groups that compete with each other as teams. Fincher (2002) reports on the problem of allotting shared credit for the product of group collaboration, noting that

> students and staff alike are reluctant to reward group members who do not contribute (although some groups are perfectly happy to 'carry' a hitch-hiker). In either case, it is impossible for staff to know precisely how much work each team member did: only the students involved know this (p. 29).

The solution, Fincher argues is to 'find a mechanism which devolves some control over the performance of group members to the groups themselves' (p. 32).[13] Two dimensions of the organization of project work at UNZA in psychology were borrowed from the professional practices of academia: conference presentations, and research reports. To some extent this may represent an attempt by staff to treat students as apprentices for the profession of scholarship. But they also seem to be well-suited to an important pedagogical aspect of project work: the motivation to earn the respect of one's peers. Universities in Anglophone Africa have a tradition of inviting faculty of other Universities to serve as External Examiners with a mandate to assist in the moderation of undergraduate examination results. When serving in this capacity at the Psychology Departments of the University of Lagos, Nigeria (1974–1976), the University of Malawi (1985–1987), and the University of Zimbabwe (1990–1992), I became aware of the high level of importance attached by students and staff to project work. Occasionally, I was accorded the opportunity to interview a sample of graduating students at those institutions, and fell into the habit of asking them to tell me which of the courses they had taken they regarded as having been most beneficial to their education. Consistently, students testified that the project course was the one in which they learned most across their entire period of full-time study.

Fincher (2002) too noted that student motivation is exceptionally high in project work, often leading to students investing a level of effort in their project that is disproportionate to the amount of credit that the grade carries in the overall assessment of their degree. At the University of Zambia, this phenomenon was reported at a meeting of the Senate Examinations Committee in 2005, when the School of Medicine was challenged to explain why the grade distribution for a project-based course in Community-Based Education was skewed relative to the grade distribution for other courses taken by the same cohort of students. Within the School, it is apparently common knowledge that most students make an exceptional commitment to their projects and generate reports of consistently high quality.

One way of understanding why this happens is that students experience a greater sense of personal agency in project work and thus appropriate the deeper value of the material than is common in taught courses. Indeed, students often express in their project reports a sense of having contributed to the growth of knowledge, sometimes reflected in a rather grandiose style of writing. The quality of learning outcomes from project work is often manifested in conference presentations, which are typically ephemeral. However, in this era of poster presentations and power-point handouts, some of the substance can be captured in a more enduring form and archived as a resource for future generations of students. In some cases departmental libraries also maintain a collection of bound project reports for student reference. A significant limitation of such documents is their relatively static representation of a learning process that is dynamic. The data reported at the end of a student project may be less informative about what was learned than the various changes in the student's thinking generated over the course of its implementation. Portfolios, as explained by Gardner (1991) and Waters (n.d.) are an attractive format for documenting such changes, and can be structured by both academic staff and students in creative ways to address a wide variety of educational objectives.

The concept of student project work is not new to the undergraduate curriculum structure of African universities. But in the current climate of economic stringency at UNZA, when budgets are being squeezed, it has become somewhat at risk for elimination or at best marginalization, on the grounds that it is an 'optional extra' that is relatively expensive to sponsor, by comparison with classroom activities. My argument here is that, far from being a good candidate for streamlining out of the curriculum, the project is a critically important element of good quality higher education, especially in Africa. I hope that the various reasons I have advanced for believing this to be so will serve in some measure as arguments against its abolition from the list of essential elements of higher education that must be sponsored financially.

Conclusions

Students embark on the journey of higher education with a view to adaptation to a future world of which their teachers have only partial knowledge and understanding. University curricula should therefore afford opportunities for students to test existing theories against reality, and to prepare for practical challenges in the world of work. The university tradition of scholarship centres on the power of systematic inquiry to enable the discovery of truth and justice. Universities should therefore cultivate in their students the spirit of inquiry and the egalitarian mode of discourse that ensures its validation. African universities have inherited from the west a number of institutuionalized arrangements for learning that are imperfectly designed for promoting genuine appropriation by students of the literacy, science and technology that will empower them to transform the world and pioneer social progress. Project assignments that require students to engage with the world outside the walls of the campus are conducive to situated learning and afford students opportunities to compare and integrate academic theories with indigenous interpretations of experience. They are thus both pedagogically and socioculturally essential elements of a curriculum responsive to the demands of a rapidly changing African society committed to progressive social change.

Notes

1. As Bruner (1986, p. 48) has observed, although the role of metaphors is often acknowledged as a part of theoretical model-making, there is a tendency to treat them as 'crutches to get us up the abstract mountain', to be later discarded 'in favour of a formal, consistent theory', and 'made not part of science but part of the history of science'. Yet, in many ways we 'live by' the metaphors that inform our conception of the world (Lakoff & Johnson, 1980). Moreover, the semantic device of metaphor is essential to any kind of innovative communication (Barfield, 1947).
2. The concept of restricted literacy has been debated (Goody, 1977; Street, 1984). My use of the expression in this context refers, not to different levels of intellectual sophistication, but rather to different levels of complexity of the repertoire of activities across which literacy is applied as a tool of thought. In many Zambian families, literacy is used almost exclusively for religious and commercial purposes (cf. Wells, 1990, on different modes of engagement with texts).
3. Luangala (2004) takes this argument a step further, arguing that Zambian society lacks 'a reading culture', and that the promotion of such a culture is an appropriate part of the national agenda of acquiring new modes of thinking as an adaptive response to the evolving global culture. I find his interpretation of various contemporary cultural phenomena in our society insightful about the prevailing character of adult literacy. But I do not agree with him that the restricted uses of literacy that prevail in contemporary Zambian society show that the culture of Zambian society is under-developed with respect to self-regulation, nor that Zambians are a 'primitive' species of humans. I have argued elsewhere, in response to Scribner's (1985) analysis of Vygotsky's 'uses of history', that it is inappropriate to portray the processes of change over time in biological evolution as homologous with those involved in social history (Serpell, 1995).
4. I am grateful to the following colleagues for their contributions to this survey: Mr Chitundu Kasase, Acting Head, Department of Food Science and Technology, School of Agricultural Sciences; Dr C. K .Wamukwamba, Dean, School of Engineering; Dr Musonda Lemba, Senior Lecturer, Department of Social Development Studies, School of Humanities and Social Sciences; Dr G. Silwamba, Department of Community Medicine, School of Medicine; Dr S. Kambani, Dean, School of Mines; Dr Mulenga, Head of Department of Geography, School of Natural Sciences.
5. Giddens (1999) argues that in the contemporary era of globalization, multiple forces 'are creating something that has never existed before, a global cosmopolitan society. We are the first generation to live in this society, whose contours we can as yet only dimly see. It is shaking up our existing ways of life, no matter where we happen to be. This is not—at least at the moment—a global order driven by collective human will. Instead, it is emerging in an anarchic, haphazard, fashion, carried along by a mixture of economic, technological and cultural imperatives. It is not settled or secure, but fraught with anxieties, as well as scarred by deep divisions. Many of us feel in the grip of forces over which we have no control. Can we re-impose our will upon them? I believe we can. The powerlessness we experience is not a sign of personal failings, but reflects the incapacities of our institutions. We need to reconstruct those we have, or create new ones, in ways appropriate to the global age'. The university is clearly one candidate institution for such adaptive reconstruction. Giddens (1999) also cites the insightful observation of

the American sociologist Daniel Bell that, in this era of globalization, the nation state becomes too small to solve the big problems, but also too large to solve the small ones.

6. See, for instance, the work of the Institute for the Study of Islamic Thought in Africa, located at the Programme of African Studies, Northwestern University, inaugurated in January 2001 (http://www.isita.org).

7. This account of the origins of contemporary university education draws on my address to the 34th Graduation Ceremony of the University of Zambia in June 2004.

8. Douglass was born into slavery in Maryland, USA, largely self-educated under adverse conditions, an ardent believer in the enlightening power of literacy, and a leading figure in the Abolitionist movement, eventually rising to be appointed the first person of African descent to serve as US Ambassador, and in old age an activist on behalf of women's emancipation. Anderson was born into the family of a professional Englishman, and inspired by her father's work to enter the medical profession. With the (initially reluctant) support of her father, she worked her way around the barriers against women erected by the medical guild in Britain to win eventual accreditation as a medical practitioner, and went on to become a pioneer of women's admission to the medical profession. Gandhi was born into a high caste family in India and sent to Britain to receive training as a barrister in the London Inns of Law. Graduating with distinction, he went to South Africa where he encountered crass racial discrimination, and launched some early protests against institutionalized racism. Moving back to his home country in his thirties, he embarked on a forty-year campaign against British imperialism that eventuated in the collapse of the Raj in 1948. The expulsion of the British from India inspired the struggle for decolonization in Africa in the 1950s and 1960s.

9. This checklist was presented and somewhat elaborated in my address to the 36th Graduation Ceremony of the University of Zambia in June 2006 (Serpell, 2006).

10. SAUVCA was renamed HESA (the Higher Education Association of South Africa) in 2005.

11. I have discussed elsewhere several different ways in which the cultural-political agenda of affirmative Afrocentrism can be applied in the field of developmental psychology (Serpell, 1992).

12. The tension between academic rigour and local relevance is sometimes expressed in the form of advocacy by academic staff for greater formalization. But in my view this is a hazardous direction in which to move the curriculum. In the Extension Services courses offered at UNZA's provincial centres I have observed a related danger of lecturers bowing to pressure from their student clientele to introduce a greater element of professionalism into the courses they offer. This pressure is driven by credentialism rather than by the deeper agenda of extension education.

    A similar debate is ongoing in Zambia about how the Clinical Officer training relates to career progression in the health services and to the accessibility of quality health care to the widely dispersed rural population. Recently, the UNZA School of Medicine has endorsed the launching of a Licentiate degree at the Health Sciences College, which stands as an intermediary qualification between that of the Clinical Officer Diploma and the full medical degree, MB ChB, offered by the University.

    Prof. Dickson Mwansa has problematized the same issue in the context of adult literacy and Adult Education programmes in Zambia. The original rationale for such programmes was to broaden access to education beyond the narrowing staircase model of provision within the mainstream of the public school system (Serpell, 1993a), and beyond the first two decades of the lifespan, and to empower adults who missed out on that provision in their earlier years by offering them opportunities to achieve functional literacy and access to those aspects of humanity's cultural heritage that are stored in written texts. By offering such courses to older students without formal educational credentials, such programmes have the potential to counteract the socially extractive tendencies of the elitist narrowing staircase model. But if excessive emphasis is placed on formal certification, the courses are liable to be co-opted as back-door entry routes to the extractive and elitist model they were designed to counteract.

13. Fincher (2002) describes as follows an ingenious management tool for students on a cooperative project assignment to share responsibility for early detection of freeloading and formative guidance to bring deviants back into fuller participation:

'Red Card/Yellow Card *(aka 'La Coupe du Monde 1998')*
Bundle body

- *This bundle* gives students some control over the behaviour of members of their project group and allows their non-performance to be factored into assessment.
- *The way it works is* that students are allowed to issue others in their project group with yellow, and in extremis, red cards. A yellow card is "shown" to a student who is deficient in effort or attitude or in other ways not making a full contribution to the group and is then lodged with the project supervisor. Being "shown a yellow card" results in a known penalty being applied to the student (for example, a fixed number of marks lost), though a yellow card may be cancelled by increased effort, or at a boundary between phases of the project, or after a set time. A student who attracts the maximum number of yellow cards can be "shown a red card", which excludes the student from the rest of the project and sets the mark awarded to zero. There is no recovery from a red card.

Bundle conditionals

- *It works better if* staff set the parameters of control (the penalty, the number of yellow cards that can be carried)
- *It doesn't work if* the system leads to the frivolous use of penalties. It doesn't work unless day-to-day management of the resource/role allocation is in the hands of the group themselves'. (pp. 30–31)

Notes on contributors

Robert Serpell, born and raised in England, naturalised citizen of Zambia since 1979, received his B.A. degree (Psychology & Philosophy) from Oxford in 1965 and D.Phil (Experimental Psychology) from Sussex in 1969. He has held academic posts at the Universities of Zambia (1969–1971, 1972–1989), Manchester (UK, 1971–1972), and Maryland, Baltimore County (USA, 1989–2002) where he was Director of the doctoral studies programme in Applied Developmental Psychology, returning to Zambia as Vice-Chancellor in 2003. His research and publications have centred around human development in sociocultural context, with particular attention to the design of methods of assessment and education.

References

Anderson, C. W. (1993) *Prescribing the life of mind: an essay on the purpose of the University, the aims of liberal education, the competence of citizens and the cultivation of practical reason* (Madison, WI, University of Wisconsin Press).

Aptekar, L. & Ciano, L. (1999) Street children in Nairobi, Kenya: Gender differences and mental health, in: M. Rafaelli & R. Larson (Eds) *Developmental issues among homeless and working street youth: new directions in childhood development* (San Francisco, CA, Jossey Bass), 35–46.

Aptekar, L. & Stocklin, D. (1997) Growing up in particularly difficult circumstances: a cross-cultural perspective, in: J. W. Berry, P. R. Dasen & T. M. Saraswathi (Eds) *Handbook of cross-cultural psychology* (2nd edn), Volume 2 (Boston, MA, Allyn & Bacon), 377–412.

Ardila, R. (1982) International psychology, *American Psychologist*, 37, 323–329.

Azuma, H. (1984) Psychology in a non-western country, *International Journal of Psychology*, 19, 45–55.

Barfield, O. (1947) Poetic diction and legal fiction, in: M. Black (Ed.) *The importance of language* (Englewood Cliffs, NJ, Prentice-Hall), 51–71.

Berlin, I. (1956). Introduction, in: I. Berlin (Ed.) *The age of enlightenment* (New York, Mentor).

Bourdieu, P. & Passeron, J.-C. (1964) *Les heritiers* [The inheritors: French students and their relations to culture] (Paris, France, Minuit) (English translation published by University of Chicago Press, 1979).

Bruner, J. S. (1986) *Actual minds, possible worlds* (Cambridge, MA, Harvard University Press).

Cole, M (1996) *Cultural psychology: a once and future discipline* (Cambridge, MA, Harvard University Press).

Descartes, R. (1637) *Le discourse de la methode* [Discourse on method] (Amsterdam, Netherlands, Elsevier).

Fincher, S. (2002) Project work in the computing curriculum. Power-point presentation to the *15th Annual NACCQ Conference*, Hamilton, New Zealand, July 2002. Available online at: www.ukc.ac.uk/people/staff/suf/nacq.ppt (accessed on 15 August 2006).

Fincher, S., Clear, T., Perova, K., Hoskin, K., Birch, R. Claxton, G. & Wieck, M. (2004) Cooperative education in information technology, in: R. K. Coll & C. Eames (Eds) *International Handbook for Cooperative Education: an international perspective of the theory, research and practice of work integrated learning* (Boston MA, World Association for Cooperative Education) 111–121.

Fortes, M. (1938) Social and psychological apsects of education in Taleland, *Africa*, 11(4), 1–64 (Supplement).

Gardner, H. (1991) *The unschooled mind: how children think and how schools should teach* (New York, NY, Basic Books).

Gibson, E. J. (1982) The concept of affordances: the renascence of functionalism, in: A. Collins (Ed.) *The concept of development: the Minnesota symposia on child development (Vol 15)* (Hillsdale, NJ, Erlbaum), 55–81.

Giddens, A. (1999) *Runaway world: lecture 1.* Reith Lectures. (London, BBC). Available online at: http://news.bbc.co.uk/hi/english/static/events/reith_99/week1/week1.htm (accessed on 20 August 2006).

Goody, J. (1977) *The domestication of the savage mind* (Cambridge, Cambridge University Press).

Greenfield, P. M. & Lave, J. (1982) Cognitive aspects of informal education, in: D. A. Wagner & H. W. Stevenson (Eds) *Cultural perspectives on child development* (San Francisco, CA, Freeman), 181–207.

Habermas, J. (1984) *The theory of communicative action, vol 1: Reason and the rationalisation of society* (Trans. T. McCarthy) (Boston, Beacon Press).

Jenkins, P. (1996–2002) *Essays on geopolitics history and the future. 37, Free choice.* Available online at: http://www.palden.co.uk/hhn/essays/hhn-37.html (accessed 4 February 2007).

Kleibard, W. (1975) Metaphorical roots of curriculum design, in: W. Pinar (Ed.) *Curriculum theorising: the reconceptualists* (Berkeley CA, McCutchan), 84–85.

Lakoff, G. & Johnson, M. (1980) *Metaphors we live by* (Chicago, IL, University of Chicago Press).

Lave, J. & Wenger, E. (1991) *Situated learning: legitimate peripheral participation* (Cambridge, Cambridge University Press).

Luangala, J. R. (2004) A reading culture in Zambia: an alternative explanation of its absence, *Journal of Humanities*, 4, 41–52.

Moja, T. (2004) Globalization: a challenge for curriculum responsiveness, in: H. Griesel (Ed.) *Curriculum responsiveness: case studies in higher education* (Pretoria, South Africa, South African Universities Vice-Chancellors Association), 21–38.

Moll, I. (2004) Curriculum responsiveness: the anatomy of a concept, in: H. Griesel (Ed.) *Curriculum responsiveness: case studies in higher education* (Pretoria, South Africa, South African Universities Vice-Chancellors Association), 1–19.

Msolla, P. M., Rutatora, D. F. & Mattee, A. Z. (2005) Towards making university training more relevant: the case of the B. Sc. Agricultural education and extension curriculum at Sokoine Univesity of Agriculture, Morogoro, Tanzania, in: DAAD (Eds) *Quality assurance through curriculum design: a case study of higher education management in East Africa (3rd Dialogue on Innovative Higher Education Strategies (DIES III) Conference documentation)* (Kampala, Uganda, Inter-University Council for East Africa (IUCEA), 74–86.

Mwanalushi, M. (2006) *Cultivating a sense of responsibility in university students towards their heritage.* Chancellor's Address to the 15th Graduation Ceremony of the Copperbelt University. (Kitwe, Zambia, Copperbelt University).

Neisser, U. (1976) *Cognition and reality* (San Francisco, Freeman).

Nsamenang, A. B. (1992) *Human development in cultural context: a third world perspective* (New York, Sage).

Ogunnaike, O. A. & Houser, R. F. (2002) Yoruba toddlers' engagement in errands and cognitive performance on the Yoruba Mental Subscale, *International Journal of Behavioral Development,* 26, 145–153.

Packer, M. (1993). Away from internalization, in: E. Forman, N. Minick & A. Stone (Eds) *Contexts for learning: sociocultural dynamics* (New York, Oxford University Press), 357–368.

Piaget, J. (1971) *The construction of reality in the child* (New York, Ballantine).

Rogoff, B. (1990) *Apprenticeship in thinking* (New York, Oxford University Press.

Rogoff, B. (1993) Children's guided participation and participatory appropriation in sociocultural activity, in: R. Wozniak & K. Fischer (Eds) *Development in context: acting and thinking in specific environments* (Hillsdale, NJ, Erlbaum), 121–153.

Scheper-Hughes, N. (1990) Mother love and child death in northeast Brazil, in: J. W. Stigler, R. A. Shweder & G. Herdt (Eds) *Cultural psychology: essays on comparative human development* (New York, Cambridge University Press), 542–565.

Schon, D. (1983) *The reflective practitioner* (New York, Basic Books).

Scribner, S. (1985) Vygotsky's uses of history, in: J. Wertsch (Ed.) *Culture, communication, and cognition: Vygotskian perspectives* (Cambridge, Cambridge University Press), 119–145.

Scribner, S. & Cole, M. (1981) *The psychology of literacy* (Cambridge, MA, Harvard University Press).

Serpell, R. (1990) Audience, culture and psychological explanation: a reformulation of the emic-etic problem in cross-cultural psychology, *Quarterly Newsletter of the Laboratory of Comparative Human Cognition,* 12(3), 99–132.

Serpell, R. (1992) Afrocentrism: what contribution to the science of developmental psychology ? Paper presented at the *Yaounde International Workshop on Child Development and National Development in Africa* held in Yaounde, Cameroon, 6–10 April.

Serpell, R. (1993a) *The significance of schooling: life-journeys in an African society* (Cambridge, Cambridge University Press).

Serpell, R. (1993b) Interaction of context with development: theoretical constructs for the design of early childhood intervention programmes, in: L. Eldering & P. Leseman (Eds) *Early intervention and culture* (Paris, UNESCO), 23–43.

Serpell, R. (1993c) Interface between sociocultural and psychological aspects of cognition: a commentary, in: E. Forman, N. Minick & A. Stone (Eds) *Contexts for learning: sociocultural dynamics* (Oxford, Oxford University Press), 357–368.

Serpell, R. (1994) The cultural construction of intelligence, in: W. J. Lonner & R. S. Malpass (Eds) *Readings in psychology and culture* (Boston, Allyn & Bacon), 157–163.

Serpell, R. (1995) Situated theory as a bridge between experimental research and political analysis, in: L. Martin, K. Nelson, & E. Tobach (Eds) *Cultural psychology and activity theory: essays in honor of Sylvia Scribner* (New York, Cambridge University Press), 21–42.

Serpell, R. (1998) Participatory appropriation in sociocultural context: a multilevel strategy for applied developmental science. Keynote address to the *4th Regional African Workshop of the International Society for the Study of Behavioural Development (ISSBD).* Windhoek, Namibia, July 1998.

Serpell, R. (1999) Theoretical conceptions of human development, in: L. Eldering & P. Leseman (Eds) *Effective early intervention: cross-cultural perspectives* (New York, Falmer), 41–66

Serpell, R. (2001) Cultural dimensions of literacy promotion and schooling, in: L. Verhoeven & C. Snow (Eds) *Literacy and motivation* (Mahwah, NJ, Erlbaum), 243–273.

Serpell, R. (2006) *Public accountability of the University.* Vice-Chancellor's address to the 36th Graduation ceremony of the University of Zambia (Lusaka, University of Zambia).

Serpell, R., Baker, L. & Sonnenschein, S. (2005) *Becoming literate in the city: the Baltimore Early Childhood Project* (New York, Cambridge University Press).

Serpell, R., Baker, L., Sonnenschein, S. & Hill, S. (1991) Caregiver ethnotheories of children's emergent literacy and numeracy. Paper presented at a symposium on the sociocultural context of development, *11th Biennial Meeting of the International Society for the Study of Behavioural Development (ISSBD)*. (Minneapolis, MN, USA) 3–7 July.

Serpell, R. & Hatano, G. (1997) Education, literacy and schooling in cross-cultural perspective, in: J. W. Berry, P. R. Dasen & T. M. Saraswathi (Eds) *Handbook of cross-cultural psychology (2nd edition), volume 2,* (Boston, MA, Allyn & Bacon), 345–382.

Serpell, R. & Mwape, G. (1998/99) Participatory appropriation of health science and technology: a case study of innovation in basic education in a rural district of Zambia, *African Social Research,* 41/42, 60–89.

Service-Learning Club (2006) *University of Zambia-San Jose State University Service Learning Project* (Lusaka, Zambia, University of Zambia, Psychology Department, unpublished, limited circulation document).

Slominsky, L. & Shalem, Y. (2004) Pedagogic responsiveness for academic depth, in: H. Griesel (Ed.) *Curriculum responsiveness: case studies in higher education* (Pretoria, South Africa, South African Universities Vice-Chancellors Association), 81–101.

Spiro, M. E. (1990) On the strange and the familiar in recent anthropological thought, in: J. W. Stigler, R. A. Shweder & G. Herdt (Eds) *Cultural psychology: essays on comparative human development* (New York, Cambridge University Press), 47–61.

Street, B (1984) *Literacy in theory and practice* (New York, Cambridge University Press).

Tharp, R. G. & Gallimore, R. (1988) *Rousing minds to life: teaching, learning, and schooling in social context* (New York, Cambridge University Press).

Udell, C. (2003) *Early literacy tutoring after school* unpublished PhD dissertation, University of Maryland Baltimore.

Valsiner, J. (1987) *Culture and the development of children's action* (Chichester, England, Wiley).

Vygotsky, L. (1978) *Mind in society: the development of higher psychological processes* (Cambridge, MA, Harvard University Press).

Waters, J. (n.d.) *Project zero: the uses of portfolios* (Cambridge, MA, Harvard University). Unpublished, limited circulation document.

Wells, G. (1990) Talk about text: where literacy is learned and taught, *Curriculum Inquiry,* 20(4), 369–405.

Wertsch, J. V. (1985) *Vygotsky and the social formation of mind* (Cambridge, MA, Harvard University Press).

Wertsch, J. V. (1991) Sociocultural setting and the zone of proximal development: the problem of text-based realities, in: L. Tolchinsky-Landsmann (Ed.) *Culture, schooling and psychological development* (Norwood, NJ, Ablex), 71–86.

Wrigley, H. S. (1999) *Knowledge in action: the promise of project-based learning.* Available online at: http://www.ncsall.net/?id=384 (accessed on 18 August 2006).

ZAWECA (2005) *Report of a collaborative project of HIV/AIDS peer counseling at the University of Zambia and the University of the Western Cape, South Africa* (Cape Town, South Africa, University of the Western Cape).

Orthodoxy, cultural compatibility, and universals in education

Roland G. Tharp and Stephanie Stoll Dalton

Are western psychological and educational theory and educational practice truly applicable to a range of diverse settings around the world? Should our international students be encouraged to believe that our orthodoxies will inform best practice on their return home? We will address these questions by considering first the nature of the dominant pedagogical orthodoxy, and continue by proposing an alternative that aspires directly and by design toward universal applicability.

The dominant orthodoxy: a transnational culture of the school

Is there a dominant transnational school orthodoxy? What are the major findings from the recent seven-nation TIMSS 1999 video study of eighth-grade mathematics teaching? 'The comparative nature of this study tends to draw attention to the ways in which it is clear that all seven countries shared common ways of teaching eighth-grade mathematics. Viewed from this perspective, some similarities are striking' (Hiebert *et al.*, 2003), and are listed below:

(1)   In all of the countries, eighth-grade mathematics was often taught through solving problems; at least 80 percent of lesson time, on average, was devoted to solving mathematics problems.

(2)   Eighth-grade mathematics lessons in all seven countries were organized to include some public, whole-class work and some private, individual or small-group work. During the time that students worked privately, the most common pattern across the countries was for students to work individually, rather than in pairs or groups.

(3)   On average, lessons in all of the countries included some review of previous content as well as some attention to new content.

(4)   At least 90 percent of lessons in all the countries made use of a textbook or worksheet of some kind.

(5)   Teachers in all of the countries talked more than students, at a ratio of at least 8:1 words, respectively. (Hiebert *et al.*, 2003, p. 4).

In a recent analytic paper (Givvin *et al.*, 2005), a systematic search was undertaken for distinctive national differences in those TIMSS videotapes. Of course there were some discernible variations across nations, but the authors concluded that their very careful study could not resolve the dispute about whether there are significant national differences or merely variations on a common pattern. Our own interpretation is that the differences are truly variations on a common pedagogic system, and that the similarities bespeak an underlying transnational orthodoxy.[1] Contrast it to the alternative pedagogic system proposed below, and transnational differences are seen as minor.

We first proposed the concept of the 'transnational culture of the school' in 1979 (Jordan & Tharp, 1979), responding to the remarkable similarity of classrooms for youth across the cultures then known to us. This form of pedagogy is often taken to be 'western', though the TIMSS research suggests a different origin, perhaps a transnational response to common circumstances. But regardless of historical influences, schools around the world appear more alike than different. We speculate that the model arose from two sources: common-sense ideas of economy, and a flawed common-sense theory of psychology.

The economies of bringing youth together into a dedicated space with roof and rooms and small numbers of supervising adults lead easily into rooms-full of age-sorted students, age being the most visible likely marker of developmental progress. The psychological notion of teaching-through-transmission (and learning by absorption and practice) also matches this pedagogy of apparent efficiency. Thus teachers perform and direct 'classes'—large groups of students treated with little variation by a teacher whose transmissions they passively receive, practice, and are tested on. Assign, lecture, test; assign, lecture, test; on and on for 16 years, or until school or student despairs and terminates.

As we will elucidate below, even the economies of the transnational model are unpersuasive, there being alternative pedagogical systems of no greater cost. And the common-sense psychological theory of cognitive development through transmission and practice is grossly inadequate if not false.

If this is so, how has the transnational model persisted for so long and so broadly? During the pre-industrial and industrial eras, the model worked well enough to supply workforces for most of the societies that employed it; and of more probable impact, its most successful products perpetuate the transnational model. Professors, educational researchers, policy-makers, administrators: we not only succeeded in school, we excelled and elected to stay in them. We are the least likely to know or notice the system's shortcomings. Even now, when gross disparities are too evident to ignore—witness in the US the 'achievement gaps' among races, cultures, social classes, and language groups—we educators and professors of education are inclined toward tinkering, polishing, and driving the system ever harder.

Exceptions exist, and are the topic of this paper. We will mention several, but we report primarily on our own work in a thirty-seven-year-long programme of research and development, and the alternative pedagogical system it has produced. It is not transnational, and is neither western nor non-western, it is both.

The development of an alternative system of pedagogy

As Vygotsky has taught us, we understand a person, event, or process only by understanding its developmental history. In that spirit we provide an overview of the developmental history of the pedagogical system to be elucidated.

Forty years ago, systematic failures became obvious in the traditional model. When equal education became a civil right, the inability of schools to deliver equal outcomes across social groups forced attention. Our own work began with a research and development effort to devise an educational system in which Native Hawaiian students would improve literacy learning from abysmal to nationally competitive levels. The story of the Kamehameha Early Education Program (KEEP)'s success has been well told in hundreds of publications; summary documents include Tharp *et al.*, 1984; Au *et al*, 1985; Tharp & Gallimore, 1989. It suffices here to summarize briefly. Raising those achievement levels required the design of an alternative pedagogy that afforded opportunities for teachers and students to employ elements of Hawaiian culture— primarily social and linguistic—in a variety of teaching and learning activities. This cultural compatibility between school and home culture was only enabled by a system of instruction far different from the transnational model with which we began.

It was in the culturally compatible teacher–student and student–student exchanges that assistance in student performance occurred; following Vygotsky, we defined *teaching* as *providing assistance in the Zone of Proximal Development* (Tharp & Gallimore, 1989). However, providing ample assistance required a transformation of the structure of classroom events, and for that structure we began to use the term *pedagogy*, by which we mean *the system of instructional activity*. An ideal pedagogy facilitates and intensifies teaching by maximizing opportunities for teachers to assist students in their zones of proximal development (ZPDs), while ensuring that sufficient peer engagement and practice occur (Dalton, in press).

Those acts of assistance (from various means and sources) were culturally conditioned in the KEEP programme, since both psychological and social planes are formed by culture (Cole, 1985). To understand better that conditionality, we took the same KEEP pedagogical system to another culture, the American Indian Navajo nation of the US southwest. Chosen because of the many sharp differences in cultural style evident in published ethnographies of Hawaii and Navajo, we expected, found, and employed several sharply different sociolinguistic, cognitive, and social organizational variables to maximize student engagement, linguistic and cognitive processing, and the provision of teaching assistance. In surface appearance, the Hawaiian and Navajo classrooms' common pedagogical system made for instant recognition as sister programmes. The more subtle differences in *teaching* were equally important (White *et al*, 1989; Vogt *et al.*, 1992; Tharp, 1994; Jordan, 1995).

A few examples may clarify.

(1) Although the Instructional Conversation was a daily, central instructional setting in both, the sociolinguistic patterns engaging for Navajo children included longer speech turns, and longer wait times between turns; for Hawaiian children, rapid overlapping speech turns and co-narration were characteristic. Both were 'imported' from cultural conventions and courtesies of conversation.

(2) Though small group classroom organization was characteristic in both, effective assistance in peer interaction required smaller groups in Navajo than in Hawaii, and same-sex grouping in the (gender-graded) Navajo society, whereas in the (age-graded) Hawaiian society, mixed gender student groups produce more mutual assistance.

(3) In both groups, cognitive processing during dialogue was frequent and deep. However, a more holistic cognitive style was employed in Navajo; American Indian cognition has been long and widely reported as holistic in style.

Elaborations and analyses of these differences can be found in Vogt, Jordan & Tharp (1992).

By the mid-1980s, studies of meaningful compatibilities between cultures and classrooms had reaped a good harvest. In a review of the literature in 1987, hundreds of reports were available, and patterns emerged. Programmes reported as successful by their authors—across all cultures—foregrounded two features: *language development* and *contextualization* of schooling in the individual and community lives of the students.

In addition, four variable cultural features were regularly considered in these reports: *motivation* (individual or collective); *cognition* (holistic or analytic); *sociolinguistics* (courtesies and conventions of conversation); and *social organization* (age, gender, and adult–child relationships). These categories emerged from inductive analysis of published reports, and so demonstrated a strong concurrence among independent research and development teams (Tharp, 1989). Thus we had available a rough protocol for tailoring educational settings for compatibility with a specific culture.

Therein, of course, also lay the problem. What would one do with a classroom half Hawaiian and half Navajo? By 1990 the multicultural, multilingual classroom was commonplace, and is now typical in the US. Our research group's next approach was to re-examine that same research and development literature, by rotating the kaleidoscope and searching not for differences, but similarities across culturally based solutions. Two had already been identified: (1) *language development,* and (2) *contextualization* of instruction were present in virtually all reports of successful programmes for at-risk populations. In addition, three other features of these programmes were held in common: (3) *joint productive activity* between teacher and students (in contrast to individual work); (4) *teaching through dialogue* (in contrast to a dominance of teacher talk and transmission); and (5) *teaching for cognitive complexity* (in contrast to predominance of basic skills and command of facts). Thus these five may be offered as descriptors of the potent features for educational success of diverse at-risk populations, and thus as standards to meet in classroom teaching.

- Standard I: Teachers and Students Producing Together. (Joint Productive Activity, JPA). *Facilitate learning through joint productive activity between teacher and students.*
- Standard II: Developing Language and Literacy Across the Curriculum (LL). *Develop competence in the language(s) of instruction and of the disciplines throughout the day.*
- Standard III: Making Meaning—Connecting School to Students' Lives (Contextualization, CTX). *Embed curricular instruction in the interests, experiences and skills of students' families and communities.*
- Standard IV: Teaching Complex Thinking (CC) *Challenge students toward cognitive complexity.*
- Standard V: Teaching Through Instructional Conversation. (IC) *Engage students through dialogue.*

These Standards do not preclude activities of direct instruction nor any other effective strategies. Indeed, teachers who use the Standards at higher rates are more likely to use a variety of other effective teaching strategies (Doherty *et al.*, 2003).

It is important to understand that these five elements were empirically derived through the method of analytic deduction; that is, by extraction from a specific domain of knowledge, namely, published reports of educational programmes designed for cultural and/or linguistic minority students deemed successful by those reporting them (using various criteria and methods of assessment). Propositions derived in this way can only be provisional.

To move toward greater certitude requires the *method of universals* (Lindesmith, 1957; Athens, 1992, 1997; Rhodes, 1999) which '…requires the researcher to attempt to formulate propositions which apply to all instances without exception. Crystallized, the advantages of this method are: (1) theories can be disproved and compared against evidence; (2) knowledge can grow as old propositions are revised in the light of negative evidence; and (3) it requires the investigator to link closely theory and fact, as exceptions demand revision' (Znaniecki, 1934, quoted in Lindesmith, 1957, p. 19). The logic of the method is that of William James's White Crow test. '(I)f you wish to upset the law that all crows are black, you must not seek to show that no crows are; it is enough if you prove one single crow to be white' (Murphy & Ballou, [1890] 1969, p. 41). Surely this most unforgiving of methods imposes the greatest discipline on theorists/researchers: diligently to seek exceptions to propositions, thus striving to prove ourselves wrong, by which we are able to formulate more refined, more accurately phrased propositions.

In the early 1990s our group accepted this challenge, and offered these 'Five Standards for Effective Pedagogy' as universally potent features. We pursued, in a continual review of the literature, in conversation and correspondence, to search for exceptions. Simultaneously we embarked on a fifteen-year programme of research and development studies designed better to understand and refine the concepts of these Standards. These forty or so studies were carried out in communities of most cultural and linguistic minority groups in the US.[2] While we have not discovered exceptions at the conceptual level, we have continually corrected and refined our descriptors and indicators of the concepts.

As confidence grew in the Five Standards proposition, we turned attention to the task of designing a full pedagogical system that would allow the maximum enactments of the five elements simultaneously (Tharp *et al.*, 2000). In brief, the pedagogy system involves both collaborative group and individual work; activities linking curriculum to the strengths, needs and interests of local communities; and the rich dialogic language environments of multiple, simultaneous classroom activity settings. Our original KEEP Hawaiian and Navajo classrooms can be recognized as prototypes, though our current understanding—both theoretical and operational— has allowed considerable refinement. A highly abstracted model of a classroom using the Five Standards consists of a teacher and a small group of students having an instructional conversation while collaborating on a cognitively challenging activity connected to students' knowledge and experience, while other student groups are working in a variety of supportive instructional activities. The overarching goals of instruction are to foster complex thinking by all students, and language and literacy development in the language of instruction, as well as in the content domains.

The Five Standards for Effective Pedagogy provided a lens for disaggregating pedagogy from teaching. This view clarified pedagogy's functional value for strengthening teaching. For example, if only the personal and individual levels of learning are activated (as in traditional US classrooms and most transnational models), interpersonal and social levels of learning will not be—as they are in the Five Standards mode. A systematic pedagogy is needed to support this richness and variety of instructional activity and interaction (Dalton, in press).

During the later CREDE years, fully operational models of the Five Standards pedagogy system offered proofs of concept, in three demonstration schools— preschool, elementary, and high school, serving at-risk minority communities.

Our next intellectual challenge to be faced was (is) inherent in the method of universals. A proposition may be universally correct yet insignificant in consequences. To test for the power and significance of universalist propositions, they must—like all others—be tested by probabilities as well as observations. So we then put the Five Standards for Effective Pedagogy to a variety of tests, using experimental, quasi-experimental, and correlational designs, along with qualitative reports, on partial and full implementations of the system. The results of these studies have all been favourable, allowing the generalization that the greater the degree of implementation of the

Five Standards, the higher the achievement scores of students on standardized high-stakes tests, as well as on other measures of efficacy (see below).

Currently we are returning to research and development studies of teacher preparation programmes, modelling education in and by the Five Standards pedagogical system. In a study of pre-service teacher preparation based on effective pedagogy standards as implemented at KEEP, pre-service teachers engaged, enacted, and reflected their preparation through formal learning, but also through critical collegial relationships with a variety of mentors in the community of practice. The relational and activity-based processes of teacher preparation that produced professionally knowledgeable, quality teachers depended on the congruence in what the programme teaches with what actually happens in K–12 classrooms (Dalton & Tharp, 2002). It being difficult to teach using methods by which one has never learned, we are attempting a transformation of the pedagogical system of higher education using the Five Standards, in undergraduate arts and sciences courses and in teacher preparation courses, as well as in beginning teacher classroom placements and induction programmes.[3]

Evaluation evidence for effectiveness of the Standards for Effective Pedagogy

Classroom practices

Recent research has examined teachers' use of the Five Standards, both separately and in combination, with multi methods including case studies of multiple classrooms, short-term randomized designs, and quasi-experimentation in single classrooms, and longitudinal studies of entire schools. All studies have shown positive relationships between teachers' use of the Five Standards and student achievement and other favourable outcomes.

Several studies by the Saunders & Goldenberg group (Saunders *et al.*, 1998; Saunders, 1999; Saunders & Goldenberg, 1999a, b) have found Standard Five (Instructional Conversation, IC) positively related to students' acquisition of thematic understanding of literature while doing no harm to the development of literal comprehension. When IC was combined with Standard Three (Contextualization), those same effects were positive for all students, but even more sharply for English Language Learners (ELL).

Doherty and Pinal (2002) used the Standards Performance Continuum (Doherty, *et al*, 2002) to measure teachers' use of joint productive activity (JPA) during language arts instruction. JPA fostered the meta-cognitive development of predominantly Latino ELL students, increasing student use of effective reading strategies, which in turn predicted achievement gains on standardized comprehension tests, whereas ineffective strategy use, unrelated to JPA, predicted declines in comprehension achievement.

A set of studies by Estrada over a four-year period has consistently shown a positive relation between use of the Five Standards and positive outcomes in 1st and 4th grades. Stronger implementation of the Five Standards produced higher student scores on tests of reading and the language of instruction. The vast majority of students in strong implementers' classrooms reached grade level in reading, whereas less than half did so in weaker implementers' classrooms. Virtually all students reached grade level in reading in strong implementers' classes, whereas 69% did so in weaker implementers' classrooms (Estrada, 2004; 2005).

Hilberg *et al.*, (2000) examined the efficacy of the Five Standards in mathematics instruction. Two groups of American Indian eighth grade students were randomly assigned to either Five Standards or traditional pedagogy for a one-week unit on fractions, decimals, and percentages. Students in the Five Standards condition outperformed controls on tests of conceptual learning at the end of the study and better retention of unit content two weeks later.

Several studies recently conducted at one of CREDE's Research and Demonstration Schools (serving low-income Latino ELLs) document the effects of teachers' use of the Five Standards and student achievement. The Standards Performance Continuum (SPC), a rubric with excellent psychometric properties of inter-observer reliabilities and validities (Doherty *et al.*, 2002), measures the degree of Five Standards use quantitatively. Student achievement gains were estimated from standardized test scores (SAT-9) from two consecutive years. Teachers' overall use of the standards reliably predicted achievement gains in comprehension, language, reading, spelling, and vocabulary (Doherty *et al.*, 2003). Students whose teachers used the Five Standards extensively *and* experienced classroom organization consisting of multiple, simultaneous, diversified activity settings as specified in the pedagogy model (Tharp *et al.* 2000) showed significantly greater achievement gains on all SAT-9 tests than students whose teachers had not similarly transformed their teaching. Doherty *et al* (2002) in a quasi-experimental design that used a school in an adjacent catchment area as an untreated control group, showed the same patterns of vocabulary gains, exceeding a half a standard deviation in normal curve equivalent scores.

Teachers' use of the Five Standards has been linked to factors critical to school performance such as motivation, perceptions, attitudes, and inclusion. In an isolated Native American community, students participating in activities guided by the Standards increased their academic engagement. Teachers, together with peers and parents, enacted and reflected on the rationales, strategies and specific activities of the Standards to develop classroom communities of effective practice (Dalton & Youpa, 1998). Predominantly Latino ELL students in classrooms where the Five Standards were used only slightly or moderately spent more time on-task, perceived greater cohesion in their classrooms, and perceived themselves as better readers having less difficulty with their work, as compared to classrooms where the Standards were not present at all (Padron & Waxman, 1999). American Indian students in mathematics classes integrating the Five Standards reported more positive attitudes toward mathematics (Hilberg *et al.*, 2000). Findings, replicated over two years with two cohorts of students indicated that, across language programmes, peer inclusion in social choices was greater in classrooms in which students participated in more peer joint productive activities (or peer collaboration) (Estrada, 2004, 2005).

Explaining the efficacy of Five Standards pedagogy

The effects of this pedagogy may reasonably be attributed to the increased frequency of assisted performance in the ZPD; increased student use of language (writing, speaking, listening); increased frequency of cognitive processing of concepts; increased positive affective loading of learning due to the increased personal relationships of teachers and students; and increased contextualization of learning, leading to the broad relating of school learning to the learner's apperceptive mass across the psychological planes of individual, interpersonal and community.

Most writers discuss these effects in the conceptual vocabulary of cultural-historical-activity theory (CHAT), because of CHAT's power to relate the personal to the cultural, and its general developmental orientation, all of which allow teacher, learner, classroom, community and culture to be understood in their complex overlaps and dynamics. Others prefer a cognitive science approach, many propositions of which would also predict greater efficacy for this pedagogy as compared to the traditional transnational model. For example, greater conceptual retention is provided by the extensive cognitive processing provided through instructional dialogue and connection to previously understood material. Likewise, Rueda (2006) has discussed the efficacy of contextualization and cultural compatibilities in terms of *cognitive load theory*, which invokes basic concepts in information processing and the capacities of working memory.

Indeed it would be surprising should not this increased efficacy exist. The general pattern of early socialization for most of the millennia of *Homo sapiens* has been caretaker-child joint meaningful activity (with increasing child participation) accompanied by language exchanges carrying both information and affect. In the early school years, a Five Standards classroom provides an emulation of the rich language environment provided by the homes of professional and middle-class caretakers that prepare their babies and toddlers so well for subsequent schooling (Hart & Risley, 1995; Tharp & Entz, 2003). Certainly in the US, the most successful portions of the educational system are preschool, vocational education, on-the-job education, and university graduate school; and these are the systems in which the standards for effective pedagogy are most likely to be seen. In post-industrial economies, the most desired capacities for an entering work force are language, literacy and conceptual abilities, the capacities for working effectively both alone and in small teams of flexible size and flexible leadership, with a valuation of creativity and problem-solving rather than waiting for detailed instructions. Even armies like that description. Ironically, across all major social environments, it is in K–12 schools that those performances are least likely to occur.

The current developmental stage of Five Standards pedagogy

Pedagogy and content

There is high consistency between the Five Standards and those issued by other national standards groups, to the extent that they discuss pedagogy (e.g., for mathematics, National Council of Teachers of Mathematics (2000) *Principles and Standards for School Mathematics*; for science, National Research Council's National Committee on Science Education Standards and Assessment, (1996); and for general teaching standards, the various publications of the National Board for Professional Teaching Standards. The pedagogy standards have been endorsed by the National Bilingual Education Association, and the International Reading Association.

A current thrust of CREDE work is the more detailed development of the Standards in content-specific contexts. Most of our research has been in literacy in the early grades, and so in that domain our indicators and exemplars are the best developed. In research, the integration of the Five Standards into elementary science education has shown positive effects on achievement for students of limited English proficiency (LEP) (Stoddart, 1999; 2004; Stoddart *et al.*, 2002). This programme of inquiry science implemented a pedagogy that integrated language development, joint productive activity, and instructional conversation in a culturally contextualized and cognitively demanding science curriculum. Students showed significant achievement gains using both performance-based and standardized assessment. In three consecutive summer sessions, 1200 LEP students made significant gains in academic language and science concepts measured on the Woodcock Munoz standardized assessment of academic language and concept maps (Stoddart, 1999). In two participating schools districts, students who were in this programme for one or for two years scored significantly higher on the SAT-9 in reading, language and science than controls. At the present time, we are further refining that programme and subjecting it to experimental tests. Our longer-term plans are to address mathematics instruction similarly.

The pedagogy system and its variants

Published schematics of the implementation of the pedagogy system describe progressions through lessons, class periods, and semesters as organizational patterns of classroom instructional activities (Tharp, *et al.*, 2000). These sketches can be used to plan and organize the several elements of the multi-tasking system. Derived primarily from experiences in K–6 classrooms, these schematics are elastic enough to fit generally over Five Standards classrooms in preschool, middle school, high school and higher education, but development is underway to enlarge our understanding of those specifics. For example, the pedagogical system must be responsive to preschool's higher teacher/student ratio, shorter student attention spans, and the provision for language and literacy development during play (Tharp & Entz, 2003). In university classes numbering hundreds of students, the opportunities for instructional conversation and other dialogic approaches may require scheduling varied activities with an instructional week–not a single day's class–as the unit (Ball & Wells, 2005). In a field-study based science-oriented high school, each day of the week may differ in the rhythms and types of activity (Yamauchi, 2003). In graduate seminars and classes in teacher education, crucial decisions are made about which

instructional activities are to be held during scheduled class time, and which are to be scheduled on other days, hours and settings. These variants are exciting challenges for educational design. Our group continues to find the Five Standards for Effective Pedagogy to be vital quality filters for the design of instructional activity in all these settings.

The place of the Five Standards in the panoply of educational reform programmes

In our view, for maximizing the educational achievement of the members of most if not all cultures, the Five Standards are a necessary but not sufficient condition. Other reform efforts focus on other necessary conditions: good finance, good buildings, good curriculum, safety, and a deep teacher knowledge of subject-matter. We emphasize especially the necessary condition for effective teaching and learning of a solid assessment system—not the standardized achievement tests of summative evaluation, but an ongoing system of assessment of students' mastery of the goals of instruction, so that teaching can be adjusted responsively and continuously by that feedback. Our own work features pedagogy and teaching, not because it is sufficient, but because the final common pathway of all reform is the interaction during activity among teachers and students.

Among other reform programmes featuring teaching, the distinction of the Five Standards pedagogy does not lie in our emphases on literacy development, active student involvement, contextualization, challenging instruction, and dialogue; these are hardly exclusive. Many well-known programmes include one or more of these elements: *Cognitively Guided Instruction* (Carpenter *et al.*, 1996) is a programme that assists teachers to create elementary mathematics classes. *Complex instruction* (Bower, 1997; Cohen & Lotan, 1997), features cognitively challenging activities, which require varied abilities, in a small-group, multiple-activity format. In *Authentic Instruction*, teachers help to construct knowledge through the use of disciplined inquiry (connecting students' previous knowledge to their expressions of current material, including those beyond the classroom (Newmann *et al.*, 1995; Newmann, 1996). *Reciprocal Teaching* employs small-group discussion as a basis for teaching reading (Palinscar, 1984); *Instructional Congruence* (Lee & Fradd, 1998) interweaves science and literacy teaching emphasizing contextualization, language and literacy development, and challenging instruction; and Carol D. Lee's classrooms teach *literary criticism* to African American adolescents (Lee, 1993, 1995) employing contextualization (beginning with critiques of rap lyrics, ending with Shakespeare). Our characterizations of these programmes are drawn from the emphases in the authors' own programme descriptions, but we have no doubt that were good instances of these classrooms to be measured with the Standards Performance Continuum, their scores would be high on many of the Five Standards. The obvious overlap with programmes such as these lends credibility to our universalist propositions.

Reasoning directly from cultural–historical–activity theory, several writers have proposed teaching strategies congruent with the Five Standards, and in many cases

using the same or similar terminology. Among them are Wells' (1999) explanation of 'the spiral of knowing' where 'knowledge grows out of and has value for action' (*passim*); and Ball & Wells (2005) high-enrolment university courses that employ a variety of activity settings. And many writers have proposed that cooperative, productive learning activity has to be implemented in any worthwhile thinking curriculum (Davydov, 1988; Engestrom, 1990; van Oers, 1990a,b; Carpay & van Oers, 1999). This is unsurprising, since the labels of the Standards have been drawn from the cultural-historical-activity theory lexicon, and we too are continually guided by that theory in correcting and refining our understanding.

The specific distinctions of the Five Standards pedagogy lie in its developmental history and systematicity. As for the latter: as a consequence of our professional development activity, guidelines are available for transforming instruction from traditional to Five Standards, that include suggestions for sequencing the several dimensions of change, and full discussions of the pertinent elements of contextualization in the specifics of classrooms and communities. These systematic guides are useful to beginners and for solving recalcitrant problems (Tharp *et al.*, 2000). The art of teaching is not thereby eliminated; on the contrary, the guidance of the pedagogy standards promotes creative, responsive and enriched teaching.

The developmental history of the Five Standards Pedagogy offers the distinction of a long history of research and development across a variety of cultures, languages, and socio-economic groups, including the mixed-culture classrooms that are becoming the norm in the developed world; evaluated by a significant accumulation of evidence garnered through multi-methods: universals, experimentation and qualitative approaches, and justified by a continuous alignment against theory.

It is important to note that while additional resources might always be welcome, a fully-enacted Five Standards classroom can be achieved without increasing any costs over traditional classrooms nor necessarily requiring reduced class size. Five Standards classrooms routinely have had thirty or more students; a larger number may increase student-to-student resources of assistance and enrichment in small group joint activity.

Limitations of Five Standards pedagogy

The limitation of this pedagogical system is *incompleteness*. The open-ended nature of the method of universals requires a continual search for exceptions, and the consequent required revisions. The limitation on the method of analytic deduction is closely aligned: extracting the Five Standards from the existing literature on at-risk, diverse populations provides no evidence beyond that literature. Thus educational operations of potentially great power, if not yet researched, cannot appear. We have encountered this problem in a recognizable form in the following example. In our original extraction, the subset of studies on cultures of Native Americans/Canadians, Native Alaskans, and Inuit peoples of the circumpolar North yielded (*in addition* to the Five Standards) two other strong consistencies among successful programmes. These are: (1) learning through observation, teaching by modelling; and (2) student

choice and initiative in the selection and/or design of instructional activities. Among those cultural groups, these two features of traditional community life are the most robust in ethnographic and educational literature (Tharp, 1994; Hoem & Darnell, 1996). However, the features rarely appear in work among other cultures, including mainstream Euro-American. Will these two features, when broadly and sufficiently researched, emerge as two additional Pedagogy Standards? In the meantime there is every theoretical, ethnographic, and research reason to treat the pedagogical systems for Native Americans/Canadians, Native Alaskans, and Inuit peoples of the circumpolar North as containing *Seven* Standards.

Of course, the method of analytic deduction can be used on ever-expanding domains of observational data. In this spirit, we have explored the explanatory value of the Five Standards for non-formal education, from primary socialization to indoctrination of captives (Tharp, 2006). Our current research in teacher preparation and other higher education applications will provide new knowledge about other cultural groups and other institutions. There must be new grist for the mills of analytic deduction and the method of universals; they can grind, but they do not plant.

The same limitation is present also with respect to powerful educational interventions not yet researched nor dreamed of. So incompleteness is an existential condition of the universalist enterprise. We do not claim the adjective *universal*. That remains to be seen, and if at all, awarded by others at some later stage of development. Universalism is a process, and not often an achieved goal. This is why we claim for our system the adjective *universalist*, thereby emphasizing the method of its derivation and continual testing. Nor is the method of universals a sufficient process, as we hope our developmental account has demonstrated. Invention, experimentation and tinkering provide the discoveries and weigh them; theory justifies them; and the evidence then joins the profession's body of knowledge, against which it must be inspected in the everlasting search for the white crow.

Is a universal effective pedagogy feasible?

The answer to that question is complex. First let us distinguish universally validated propositions from the method of universals. The method itself remains invaluable in the pursuit of propositions with the highest generality and the highest utility. As for a universal pedagogy itself, we suggest that it is much more likely to be found than ordinarily assumed, but perhaps not totally achievable.

We make these judgements, of course, in the light of our own work; other and future pedagogical standards and principles may have different prospects. In the present case, we have not yet encountered a cultural group for which the system is inappropriate or has failed. This broad applicability is due to Standard Three, Contextualization, which calls for instruction to be connected to the values and concerns of students, their families and communities. Little in human repertoires is not conditioned by culture—contextualization implies employing community courtesies and conventions of conversation, patterns of adult-child relationships, and preferences for social organization, as well as connecting curriculum content to local environments. This means that the third (middle) standard acts as a fulcrum for the other four, so that patterns of activity, language development, complex problem solving, and dialogue are expressed in local cultural needs, mores, and strengths. (Our Chinese students say that the Five Standards system is enjoyable for them, but not necessary: the traditional system works fine, thank you, being culturally congruent with a Confucian society.) Thus a central aspect of universalism is that the best education is culturally realized, and thus to a degree localized. In this light, we may consider the earlier question: what would one do with a classroom half Hawaiian and half Navajo? Or indeed, with multicultural, multilingual classrooms? The Five Standards system is supple enough to manage multicultural and multilingual classrooms through its multiple activity settings and rolling groupings that allow both uni-cultural and cross-cultural collaborative activity. The weaving of these student relationships also builds a whole class learning community, the shared experiences of which become another meaningful reference for contextualization of instruction.

Of course there comes a time—ordinarily at university or in the run-up to it, when education becomes an enculturation, into the new culture of 'the educated' or of the professions. But even there, making learning meaningful in the context of student ambitions and values remains a prescription for full engagement.

However, we do see a limit to the potential for full universalism in our own system. The emphasis on teaching complex, critical thinking is a preparation for democratic and capable citizenship.

In conclusion, we return to the questions that animate this paper and this volume: are western psychological and educational theory and educational practice truly applicable to a range of diverse settings around the world? Should our international students be encouraged to believe that our orthodoxy, our theories, or our science will inform best practice on their return home? We need to develop answers with those students, through an effective teaching and learning process. The topics are too long for a lecture, and so complex and particularized that they would be managed best in dialogical pedagogy—supported by some joint projects connecting the goals to each of our own cultures and concerns.

Authors' note

This article was written by the second author in her private capacity. The views expressed in the article do not necessarily represent the views of the US Department of Education or the United States

Notes

1. A parallel TIMSS study of international science lessons (released after this paper was completed) appears also to support this conclusion (Roth *et al.*, 2006).
2. Under the auspices of two successive National Research Centre contracts to the University of California, Santa Cruz, from the US Department of Education: The Centre for Research on Education, Diversity and Excellence (CREDE); and earlier, The National Centre for Research on Cultural Diversity and English Language Learning.

3. Our group is currently at the Centre for Research on Education, Diversity and Excellence (CREDE), at the Graduate School of Education, University of California, Berkeley.

Notes on contributors

Roland G. Tharp is research professor and director of the Centre for Research on Education, Diversity & Excellence (CREDE), Graduate School of Education, University of California, Berkeley. He has published widely for many years in educational, developmental, cultural, and clinical psychology. He is a laureate of the Grawemeyer Award in Education.

Stephanie Stoll Dalton's career spans teacher preparation and development, studies of effective practice in diverse classrooms, and classroom teaching from kindergarten through graduate studies.

References

Athens, L. (1992) *The creation of dangerous violent criminals* (Urbana, University of Illinois Press).

Athens, L. (1997) *Violent criminal acts and actors revisited* (Urbana, University of Illinois Press).

Au, K. H., Tharp, R. G., Crowell, D. C., Jordan, C., Speidel, G. E. & Calkins, R. P. (1985) The role of research in the development of a successful reading programme, in: J. Osborn, P. Wilson, & R. Anderson (Eds) *Reading education: foundations for a literate America* (Lexington, MA., D. C. Heath & Co), 275–292.

Ball, T. & Wells, G. (2005) *Walking the talk: the complexities of teaching about teaching* (Education Department, University of California, Santa Cruz, CA 95064).

Bower, B. (1997) Effects of the multiple-ability curriculum in secondary social studies classrooms, in: E. G. Cohen & R. A. Lotan (Eds) *Working for equity in heterogeneous classrooms: sociological theory in practice* (New York, Teachers College Press) no pp. nos. available.

Carpay, J. A. M. & van Oers, B. (1999) Didactic models and the problem of intertextuality and polyphony, in: Y. Engeström, R. Miettinen & R. L. Punamäki (Eds) *Perspectives on activity theory* (Cambridge, Cambridge University Press), 298–313.

Carpenter, T., Fennema, E. & Franke, M. (1996) Cognitively guided instruction: a knowledge base for reform in primary mathematics instruction, *Elementary School Journal*, 97, 3–20.

Cohen, E. G. & Lotan, R A. (Eds) (1997) *Working for equity in heterogeneous classrooms: sociological theory in practice* (New York, Teachers College Press).

Cole, M. (1985) The Zone of proximal development: where culture and cognition create each other, in: J. V. Wertsch (Ed.) *Culture, communication and cognition: Vygotskian perspectives* (Cambridge, Cambridge University Press), 146–161.

Dalton, S. S. (in preparation) *Pedagogy as system, teaching as assistance*.

Dalton, S. S. (in press) *Five standards for effective teaching: how to succeed with all learners* (San Francisco, Jossey-Bass).

Dalton, S. S. & Tharp, R. (2002) How do preservice teachers learn? in: L. Minaya-Rowe (Ed) *Effective pedagogy and teacher training* (Greenwich, CT, Information Age Publishing Inc.), 93–117.

Dalton, S. S. & Youpa, D. (1998) School reform in Zuni Pueblo middle and high schools, *Journal of Equity and Excellence in Education*, 31(1), 55–68.

Davydov, V. V. (1988) Problems of developmental teaching: the experience of theoretical and empirical psychological research, *Soviet Education, Part I:* 30(8), 15–97; *Part II: 30*(9), 3–28; *Part III:* 30(10), 3–77.

Doherty, R. W., Hilberg, R. S., Epaloose, G. & Tharp, R. G. (2002) Standards performance continuum: development and validation of a measure of effective pedagogy, *Journal of Educational Research*, 96(2), 78–89.

Doherty, R. W., Hilberg, R. S., Pinal, A. & Tharp, R. G. (2003) Five standards and student achievement, *NABE Journal of Research and Practice*, 1(1), 1–24.

Doherty, R. W. & Pinal, A. (2002) Joint productive activity, cognitive reading strategies, and achievement. Paper presented at the *Annual Meeting of the National Council of Teachers of English*, Atlanta, GA, November 2002.

Engestrom, Y. (1990) *Learning, working and imagining: twelve studies in activity theory* (Helsinki, Orienta-Konsultit).

Estrada, P. (2004) Patterns of language arts instructional activity and excellence in first and fourth grade culturally and linguistically diverse classrooms, in: H. Waxman, R. G. Tharp & R. Hillberg (Eds) *Observational research in U.S. classrooms: new approaches for understanding cultural and linguistic diversity* (Cambridge, MA, Cambridge University Press), 122–143.

Estrada, P. (2005) The courage to grow: a researcher and teacher linking professional development with small-group reading instruction and student achievement, *Research in the Teaching of English*, 39, 320–264.

Givvin, K. B., Hiebert, J., Jacobs, J. K., Hollingsworth, H. & Gallimore, R. (2005) Are there national patterns of teaching? Evidence from the TIMSS 1999 Video Study, *Comparative Education Review*, 49(3), 311–343.

Hart, B. & Risley, T. R. (1995) *Meaningful differences in the everyday experience of young American children* (Baltimore, MD, Paul H. Brookes Publishing).

Hiebert, J., Gallimore, R., Garnier, H., Givvin, K. B., Hollingsworth, H., Jacobs, J., *et al.* (2003) *Teaching mathematics in seven countries: results from the TIMSS 1999 Video Study (NCES 2003–013)* (Washington, DC, US Department of Education, National Centre for Education Statistics).

Hilberg, R. S., Tharp, R. G. & DeGeest, L. (2000) The efficacy of CREDE's standards-based instruction in American Indian mathematics classes, *Equity and Excellence in Education*, 33(2), 32–39.

Hoem, A. & Darnell, F. (1996) *Taken to extremes: education in the far north* (Cambridge, MA, Scandinavian University Press North America).

Jordan, C. (1995) Creating cultures of schooling: historical and conceptual background of the KEEP/Rough Rock Project, *The Bilingual Research Journal*, 19(1), 83–100.

Jordan, C. & Tharp, R. G. (1979) Culture and education, in: A. J. Marsella, R. G. Tharp & T. Ciborowski (Eds) *Perspectives in cross-cultural psychology* (New York, Academic Press), 265–285

Lee, C. D. (1993) *Signifying as a scaffold for literary interpretation: the pedagogical implications of an African American discourse genre* (Urbana, IL, National Council of Teachers of English).

Lee, C. D. (1995) A culturally based cognitive apprenticeship: teaching African American high school students skills in literacy interpretation, *Reading Research Quarterly*, 30, 608–630.

Lee, O. & Fradd, S. H. (1998) Science for all, including students from non-English-language backgrounds, *Educational Researcher*, 27(4), 12–21.

Lindesmith, A. R. (1957) *Opiate addiction* (Evanston, Principia Press of Illinois).

Murphy, G. & Ballou, R. O. (Eds) ([1890] 1969) *William James on psychical research* (New York, Viking) 25–47.

National Council of Teachers of Mathematics (2000) *Principles and standards for school mathematics*. Available online at: http://standards.nctm.org/ (accessed on 29 November 2006).

National Research Council's National Committee on Science Education Standards and Assessment (1996) *National Science Education Standards*. Available online at: http://www.nsta.org/standards (accessed on 29 November 2006).

Newmann, F. M. (Ed.) (1996) *Authentic achievement: restructuring schools for intellectual quality* (San Francisco, Jossey Bass).

Newmann, F. M., Secada, W. G. & Wehlage, G. (1995) *A guide to authentic instruction and assessment: vision, standards, and scoring* (Madison, WI, Wisconsin Centre for Educational Research at the University of Wisconsin).

Oers, B. van (1990a) The development of mathematical thinking in school: a comparison of the action-psychological and information-processing approaches, *International Journal of Educational Research*, 14(1), 51–66.

Oers, B. van (1990b) The dynamics of school learning, in: J. Valsiner & H.-G. Voss (Eds) *The structure of learning* (New York, Ablex), 205–228.

Padron, Y. N. & Waxman, H. C. (1999) Classroom observations of the Five Standards of Effective Teaching in urban classrooms with English language learners, *Teaching and Change*, 7(1), 79–100.

Palinscar, A. (1984) *Teaching reading as thinking* (Alexandria, VA., Association for Supervision and Curriculum Development).

Rhodes, R. (1999) *Why they kill: the discoveries of a maverick criminologist* (New York, Knopf).

Roth, K. J., Druker, S. L., Garnier, H., Lemmens, M., Chen, C., Kawanaka, T., *et al.* (2006) *Teaching science in five countries: results from the TIMSS 1999 Video Study. (NCES 2006–011)* (Washington, DC, US Department of Education, National Centre for Education Statistics).

Rueda, R. (2006) Motivational and cognitive aspects of culturally accommodated instruction: the case of reading comprehension, in: D. M. McInerney, M. Dowson & S. Van Etten (Eds) *Effective Schools* (Greenwich CN., Information Age), 129–150.

Saunders, W. (1999) Improving literacy achievement for English learners in transitional bilingual programs, *Educational Research and Evaluation*, 5(4), 345–381.

Saunders, W. & Goldenberg, C. (1999a) The effects of instructional conversations and literature logs on limited- and fluent-English proficient students' story comprehension and thematic understanding, *Elementary School Journal*, 99(4), 277–301.

Saunders, W. & Goldenberg, C. (1999b) *The effects of comprehensive Language Arts/Transition Program on the literacy development of English learners (Technical Report)* (Santa Cruz, CA, Centre for Research, Diversity & Excellence, University of California).

Saunders, W., O'Brien, G., Lennon, D. & McLean, J. (1998) Making the transition to English literacy successful: effective strategies for studying literature with transition students, in: R. Gersten & R. Jimenez (Eds) *Promoting learning for culturally and linguistically diverse students* (Monterey, CA., Brooks Cole Publishers), 99–132.

Stoddart, T. (1999) Language acquisition through science inquiry. Paper presented at the annual meeting of the *American Educational Research Association*, Montreal, April 1999.

Stoddart, T. (2004) *Improving student achievement with the CREDE Five Standards Pedagogy* (Santa Cruz, CA, University of California, Center for Research on Education, Diversity and Excellence).

Stoddart, T., Pinales, A., Latzke, M. & Canaday, D. (2002) Integrating inquiry science and language development for English Language Learners, *Journal of Research in Science Teaching*, 30(8), 664–687.

Tharp, R. G. (1989) Psychocultural variables and constants: effects on teaching and learning in schools, *American Psychologist*, 44, 349–359.

Tharp, R. G. (1994) Intergroup differences among Native Americans in socialization and child cognition: an ethnogenetic analysis, in: P. Greenfield & R. Cocking, (Eds) *Cross-cultural roots of minority child development*, (Hillsdale, NJ., Lawrence Erlbaum Associates), 87–105.

Tharp, R. G. (2006) Four hundred years of evidence: culture, pedagogy and Native America, *Journal of American Indian Education*, 45(2), 8–25.

Tharp, R. G. & Entz, S. (2003) From high chair to high school: research-based principles for teaching complex thinking, *Young Children*, September, 38–43.

Tharp, R. G., Estrada, P., Dalton, S. S. & Yamauchi, L.A. (2000) *Teaching transformed: achieving excellence, fairness, inclusion and harmony*, (Boulder, CO., Westview Press).

Tharp, R. G. & Gallimore, R. (1989) *Rousing minds to life: teaching and learning in social context* (New York, Cambridge University Press).

Tharp, R. G., Jordan, C., Speidel, G. E., Au, K. H., Klein, T. W., Calkins, *et al.* (1984) Product and process in applied developmental research: education and the children of a minority, in: M. E. Lamb, A. L., Brown, & B. Rogoff (Eds) *Advances in developmental psychology, Vol. III)* (Hillsdale, NJ., Lawrence Erlbaum & Associates Inc.), 91–141

Vogt, L. A., Jordan, C. & Tharp, R. G. (1992) Explaining school failure, producing school success: two cases, in: E. Jacob & C. Jordan (Eds) *Minority education: anthropological perspectives,* (Norwood, NJ, Ablex), 53–66. (Reprinted from *Anthropology & Education Quarterly,* 18, 276–286.

Wells, G. (1999) *Dialogic inquiry: towards a sociocultural practice and theory of education,* (Cambridge, Cambridge University Press).

White, S., Tharp, R. G., Jordan, C. & Vogt, L. (1989) Cultural patterns of cognition reflected in the questioning styles of Anglo and Navajo teachers, in: D. Topping, V. Kobayashi, & D. C. Crowell, (Eds) *Thinking across cultures: the third international conference on thinking* (Hillsdale, NJ, Lawrence Erlbaum Associates), 79–91.

Yamauchi, L. A. (2003) Making school relevant for at-risk students: the Wai'anae High School Hawaiian Studies Program, *Journal of Education for Students Placed At Risk,* 8(4), 379–390.

Western influences on Chinese educational testing

Weihua Niu

Chinese students have impressed the world with their extraordinary abilities to achieve high scores in various educational tests, no matter whether these are international scientific Olympic exams, graduate record examinations, or simply second language proficiency exams. What motivates Chinese students to succeed in these educational tests? What has caused the myth (or the reality) that Chinese students can score highly on all tests yet may stumble in academic pursuits that require creative thinking and independent inquiry? How have Chinese educational testing systems, influenced by the west, affected contemporary Chinese people's lives and their futures?

When I visited my hometown of Beijing in the summer of 2006, I found that in almost every household there was at least one member who had either just taken an exam or was waiting to take an exam. An example is my 17-year-old nephew, who had recently finished the high school graduation exams and a 2-day mock test for the National College Entrance Exam (NCEE). After taking just a week-long break from study, which was actually a semi-military training camp organized by his school, he recharged himself with the 'correct' studying energy and began the countdown to the real NCEE that will take place next June. Even though it was summer and all schools were closed, like most of his peers, my nephew made it his goal to spend at least10 hours a day, seven days a week, studying NCEE-related materials. His schoolteachers also kept in close contact with him and all his other peers, via the Internet or telephone, in order to help these youngsters remain focused so that they could immediately embark on a nine-month non-stop NCEE preparation sprint once the summer ended.

My nephew was not the only person in my family who was preparing for exams. My 20-year-old niece, a creative high school drop-out who likes to write fiction to entertain herself and others, was also preparing for an exam to secure a job as a cashier in a local clothing store. My sister, who works at a government-owned railroad company as a technical manager, was preparing for one of numerous exams to acquire various certificates as a technical supervisor and professional business manager.

In addition to my family, a close friend of mine, a nurse who used to work in a major hospital in Beijing, but left there 10 years ago to study law at an adult college, was embarking on her third try for the national bar exam to acquire a licence to practise law. My college classmate, who owns a small consulting company, was preparing for a test to become a professional counsellor, and his wife, a college professor, was taking an exam for English proficiency to apply for a scholarly-exchange grant as a visiting scholar in an American institute next year; having this work experience abroad was important for her promotion, as was passing this exam.

Perhaps, unlike any other time in Chinese history, during the first few years of the twenty-first century, one witnesses a whole society that is obsessed with various kinds of educational tests. Chinese websites and newspapers contain an overwhelming number of advertisements for various educational programmes, all of which require different forms of examination. For example, among the top five links from the homepage of sina.com—one of the most popular websites in China—four have a section devoted to educational testing. These five links are: (1) daily news for applying to schools in North America, (2) commercial and business directories, (3) applying for graduate schools of the Chinese Academy of Sciences, (4) exam preparation for human resources investment programmes of Beijing University, and (5) the EMBA programmes for advanced Chief Executive Officer training at Beijing University. In China, educational testing has become so commonplace that preparation for an exam has become a popular topic in daily conversation among people of all ages and professions.

What motivates Chinese people to work so hard to prepare for exams like the NCEE? What happened during the twentieth century to change the way China now views testing and create a societal obsession with these tests?

Chinese educational testing systems during the twentieth century

The Chinese educational testing system during the twentieth century was unlike that of most countries. In the beginning of the century, China, then named Qing, abolished its long-lived traditional educational testing system, the Imperial Examination

System (IES), which had lasted for 1300 years (AD 605–1905), and decided to incorporate various western models into its educational reforms. At different times in the twentieth century, China emulated three main educational models: that of Meiji Japan (1910s), the United States (1920s and after 1980), and the Soviet Union (1950s). While greatly influential, none of these were assimilated without major modification (Reynolds, 2001) as administrators have always been reluctant to make a radical break from the old system. As will be discussed in this essay, the Chinese traditional educational system had always existed as the principal guide for all of the country's twentieth century educational reforms. For example, the National College Entrance Exam (NCEE), the remote relative of the traditional Imperial Examination (IE), the world's oldest standardized test, has become increasingly modernized and westernized in content and format. However, its core principles—centralization and the super high stakes nature in deciding Chinese students' fates—remained the same as those of the old IES. A well-known motto may best describe the strategies Chinese educational administrators used in adopting western models into its educational reforms in the twentieth century: 'Chinese learning for essential principles and western learning for practical application'.[1] China is now experiencing a radical change in its educational testing systems. While Government-controlled examinations, such as the NCEE, remain important, their influence has declined as other tests, many providing important career opportunities, become more prominent.

This article seeks to examine both traditional and western practices and influences, and to consider the overall impact of western theories on the modernization of the Chinese educational system, its testing procedures and, ultimately, on Chinese people's lives.

The traditional Chinese educational system and the imperial examination

China has one of the oldest educational systems in the world. It can be traced back to the Western Zhou Dynasty (11th century BC–771 BC), when state-owned schools were seen as a viable means of nurturing and preparing future state officials (Xiong, 1983). These schools were established only for the sons of the aristocracy who were taught by teachers employed by the central government. Thus, the Chinese educational system has from its beginning been elite-orientated and dependent upon the interests of the state administration. The core function of the ancient Chinese education system was to produce a so-called scholarly official class, called 'shih', who, it was presumed, encompassed both moral and intellectual superiority, thereby justifying their political power, higher social status, and associated economic privileges (Hu, 1984).

The traditional Chinese educational system, which lasted for over 2000 years and significantly influenced the educational systems of its neighbouring countries such as Japan and Korea, is derived from the teachings of Confucius (551–479 BC), who placed moral education and the cultivation of benevolence as the ultimate goals of education. Confucius believed in an ideal society, where everyone behaved ethically and remained in social harmony with one other. Such an ideal could only be achieved when all human beings were free from deprivation and given proper education. Ironically, although Confucius himself believed everyone possessed the same potential and all should receive a proper education, the educational system derived from his teachings was in fact elite-orientated. Only a limited number of individuals could gain access to educational resources. It is also ironic that even though Confucius emphasized teaching the individual as a whole and practised individualized teaching himself, an educational system based on his theories consisted primarily of rote learning and memorization of the Classics. The Confucian philosophy of emphasizing individuality was only applied much later, in the twentieth century, when Chinese education was under the influence of the west (Xiong, 1983).

The Chinese educational system became more stabilized and rigid around thirteen centuries ago when an increasingly elaborate and crystallized civil service examination, named the Imperial Examination (IE) (*kējǔ*), was implemented to select government servants and leaders. This was based on how much and how deeply a candidate understood the Confucian classics (Grigorenko *et al.*, 2007).

The IE system originated in the Han (206 BC–AD 220), was initiated in the Sui (AD 580–618), established in the Tang (AD 618–907), fully developed in the Song (AD 960–1279), thrived in the Ming (AD 1368–1644) and Qing dynasties (AD 1644–1911), and was officially abolished in 1905, six years before the end of imperial system of China, thus lasting continuously for 1300 years. Consistent with the imperial hierarchy, the IE system was organized as a pyramid ranging from a low-level county test to a high-level palace test. This system formed the backbone of Chinese traditional education. To reach the top of the hierarchy, applicants took the county test, provincial test, capital test, and finally the palace test which was administrated in the palace under the direct supervision of the emperor. Most students would be screened out level by level, leaving very few to take the final exam (Franke, 1960; Yuan, 1994).

The format of the IE varied in different dynasties, but consisted primarily of essay-writing (although before the Song, poetry compositions were also used in order to discourage rote memorization as a means of test preparation) (Suen & Yu, 2006). Starting from the Ming dynasty, the essay was restricted solely to argumentation, using approximately 500 words (700 words in the Qing Dynasty), strictly following the format of the eight-legged essay (*baguwen*).

The general features of the IE, included the following from the Song dynasty: firstly, all of the examination titles were chosen from original texts of the Confucian canons, consisting of *The Four Books* and *The Five Classics*. For example, a title of 'If the people do not have enough, how can the ruler have enough?' was drawn from *one of* the *Four Books, The Confucian Analects*.

Secondly, the content of the essay had to be in accordance with the commentary from the schools of teaching and documentation of Neo-Confucianism, and more specifically, the Zhu (Zhu Xi, 1130–1200), Cheng (Cheng Hao, 1032–1085; and Cheng Yi, 1033–1107) schools. Therefore, in addition to memorizing all the Confucian canons, a candidate also had to be very familiar with Zhu and Cheng's commentaries on the Classics (Kao, 1999).

Finally, there was a fixed format for the structure of the essay. This had a complex set of rules, including a requirement of four pairs of antithetic and parallel sentences in the middle of the essay, from which the term 'eight-legged' was derived. The format of the eight-legged essay was extremely important for achieving success in the examination and had to be strictly followed. In many cases, the importance of the format outweighed that of the content itself.

In addition to the exhaustive preparation that normally took years and often decades, the examination itself and the evaluation process were also extremely time-consuming. The examinations typically lasted 24 to 72 hours, and were conducted in spare, cubical, and isolated examination rooms. Because of the pressure of the exam itself and the confinement of examination rooms, some candidates developed psychological problems and a few even died during these sessions (Suen & Yu, 2006).

All the examination essays were evaluated by an appointed government official familiar with the IE format. In order to obtain some level of objectivity, candidates were identified by number rather than name, and prior to being evaluated, their answers were rewritten by a third person to prevent their handwriting revealing their identity.

Most historians and psychologists have agreed that the IE was the first standardized test in the world that selected able individuals based on their knowledge and abilities in the test area (Zhang, 1988; Suen & Yu, 2006). The IE system permitted some level of objectivity, and rendered the selection of human resources rather less problematic than through other means. The system appeared to provide an equal opportunity to any Chinese male adult, regardless of his wealth or social status, with few exceptions (for example, some people, such as those from merchant-class families were not allowed to take the IE), to become a government official by passing the test. In reality, however, since the process of studying for the examination tended to be time-consuming and costly (private tutors often had to be hired), most of the candidates came from the numerically small but relatively wealthy land-owning gentry (Yuan, 1994). In contrast, the majority of ordinary Chinese people were illiterate and retained their low social status for generations.

There are several features associated with the traditional Chinese educational system and the IE that still have a significant impact on modern Chinese education. Firstly, the traditional Chinese educational system was elite-orientated, inseparable from the interest of state administration, and therefore a part of politics.

Secondly, the stakes of the exams were extremely high as the direct consequence of the exams resulted in appointments of high-ranking officials in civic services, and only very few individuals could eventually have these honours.

Finally, traditional Chinese education was a closed system in nature, permitting very few interactions with the outside world. Since only the Confucian classics were crucial in the success of the IE system, there was no value in studying subjects other than the classics, such as mathematics and natural sciences. There was also no reward system for creativity and innovation. This feature of the examination system helped to prevent China from continuing its advances in science and technology during the Ming (1368–1644AD) and Qing dynasties (1644–1911), while Europe entered the Renaissance and marched speedily toward modernization. The IE system reached its peak of complexity and stiffness in the Qing, when western imperialism started to extend outwards to the rest the world. Under the traditional system, China, led by its so-called scholarly officials, the beneficiaries of the IE system, became increasingly isolated on the international stage. To many liberated Chinese intellectuals of independent thought, the system was awkward and needed to be changed. While there were several attempts to reform the IE system during China's past, none of them succeeded on a large scale until the twentieth century when the influence of the west began to grow.

Chinese educational testing before the People's Republic (1905–1949): the first wave of western influence

During the 100 years between the mid-nineteenth to the mid-twentieth centuries, China was torn apart by military aggression from several western empires and its neighbouring Asian country, Japan. After witnessing scientific and technological advances in the west and the successful transformation of Japan from an agrarian state to a modern industrialized nation during the Meiji period (1868–1912), the reformers of the Qing government began to realize the value of incorporating adaptations of western learning into its long-lived, yet rather anachronistic, educational system.

The first state level educational reform was initiated in 1902 and implemented in 1904, when the Qing government decided to restructure the Chinese educational system by using the western graded-form schooling system. Meiji Japan's modern educational system appealed to the Qing administration as a successful model for incorporating western learning. Largely adopting this, the Qing government introduced a grade schooling system, which included 13 years of elementary education, 4 years of secondary education, and 6 years of higher education. Although they added subjects from the west, such as foreign languages and western science, the Confucian classics were still the major part of learning in every level of school (Xiong, 1983; Wang *et al.*, 1985). Another major educational initiative at this time was the reform of the IE system (in 1898, and again in 1901) and its eventual abolition in 1905. With the demise of the IE China lost its centuries-long practice of using standardized tests for the purpose of selecting personnel for government.

After the fall of the Qing in 1911, China underwent a series of western influenced educational reforms under different political administrations. There is a large literature on western influences on Chinese education at this time such as those on: higher education (Hayhoe, 1984, 1989, 1996; Hu, 1984; Ho, 2003), the student study-abroad movement (LaFargue, 1942; Wang, 1966; Su, 1979; Liu, 1981; Dong, 1985; Wang, 1992; Hayhoe, 1996; Tian, 1996; Ni, 2002), the rural education and mass education movement (Buck, 1945), and the modernization of Chinese education (Tian, 1996; Wang 1966).

Discussions about western influences on Chinese educational testing systems have, in contrast, been sparse, and have primarily focused on the second half of the twentieth century (Yuan, 1994; Grigorenko *et al.*, 2007). There are several publications, however, which provide good overviews of the development of psychological testing in China, with the influence of the west being one major theme (Zhang, 1988; Higgins & Sun, 2002; Shi, 2004). In the following section, I will examine western influences on both psychological and educational testing in the period before the establishment of the People's Republic of China.

Introducing psychological testing from the west

Modern psychometrics originated in the west at the beginning of the twentieth century (Thorndike & Lohman, 1990). It did not take long for the Chinese to become familiar with these measures. According to Zhang (1988), the first contemporary psychological test was introduced into China by a British scholar, Creighton, in 1915, in order to assess children's memory and analytical skills in Guangdong province. In 1919, China also started to offer college courses in many universities that introduced western theories and practices in educational and psychological testing. In 1916, Bingqing Fan first translated the Binet-Simon Intelligence Test into Chinese (Song & Zhang, 1987); however, it was Zhiwei Lu[2] (Lu, 1924) and T. M. Wu (Wu, 1936) who made the concept of intelligence testing popular in China. Lu (1924) first modified the Binet-Simon Intelligence Scale to make it more suited to the Chinese context and named it the Chinese Binet Intelligence Test (I) (CBIT-I). The CBIT underwent further revisions in the 1930s, and subsequently in the late 1970s by T. M. Wu (1936, 1980), ultimately becoming a classical measure of intelligence that is still used today (Zhang, 1988; Shi, 2004).

Several other western-originated intelligence tests were introduced into China between the 1920s and 1930s. For example, in 1922, Chan-En Liu, studying psychological testing in the 1910s at Columbia University, published his dissertation on 'the non-verbal intelligence test in China' (Liu, 1922). Wei Ai and his colleagues embarked on an enormous project in 1926, revising the Intelligence Test for Primary School children (ITPSC), and seeking national standardized norms. They travelled across the country, testing more than 30,000 students. Their data collection was constantly disrupted by the eight years of the Anti-Japanese War and the subsequent three years of civil war, and it took them almost 20 years to complete the study, eventually publishing the ITPSC through the Commercial Press in 1948 (Ai, 1948; Shi, 2004).

In addition, some non-verbal tests, such as Goodenough's 'Draw a Man Test', and the Merrill-Palmer Scale for infant and younger children, were also introduced between the 1920s and 1930s (Zhang, 1988). By the early 1930s, a total of 20 intelligence and personality tests, as well as 50 educational achievement tests, had been introduced into China (for details of these measurements, see Shi, 2004). Such developments led to the establishment of The Society of Psychological Testing in 1931, and the creation of a professional journal named *Testing* in 1932 (Zhang, 1988).

The western influence on various levels of educational assessment

With the abolition of the IE system in 1905, a need for a replacement naturally arose. The eagerness for introducing western tests between the 1920s and 1930s might well have reflected such a need. However, were these suitable for assessing educational competence and personnel selection in the Chinese context in the twentieth century?

The answer to this question is anything but simple. Chinese educational reforms in the first half of the twentieth century were intertwined with a series of wars (the warlord era of 1916–1928, the Anti-Japanese war of 1937–1945, and the civil war of 1946–1949) and political instability.[3] As a result, the state could play only a limited role in planning and supervising its newly developed school systems, and was unable to implement successfully any unified curriculum, textbooks, and teaching methods at the national level. Given these circumstances, it is unsurprising that a modern standardized educational testing system did not materialize and that for the most part, schools and institutions were left to design their own tests for the purposes of admission and assessing students' educational competence.

One important exam during the first half of the twentieth century worth mentioning is the comprehensive exam given by the Office of Sending Students to Study in the US, which was held every autumn between 1908 and 1929. The purpose of the exam was to select the best students to study in the US under the Boxer Indemnity Fund (BIF). On May 25, 1908, the US Congress passed a bill to return the non-expired Boxer Indemnity Fund to China, which would be used to support about 100 Chinese students each year to study in the US between 1909 and 1937 (Ye, 1989; 2001; Ni, 2002). Because of the long distance and the high cost of study in American institutions, very few people, usually from especially wealthy families, were able to afford to study in the US. Short of educational funds, the existence of the BIF made studying in the US a new possibility that attracted many highly motivated and talented Chinese students. Selection was highly competitive; all candidates needed to be equivalent to high school graduates and to have had several years of formal training in both Chinese and western learning. They were recommended by local governments based on their academic merit and performance on a provincial comprehensive exam. They were then qualified to take part in a further exam organized by the Office of Sending Students to America in Beijing. The first exam was held in August of 1908. To ensure quality, only 47 students were selected from a total of 640 candidates. Over the years, despite having 100 slots annually, the largest group in the years between 1908 and 1929 was a mere 70 students (Li & Liu, 2000; Ye, 2001).

This exam could be said to be the most demanding during that particular historical period, as studying abroad in the earlier part of the twentieth century, especially in an American higher institution under the BIF, was a great honour for Chinese students. Since they were selected from a national applicant pool, the prestige of passing the comprehensive exam and becoming a BIF-sponsored student was comparable to passing the highest level of the IE.

The exam was similar to many modern mastery tests but with more subjects. It included Chinese, English, Chinese history, geography, physics, chemistry, biology, algebra, geometry, and trigonometry. The predictive validity of the exam was very high, as the majority of the selected students were highly committed and excelled academically in the US. Among the first three groups of students (a total of 180 students), 30 of them had received Ph.D. degrees by 1907, and most had graduated from Ivy League universities. The majority of the others finished their college degrees and eventually entered graduate school. Many of the BIF-sponsored students came back to China and became a major force in driving China to modernize, some founding modern scientific disciplines in their home country (Su, 1979; Li & Liu, 2000).

Using a comprehensive examination to select the best candidates was an approach that extended to various levels of school admission during this period. Since there was no standardized curriculum during the period of the Republic and the Nationalist governments, such exams were normally created by individual schools. Therefore, the content and the difficulty levels of these varied. The nature of the exams was the same: primarily knowledge-based in subject areas that were deemed mandatory by different administrations. Some schools incorporated psychological and aptitude tests as experiments in recruiting students, but there was never a standard educational test formed at the national level, even for college admission purposes. There was an effort, however, from the Nationalist administration in 1939, to create a set of 'Regulations of University Administration', which included a national admission system. The system was characterized by traditional centralism; a national college admission committee was to be formed by the Minister of Education, and a standardized national testing service set up to guarantee the quality of candidates for higher education (Xiong, 1983). Because of the Anti-Japanese War and resistance from western missionary universities, however, such a plan was never put into operation.

It is hard to answer empirically whether any of the Chinese educational administrations during the first half of the twentieth century sought a replacement for the IE and whether any western-born psychological and educational tests had been brought to their attention as potential replacements. One thing that is certain is that Chinese scholars first introduced various western tests into China in the 1920s, and although they were interesting and refreshing to Chinese observers, most of these were still in their infancy even in their host countries, and their format and content were also drastically different from those of Chinese traditional measures. At this time, there was simply no large-scale standardized test in existence in the world.

Educational testing systems in the first three decades of the People's Republic: China under the Soviet influence

The People's Republic of China was established in 1949, after three years of civil war between troops led by two rival political parties: the Chinese Communist Party (CCP or *Gongchandang*) and the Chinese Nationalist Party (CNP or *Guomindang*).[4] Soon after its founding, the administration of the People's Republic was keen to reform the 'old' educational systems which had been established by the Nationalist government. According to their requirements, the new model should be modern yet politically acceptable and non-western in style. The Soviet educational model presented itself as the ideal choice and was soon transplanted into the Chinese system. Despite resistance from many scholars who had either studied abroad, or under westernized educational systems established by the Republican or the Nationalist governments, the new administration successfully completed its major educational reform in the early 1950s. The ten-year effort of transplanting the Soviet educational system made a significant impact upon the modern Chinese educational system (Xiong, 1983). Although relations between the two nations deteriorated in the late 1950s due to ideological disagreements, the modern Chinese educational system in the first three decades of the People's Republic largely continued to follow the Soviet model (Sheringham, 1984), partly because its centralized system and knowledge-based emphasis was consistent with Chinese traditions. Thus, for the first time in the twentieth century, China had unified its educational curriculum into a relatively well-structured and easily managed schooling system.

Chinese education under the first 30 years of the People's Republic was one of the most centrally controlled and politically charged educational systems in the world. Each school used the same national-style curriculum and unified textbooks created by the central authority. Such a system allowed a centralized educational testing system to exist, and led to the creation of the National College Entrance Exam (NCEE) in 1952, formed by the Ministry of Education for the purpose of determining college admissions. The exam was based on a modification of the Imperial Examination System (IES) proposed by the Republic government in 1939 (Yuan, 1994). Thus, in its first form, the NCEE was a product derived from the IES and reflective of Chinese political centralism. In essence, the NCEE was not influenced by the Soviet style of education, but rather by qualities largely inherent to the Chinese tradition.

Starting in 1953, the NCEE was required to gain access to college education, and was administered at the same time each year nationwide. Similar to the IES, the quota system was used to ensure the selection of an appropriate proportion of students from each province and provide equal opportunities to all. The NCEE was designed to recruit the best candidates possessing the following characteristics: politically trustworthy, academically well-prepared, and physically healthy.

During the turbulent Cultural Revolution (1966–1976), the NCEE was discontinued. Seeking to come up with an entirely new educational model, with no influence from either foreign or traditional Chinese educational systems, China decided to dismantle the existing higher educational system (mass education remained, largely following the Soviet model), and thus there was no value in keeping the NCEE. The result was to create a vacuum in Chinese higher education between 1966 and 1967 and when the colleges and universities reopened their classes in late 1967, admission was largely based on candidates' political stance and family background rather than their academic preparation (Kan, 1970).

The main form of educational assessment at this time was non-standardized classroom assessment created by teachers to evaluate the learning progress of students. However, there was strong encouragement from political leaders to rebel against any formal educational procedure or authority, with educational assessment being seen as a key component of this. The Chinese educational testing system, like many other areas, was in serious crisis, and its rebirth did not start until the 1970s.

Revival of psychological and educational assessments in China after 1980: the second wave of western influence

After the chaotic Cultural Revolution, China found itself standing on the debris of its former educational testing system. The role of education, which had been given insignificant status during the Cultural Revolution, now needed to be amended to meet the need of the nation's rapid modernization. In 1980, under the leadership of Deng Xiaoping, China set goals for education to 'face modernization, the world, and the future' (Jing & Zhou, 1985). In order to re-establish a new educational testing system, China once again opened its door to the rest of the world. Starting from the 1980s, there was a return to western educational testing theories and practice. The means of introducing these were threefold: (1) scholarly research and development; (2) governmental initiatives for integrating western models into its educational reforms; and (3) inclusion of various western commercialized and standardized models via non-governmental avenues.

Scholarly research and development

Psychology had been an active discipline prior to the establishment of the People's Republic, and Chinese psychologists had been a major force in introducing western educational and psychological testing theories and practice. As previously mentioned, many western psychological and educational assessments had been introduced into China as early as the 1920s. In line with the Soviet model, all psychological tests were banned from the 1950s, and during the Cultural Revolution, the entire discipline of psychology was suspended. By 1978, very few of the psychological measurements that had been introduced in the 1920s–1930s were still available and these had become very dated. In response to the urgent need to reintroduce new tests and train researchers and professionals in the field of psychological and educational assessment, four universities re-established departments of psychology in 1978, adopting curricula directly borrowed from western institutions. In 1979, the first psychological test training programme was held in the Department of Psychology of Beijing Normal University. Courses on psychological testing were offered in the same department in 1980. Meanwhile, research geared to revising western psychological and educational assessments for Chinese application had begun, led by psychologists who were trained before the establishment of the People's Republic (Zhang, 1988). Western intelligence tests such as the Denver Developmental Screening Test, the Wechsler Adult Intelligence Scale, and the Peabody Picture Vocabulary Test were among the first to be introduced into China in the early 1980s. There was a boom in the introduction of western intelligence tests in the 1980s and 1990s, and by 2001, a total of 22 intelligence tests had been introduced and revised (Shi, 2004).

In addition, a variety of personality and achievement measurements was also introduced. According to a survey conducted by Hangzhou University in 1993, over 50 psychological tests were introduced from the west in the 1980s and used for diagnostic purposes in mental health and school settings (Higgins & Sun, 2002)

Developing psychological and educational assessments became a popular new area in Chinese research. For example, Zha and her colleagues developed an inventory in the 1980s to diagnose intellectually gifted children This tool, named the Cognitive Ability Test for Identifying Supernormal Children (CATISC), included subscales for assessing short-term and long-term memory, numerical, verbal, and figural analogical reasoning, and creative thinking (Zha, 1986, 1990, 1993; Shi & Zha, 2000). A further measure the Basic Cognitive Ability Test (BCAT), sought to assess cognitive development in individuals aged between 10 and 90 years (Li et al., 2001).

Governmental initiatives for reforming NCEE

Western influence can be seen in the reform of the NCEE, which resumed in the spring of 1978, immediately after the Cultural Revolution ended. Because the NCEE was an indigenous product of the centralized Chinese educational system, it retained many of the features of the old IE, which included being knowledge-driven and inseparable from state interests. It has been under the close control of the central government since its inception (before 1984, it was managed by the State Ministry of Education, and thereafter by the Examinations Administration Centre of the State Education Commission). The examination process was, like the IE, very time-consuming, and consisted of a three-day examination based on multiple subtests in six or seven subject areas (For a review, read Grigorenko et al., 2007). There was no item bank for the NCEE at the outset, nor were there sufficient psychometric studies on the test itself (e.g. examining its reliability and validity). The predictive validity of the NCEE was held to be low. For example, one study showed that the correlation between test performance and students' achievement in college was much lower than the correlation between test performance and students' achievement in high school; thus, the original NCEE reflected students' prior knowledge in high school rather more than their aptitude for college studies (Zhang, 1988).

In the early 1980s, Chinese psychologists called for the replacement of this knowledge-driven test by a more aptitude-oriented test as well as the standardization of test items. This time, China turned her eyes to the west and cautiously sought help from experts in different countries, such as the United States, Japan, and some European countries, to assist in the evaluation of the NCEE. The outcome of this was widespread recognition that the tests needed to undergo multiple changes in order to become more adequately standardized and comparable with standardized tests administered in other countries.

Since 1984, the format and content of the NCEE have undergone several serious revisions (Heyneman & Fagerlind, 1985; Wang, 1995; Grigorenko et al., 2007) under the direct supervision of the Chinese Ministry of Education. Since the 1990s, the NCEE has become increasingly aptitude-driven, and the test format has become more similar to that of general ability tests, such as the American Scholastic Aptitude Test (SAT). Multiple-choice items constitute more than 50% of test items in each subject. The rest of the items include essays and fill-in-the-blank items. A professional evaluation of test difficulty is conducted after each year's testing, and testing experts have adopted modern western testing theories to monitor test items for appropriateness. Scanning machines are widely used for scoring multiple-choice items.

The most recent large-scale modification, implemented during the summer of 2003, was referred to as the *3+X System* (Wang, 1999, 2002; China Education and Research Network, 2001). The new NCEE includes only four subtests: Chinese, mathematics, English, and one of several comprehensive tests, depending on the track a student chooses. Accordingly, this allows the examination time to be reduced from three days to two.

Although the format and the content of the NCEE are changing, the purposes of the test and its role in students' lives have not changed. Students still take this high stakes exam at a fixed time each summer. These few days generally have a tremendous impact on the lives of millions of students. For many teenagers, especially those living in rural areas, a high score on the NCEE is almost their only chance to change their life paths. For them, the amount of knowledge they have obtained, supposedly reflected in their scores, becomes less important than the scores *per se*. Both teachers and students are under intense pressure to invest long hours preparing for the exam with test-related materials, such as exams used in previous years (Seeberg, 2000). Given the limited capacity of the Chinese higher education system, only 25% of high school students can enrol in college (around 5% of all Chinese 18–21-year-olds). For this reason, the NCEE is the most competitive and, undoubtedly, the most important exam in China (Seeberg, 2000).

Table 1 compares and contrasts the four exams, IE, NCEE in the twentieth century, NCEE in the twenty-first century, and the SAT.

From Table 1, one can see that the NCEE in the twentieth century shares many features in common with that of the IE. These similarities include the purpose of the exam, exam administration, creation, and scoring, social status of degree or title laureates, sources of financial support and employment for the degree or title laureates, regional quota for admission, as well as the relationship with the government. In essence, since the purpose of both tests is to select which candidates will best serve the central administration, be it an emperor or government, individuals' fates are inevitably tied to that of the administration. Another feature shared by these tests is that they were only given once a year, each lasting for few days. Preparing for either of these tests puts a lot at stake, as performance on the test would decide an individual's future once and for all. Table 1 also shows that, with regard to test subjects and format, the NCEE is closer to the SAT than to the IE.

Table 1 shows that the NCEE has grown more distant from the IE and closer to the SAT. For example, unlike the NCEE in the twentieth century when the central government had a strong influence on administration, creation, and scoring, these rights have now been delegated to local government. Also, while college graduates in the twenty-first century are no longer allocated jobs by the central government and enjoy warranted titles as national cadres, which typically mean to receive better positions in national corporations upon graduation from college, they can now freely choose their own life paths. In essence, the central government has gradually ceded

Table 1. Comparison among Imperial Examination (IE), National College Entrance Exams (NCEE) in the twentieth and twenty-first century, and American Scholastic Aptitude Test (SAT)

Principles	Imperial Examination (IE)	NCEE[a] in the 20th century	NCEE in the 21st century	Scholastic Aptitude Test (SAT)[b]
Initial year	605 A.D.	1952 (disrupted 1966–1977); and reopened in 1978	2003	1926
Purposes of the exam or the test	An exam to determine positions in civil services	College admission for selecting and training candidates as country leaders	College admission for education and enhancing future employment of individuals	College admission for education and enhancing future employment of individuals
Test administration	By test officials from regional government or the emperor	By the State Education Commission	By government of each province or direct-controlled municipality	By Private College Board, independent from government
Test development and scoring	By test officials from regional government or the emperor	By test experts organized by central government	By test experts from each regional government	By Educational Testing Service (ETS), a private organization
Social status of degree/title laureates	Government officials	Cadres, statuses differentiate them from ordinary people	No special status, but often as prerequisite for many positions	No special status
Source of financial support after the exam	Central administration	Central government	Private and government	Private or under financial aid from different resources
Employment upon receiving degrees/award	Appointed by emperor or high rank officials	Allocated by the government, often immediately upon graduation	Not immediately ready; individuals are responsible for employment	Not immediately ready, individuals are responsible for employment
Regional quota for admission or award distributions	Awards distributed according to regional quotas	Fixed admission quota for each region	Fixed admission quota for each region	No regional quota allocation
Relationship between award/degree laureates and government	Affiliated to the government unit as higher rank officials	Affiliated to the government unit as national cadres	Often no immediate affiliation with the government	Often independent from the government

Table 1. *(Continued)*

	Imperial Examination (IE)	NCEE[a] in the 20th century	NCEE in the 21st century	Scholastic Aptitude Test (SAT)[b]
Test frequency	Once every two to three years	Once a year	Once a year	Multiple times a year (mostly six or seven times)
Duration	One to several days	Three days	Two days	Three hours and 45 minutes for SAT reasoning test. One hour for SAT subject test
Practical applications				
Test subjects	Confucian classics	Seven subject areas learned in high school	3 (Chinese, English, and Mathematics) +X (a comprehensive exam)	One reasoning test plus several subject tests
Test format	Essay writings, particularly using the form of 'eight-legged essay' since the 14th century	Essay writing, problem-solving, fill-in-blank, some multiple choice items, and other forms	Essay writing, problem-solving, fill-in-blank, more multiple choice items than the 20th century test, other forms	SAT Reasoning test consists of multiple-choice tests and an essay-writing. SAT Subject test consists of multiple choice items only

[a] NCEE: National College Entrance Examination
[b] SAT is chosen as an example of the western counterpart of IE or NCEE

control of the NCEE (and of individuals) and the purpose of college education has becoming closer to that of the west.

Other forms of educational assessments in the public school system

China passed legislation in 1986 mandating nine years of compulsory education. Each child was to receive basic education (6 years in elementary and 3 years in middle school), although in reality, funding has always been insufficient in some areas to apply the law fully. As a result, some areas have been obliged to establish self-governed schools (*Minban* school) at a low cost that inevitably reduces the quality of the education provided. Being able to go to public school often becomes a privilege for children in these areas (Gordon & Wang, 2000).

Although the goals of the system of nine-year compulsory education are multifaceted, including equipping students with basic modern knowledge systems, promoting basic skills, stimulating interest and motivation for continuing study, and nurturing good learning habits (Chinese Ministry of Education, 2003), in reality, the high stakes nature of NCEE has distorted the Chinese public educational system. Thus, Chinese students live in a sea of exams and exercises from the day they enter elementary school. Since the majority of Chinese students will not be able to attend college, and high school education is not mandatory, getting into such institutions is the first step towards sitting and passing NCEE. As a result many cities and provinces have designed their own standardized high school entrance exams for middle school graduates. As these ultimately influence their chances to attend college, or for some students, to attend better colleges, the stakes of these exams are also very high.

Although there is currently no middle school entrance exam for elementary school graduates, most school districts design their own mastery tests for each grade of students to take by the end of the school year. However, the purpose of such tests is largely to examine the educational competence of each school. These additional exams and evaluations often add pressures to school administrators and classroom teachers. Under severe pressure to have their students achieve highly on measures such as mastery tests, graduation exams, or NCEE, school staff are tempted to coach students by means of additional formal and informal exams and exercises on a regular basis. Most of these measures are still knowledge-based, assessing how much students have mastered from previous levels of education. However, influenced by the structure of achievement tests in the west, standardized test items are now being included in certain subject areas such as mathematics and English.

The surge of study abroad and inclusion of commercialized western standardized tests

With the end of the Cultural Revolution and the start of an open door policy, more and more Chinese students have chosen to study abroad in order to enhance their educational and career opportunities. Under the auspices of the Chinese Ministry of Education, more than 800,000 Chinese have studied overseas in the period 1978–2004, mostly in western countries (Chinese Ministry of Education, 2004).

This number will surpass one million in 2007 and is likely to continue to grow as studying abroad has become fashionable among Chinese youth.

In keeping with this trend, many commercial foreign language proficiency tests have become popular in China. These include the Test of English as a Foreign Language (TOFEL), the International English Language Testing System (IELTS) and the Test of English for International Communication (TOEIC). Towards the end of twentieth century, other standardized tests (primarily from the United States) such as the Graduate Record Examination (GRE), the Graduate Management Admission Test (GMAT), and the Law School Admission Test (LSAT), as well as various professional certification exams, have also become widely accepted in China. These commercialized tests are run by centres that are independent of the state government and are not under the supervision of any governmental education authority.

The existence of various western educational models and testing systems not only provides a reference point for the modern Chinese educational system, it also provides routes for Chinese students to directly enter global education and become world citizens. Despite the absence of any formal policy, the needs of Chinese society have resulted in the creation of many new exams for those seeking to acquire professional licences. With the rapid development of high technology, there is an urgent need to fill a void for many new professions, such as software engineering. The existence of these new exams also provides access to many sought-after professions such as law, accounting, and business management, without even having degrees in these fields. NCEE seems no longer to be the only exam in the twenty-first century to decide one's career path. The Chinese educational system is about to experience new changes in this new century.

Conclusion

The importance of western influence on the Chinese educational testing system and Chinese people's lives is most evident in the following two aspects: firstly, under the influence of various nations, including the United States, Germany, France, Britain, Japan, and in the 1950s, the Soviet Union, the structure of Chinese education was fundamentally altered. This directly resulted in amendments to the content of educational testing, from a focus upon Confucian classics to the inclusion of modern western subject areas, and more recently, a move from knowledge-based tests to aptitude measurements. This transition has not only deeply affected the curriculum and pedagogical techniques, but has also prompted the amendment of educational policies. For example, the Chinese Ministry of Education recently initiated the Action Scheme for Invigorating Education Towards the Twenty-first Century. Its first and most important part is the promotion of 'Essential-qualities-oriented' or 'EQO (*suzhijiaoyu*) Education Project', which makes fostering students' innovative spirits and practical abilities foremost concerns in twenty-first century education (Xie, 2002). To implement EQO education, the Act suggests reforming the NCEE and other educational assessments to include more multiple-choice questions and the use of a procedure that is perceived to be more fair and scientific (hence more westernized). Prioritizing innovation and practical skills is a big leap from the concept of Chinese traditional education, which was driven by centralized educational exams emphasizing the acquisition of basic knowledge and skills. Perhaps it is still too early to evaluate the outcome of this recent initiative. However, it is an indication that China appears more willing than ever to make use of western psychological and educational models to guide its education reforms.

Beyond broader policy, western inspired reforms have impacted upon the everyday lives of Chinese students. In the shadow of the traditional educational testing systems, students lived through the drill of preparing for various exams, all of which culminated in the NCEE. The ability to combat exam-related anxieties, and the endurance developed over years of exam-preparation may help Chinese students excel in exams in comparison with their western counterparts. However, an exam-driven knowledge-based education may result in a sacrifice of independent intellectual inquiry and creative thinking (Niu & Sternberg, 2001, 2003). Such testing systems also promote homogeneity and may diminish students' motivation to pursue their own interests rather than exam-related academic work. Furthermore, many talented students, particularly those who are gifted in other areas, or who simply cannot endure preparing for numerous exams, may never have had a chance to excel or be recognized by their society. After a century-long assimilation to western models, some new educational reforms, such as the implementation of the EQO education, may provide hope for such students, and the existence of various western commercialized educational assessments may at least present them with opportunities to gain access to global education.

It is also worth noting that although western approaches to educational testing largely exert a positive influence on the Chinese system, these are far from a panacea for the problems facing Chinese education today. Moreover, the high visibility of western tests has resulted in an obsession with exams and a false belief on the part of the general public about their effectiveness in evaluating people's real potential. Additional burdens have been added to ordinary Chinese people who now have to face more educational exams in their lives than they ever had before. Finally, it is important to recognize the limits of tests. No matter where they come from, be it the west or China, and no matter how different they look, the ability they can assess only represents a small fraction of human potential. Thus, in any society, it is dangerous to use these tests decisively for determining one's fate and social mobility.

Acknowledgement

The author would like to thank the two editors of this volume, Professors Julian Elliott and Elena Grigorenko, for their patience and helpful comments on earlier drafts of this project. Special thanks are due to Professor Julian Elliott for his invaluable editorial comments on the final draft of this article.

Notes

1.   It is taken from Zhang Zhidong's (1837–1909) *Quan xue pian* (*Exhortation to learning*). His famous statement 'Chinese learning for the fundamental principles and western learning for practical application' is widely used to illustrate the reformers' half-hearted measures for reforming China.
2.   Lu Zhiwei (also spelled as CW Luh, 1894–1970), one of the founders of psychology in China. He studied psychology at the University of Chicago in the mid-1910s and received a Ph.D. in psychology there in 1920. He then taught at Nanjing Teachers College, Southeastern University, and Yenching University until 1952, when he became a research professor in the Institute of Linguistics, the Chinese Academy of Social Science.
3.   The early Republic was established in Beijing in 1912 after the fall of Qing but soon fell into an era of repeated wars among numerous warlords and fragmented by foreign powers. The Nationalists, led by *Guomindang*, unified the country again in 1928 and took Nanjing as its national capital. Later the Nationalists were forced to move to the interior of China during the Anti-Japanese war and ultimately they withdrew to Taiwan in 1949 after the three-year civil war.
4.   The Nationalist government withdrew to Taiwan, resulting in two entirely different Chinese societies, separated by the Taiwan Straits for over a half century, with different political ideologies and two different educational systems.

Notes on contributor

Dr. Niu worked in the Institute of Psychology, the Chinese Academy of Sciences, as a research scientist between 1989 and 1998. She received her Ph.D. in cognitive psychology from Yale University in 2003, and joined the Pace faculty the same year. She teaches experimental psychology and critical thinking. Her research has been focusing on studying the processes that constitute human thinking, and designing intervention programmes to cultivate these processes in school settings. More specifically, she has studied children's mathematical thinking and creativity. She is also interested in studying cultural, historical, and social influences on human potentials.

References

Ai, W. (1948) *Ability test for elementary school children* (Shanghai, Commercial Press).

Buck. P. S. (1945) *Tell the people—mass education in China* (New York, American Council Institute of Pacific Relations).

China Education and Research Network (2001) Beijing to try new college entrance exam plan. Available online at: http://www.edu.cn/20011212/3013800.shtml (accessed 20 June 2006).

Chinese Ministry of Education (2003) The guidelines for the nine-year compulsory education (10th edn.). Available online at: http://www.plutosoftware.com/ziyr/xcxtuuxtjcxtdagh.htm (accessed 30 June

Chinese Ministry of Education (2004) The statistics of Chinese students studying abroad, 1978–2004. Available online at: http://www.jsj.edu.cn (accessed 26 February 2006).

Dong, S. (1985) *History of studying abroad movement in the Qing dynasty* (Shenyang, Liaoning Province, Liaoning People's Press).

Franke, W. (1960) *The reform and abolition of the traditional Chinese examination system* (Cambridge, Harvard University Press).

Gordon, A. & Wang, Q. (2000) *Education in rural areas of China and South Africa: comparative perspectives on policy and educational management* (Nanjing, China, UNESCO International Research and Training Centre for Rural Education (INRULED)).

Grigorenko, E. L., Jarvin, L., Niu, W. & Preiss, D. (2007, in press) Is there a standard for standardized testing?, in: P. C. Kyllonen, R. D. Roberts, & L. Stankov. (Eds) *Extending intelligence: enhancement and new constructs* (Mahwah, NJ, Lawrence Erlbaum Associates).

Hayhoe, R. (1984) A comparative analysis of Chinese–western academic exchange, *Comparative Education*, 20(1), 39–56.

Hayhoe, R. (1989) China's universities and western academic models, *Higher Education*, 18, 49–85.

Hayhoe. R. (1996) *China's universities 1895–1995: a century of cultural conflict* (New York, Garland Publishing, Inc).

Heyneman, S. P. & Fagerlind, I. (1985) University examinations and standardized testing: principles, experience, and policy options. Paper given at a Seminar on the *Uses of Standardized Tests and Selection Examinations*, Beijing, China, April.

Higgins, L. T. & Sun, C. H. (2002) The development of psychological testing in China, *International Journal of Psychology*, 37(4), 246–254.

Ho, W. (2003) Westernization and social transformations in Chinese music education, 1895–1949, *History of Education*, 32(3), 289–301.

Hu, C. T. (1984) The historical background: examinations and control in pre-modern China, *Comparative Education*, 20(1), 7–26.

Jing, S. & Zhou, N. (1985) Comparative education in China, *Comparative Educational Review*, 29(2), 240–250.

Kan, D. (1970) *The impact of the cultural revolution on the Chinese higher education*. Unpublished doctoral dissertation, University of California, Los Angeles.

Kao, M. (1999) *History of the Chinese educational system* (Taipei, Linking Books Press).

LaFargue, T. (1942) *China's first hundred: educational mission students in the United States, 1872–1881* (Pullman, State College of Washington).

Li, D., Liu, C. & Li, G. (2001) The construction of the 'basic cognitive capacity test' and its standardization, *Acata Psychologica Sinica*, 33(5), 453–460. [in Chinese]

Li, X. & Liu, J. (2000) *Modern education of Chinese students who studied in the United States* (Tianjin, Tianjin Ancient Book Publisher).

Liu, B. (1981) *American overseas Chinese history* (Taipei, Daybreak Cultural Establishment).

Liu, H. C. (1922) *Non-verbal intelligence tests for the use in China* (New York, Teachers' College, Columbia University).

Lu, Z. (1924) *Chinese-Binet intelligence test* (Shanghai, Commercial Press).

Ni, T. (2002) *The cultural experiences of Chinese students who studied in the United States during the 1930s–1940s* (Lampeter, Ceredigion, Wales, The Edwin Mellen Press, Ltd).

Niu, W. & Sternberg, R. J. (2001) Cultural influences on artistic creativity and its evaluation, *International Journal of Psychology*, 36(4) 225–241.

Niu, W. & Sternberg, R. J. (2003) Societal and school influence on students' creativity, *Psychology in the Schools*, 40, 103–114.

Reynolds, D. R. (2001) Sino-foreign interaction in education, in: G. Peterson, R. Hayhoe, & Y. Lu (Eds) *Education, culture, and identity in twentieth-century China* (Ann Arbor, The University of Michigan Press), 23–30.

Seeberg, V. (2000) *The rhetoric and reality of mass education in Mao's China* (Lewiston, Ceredigion, Wales, The Edwin Mellen Press, Ltd).

Sheringham, M. (1984) Popularisation policies in Chinese education from the 1950s to the 1970s, *Comparative Education*, 20(1), 73–79.

Shi, J. (2004) Diligence makes people smart, in: R. J. Sternberg (Ed). *International handbook of intelligence* (Cambridge, Cambridge University Press), 325–343.

Shi, J. & Zha, Z. (2000) Psychological research on and education of gifted and talented children in China, in: K. Heller, F. Moenks, R. Sternberg & R. Subotnik (Eds), *International* handbook of research and development of giftedness and talent (2nd edn.) (Oxford, Pergamon Press), 757–764.

Song, W. & Zhang, Y. (1987) *Psychology measurement* (Beijing, Science Press).

Su, Y. (1979) *Modern history of Chinese student studying abroad movement* (Taipei, Gutian Publisher).

Suen, H. K. & Yu, L. (2006) Chronic consequences of high stakes testing? Lessons from the Chinese civil service exam, *Comparative Education Review*, 50(1), 46–65.

Thorndike, R. M. & Lohman, D. F. (1990) *A century of ability testing* (Chicago, The Riverside Publishing Company).

Tian, Z. (Ed.) (1996) *Overseas students and Chinese educational modernization* (GuangZhou, Guangdong Province, Guangdong Educational Press).

Wang, B., Guo, Q. Liu, D. He, X. & Gao, Q. (1985) *A concise history of Chinese education* (Beijing, Beijing Normal University Press).

Wang, G. (1999) The application of the '3+X' in NCEE and the reform of the public high school education, *Journal of Hebei Staff and Workers University*, 1(2), 62–65. [in Chinese]

Wang, J. (1995) *The college entrance examination and the development of higher education on the Chinese Mainland* (Taipei, the Mainland Affairs Council).

Wang, Q. (1992) *The historical track of Chinese overseas students, 1872–1949* (Tongshan, HuBei, HuBei Educational Press).

Wang, X. (Ed.) (2002) *Crucial questions faced to the Chinese education* (Beijing, Economic Daily Publisher).

Wang, Y. (1966) *Chinese intellectuals and the west: overseas students and modern China (1872–1949)* (Chapel Hill, The University of North Carolina Press).

Wu, T. M. (1936) *Second revision of Chinese-Binet intelligence test* (Shanghai, Commercial Press).

Wu, T. M. (1980) The nature of intelligence, *Acata Psychologica Sinica*, 3, 259–266. [in Chinese]

Xie, X. (2002) Quality education in China: EQO (Essential-qualities-oriented) education. Available online at http://epedagog.upol.cz/eped1.2002/mimo/clanek02.htm (accessed 19 May 2006).

Xiong, Mi. (1983) *The history of Chinese higher education* (Chongqing, Chongqing Press).

Ye, W. (1989) *Crossing the cultures: the experience of Chinese students in the USA, 1900–1925.* Unpublished doctoral dissertation, Yale University, New Haven, Connecticut.

Ye, W. (2001) *Seeking modernity in China's name: Chinese students in the United States, 1900–1927* (Stanford, Stanford University Press).

Yuan, F. (1994) From the Imperial Examination to the National College Entrance Examination: the dynamics of political centralism in China's educational enterprise. Paper presented at the *Annual Meeting of the Association for the Study of Higher Education* (nineteenth Meeting). Tucson, AZ, November 10–13.

Zha, Z. (1986) *Manual of cognitive ability test for identifying supernormal children* (Beijing, Institute of Psychology, Chinese Academy of Sciences).

Zha, Z. (1990) Study on gifted and talented children in China for ten years, *Acta Psychologica Sinica* 2, 115–118. [in Chinese]

Zha, Z. (1993) *Psychology of supernormal children* (Beijing, People's Publishing House).

Zhang, H. (1988) Psychological measurement in China, *International Journal of Psychology*, 23, 101–117.

The impact of the west on post-Soviet Russian education: change and resistance to change

Julian Elliott and Jonathan Tudge

Introduction

When witnessing events, such as the collapse of the Soviet Union, that have profound social, economic and political effects, it is not easy to make sense of what is happening. In this paper we will focus on some of the ways in which the Russian education system has changed and is continuing to change since the early 1990s. Some have argued that forces associated with the 'west' (apparently defined, at least implicitly, as the United States), including advertising, consumerism, liberalism, individualism and autonomy appear to be making rapid inroads into a formerly conservative and collectivist society. There is evidence to show that this process is happening in Russian schools, as western ideas about education seem to have superseded 'outmoded' Soviet ideas. Our aim is to show that this position is too simplistic, and fails to take account of the heterogeneous nature of Soviet, Russian, and American society in general and of schools in particular. Before discussing the changes that have occurred in Russian schooling, we will introduce our theoretical perspective, as it is this perspective that has helped us to make sense of the nature of these changes.

Theoretical overview

Education is intimately connected with intervention; teachers intervene in the thought processes of the students they teach, trying to persuade them to think differently about some aspect of reality than they did before. In a world in which contact between cultures seems the rule rather than the exception, it is thus perhaps not surprising that some scholars assume that apparently successful educational methods in one culture should be applied in another culture, an interventionist strategy across cultures. Others, however, argue that approaches that are successful in one culture are unlikely to be successful in another culture, given that each has different histories, values, beliefs, and practices. These competing views, universalistic and particularistic, are linked to some basic differences of opinion about the nature of human beings and the relations between humans and the cultures in which they are raised.

In the fields of education and psychology these differences are exemplified at the theoretical level by Piaget and Vygotsky. Although Piaget clearly recognized that the social world, including culture, has a major impact on children's development, he was primarily interested in what it is that we as humans have in common, the 'epistemic' individual. He was thus less concerned with the fact that in some cultures, given particular sets of circumstances, children might move through the stages of cognitive development faster than those growing up in other cultures than with the fact that all children and adolescents, given appropriate circumstances, will go through the same stages of development in the same order. By contrast, although Vygotsky wrote about the stages of development of mathematical thinking or clearly distinct periods of childhood and adolescence, his focus was far more on the ways in which different cultures, thanks to their differing historical circumstances, are linked to different ways of thinking and behaving.

Although it may be tempting to understand these views of human development as simply reflecting different theoretical positions, they are in fact related to different paradigms (Tudge & Hogan, 2005). As Guba and Lincoln (1994) stated, a paradigm refers to 'the basic belief system or worldview that guides the investigator, not only in choices of method but in ontologically and epistemologically fundamental ways' (p. 105). This position was first put forward by Pepper in the early 1940s. Pepper (1942) argued that, within the field of human development, there are four fundamentally distinct worldviews, which he labelled mechanism, organicism, contextualism, and formism. He described each worldview as having a distinctive stance on the nature of reality, on how that reality (or realities) can be known, and as having its own appropriate methodological stance. Each worldview also has its own root metaphor—that of the machine for mechanism, the living organism for organicism, the historical event for contextualism, and similarity in the case of formism. Deriving from Pepper's initial discussion of different paradigms, a number of scholars (Overton & Reese, 1973; Overton, 1984; Guba & Lincoln, 1994; Winegar, 1997; Goldhaber, 2000; Kuczynski & Daly, 2003) have discussed the ontological, epistemological, and methodological consequences of taking seriously these different paradigms, focusing primarily on mechanism, organicism, and contextualism. The two most relevant to this paper are mechanism and contextualism.

The mechanist worldview is essentially the neo-positivist position that dominates psychology in the United States. The neo-positivist mechanist ontology involves the position that reality is not directly knowable, but that methods are available that can allow us to 'disprove' incorrect views of reality, by subjecting different claims to careful and critical examination. The relevant epistemological and methodological positions are that careful experimental control is necessary to ensure that we can make appropriate (and generalizable) claims about reality. Not surprisingly, the dominant methods are quantitative, although some use of qualitative methods is encouraged as a way of generating new hypotheses to be tested (the tests themselves are almost always quantitative) and allowing some consideration of meaning for individual subjects of the research.

By contrast, the contextualist paradigm takes a dialectical position on the nature of reality, arguing that instead of clear cause-effect relationships development arises as an emergent property of the interrelations between properties of the developing organism and the context in which the organism develops. The context, for contextualists, includes both the local setting (such as the home or school) and the broader cultural and historical contexts which help give meaning to what occurs within those local settings. Not surprisingly, when comparing this dialectical paradigm with mechanism, one should expect differing views on the nature of reality in different groups, and methodological approaches that neither attempt to create a clear separation of researcher and the participants in research, nor value careful controls as ways to establish clear causal relationships.

We are going to describe one of the major contextualist theories, that of Urie Bronfenbrenner. It is interesting, given the focus of our paper, to note that Bronfenbrenner was born in Russia but lived in the US since early childhood. As is the case with all contextualist theories, Bronfenbrenner's bioecological theory requires that simultaneous attention be paid to characteristics of individuals, the interactions those individuals have with their surrounding environment, and the broader context (both temporal and spatial) that helps to give meaning to those interactions. It should be clear at the outset, therefore, that contextualist theories do not give priority to the context, but focus on the interactions of individual and context.

Although Bronfenbrenner's theory was viewed for many years simply as one relating the impact of context on human development, this has never been his position (Tudge, *et al.*, 1997). In the decades since the publication of *The Ecology of Human Development* (1979), Bronfenbrenner progressively refined the theory and what he termed the 'PPCT model' as a way of instantiating the theory in research. This model requires one to consider the interrelations among four key concepts: Process, the Person, Context, and Time (PPCT). Of these the first, or 'proximal processes', plays the key role in development, for proximal processes are the 'primary mechanisms producing human development' (Bronfenbrenner & Morris, 1998, p. 994). Proximal processes are the core of his theory and constitute the interactions 'between an active, evolving biopsychological human organism and the persons, objects, and symbols in its immediate environment' (Bronfenbrenner, 2005, p. 6). It is these proximal processes that Bronfenbrenner repeatedly described as being the 'engines of development' (Bronfenbrenner, 1995, p. 620), because they constitute the types of everyday activities and interactions in which developing individuals engage repeatedly and in gradually more complex ways, often with more competent members of their social group. It is through these types of activities and interactions that individuals come to make sense of their world, understand their place in it, and, as we will describe below, change their world.

As Bronfenbrenner made increasingly explicit in his later writings, perhaps responding to the fact that he continued to be cited as a theorist of context, proximal processes are key to the theory, but their nature varies according to aspects of the individual and to the context (Bronfenbrenner, 1995, 1999; Bronfenbrenner & Morris, 1998). At the individual level, Bronfenbrenner acknowledged the relevance of biological and genetic factors (Bronfenbrenner & Ceci, 1994; Bronfenbrenner & Morris, 1998; Bronfenbrenner & Evans, 2000), but devoted more attention to the personal characteristics that individuals bring with them into any social situation. He divided these characteristics into three types, which he termed demand, resource, and force characteristics. Demand characteristics are those of age, gender, physical appearance, etc., whereas resource characteristics are such things as past experiences, skills, and intelligence. However, Bronfenbrenner focused more on force characteristics; these have to do with differences of temperament, motivation, persistence, and the like. According to Bronfenbrenner, two children may have equal resource characteristics, but their developmental trajectories will be quite different if one is motivated to succeed and persists in tasks and the other is not motivated and does not persist.

Thus Bronfenbrenner provided a clear sense of individuals' roles in altering proximal processes, from the relatively passive (changing the environment simply by being in it, to the extent that others react differently to individuals based on their age, gender, skin colour, and so on), to the more active (the ways in which individuals change their environments are linked to the types of physical, mental, and emotional resources they have available to them), to the most active (the extent to which individuals change the environment is linked to their motivation to do so, persistence, and so on).

Proximal processes are also profoundly influenced by the contexts ('systems') in which they occur. The two key systems for Bronfenbrenner are the microsystem and macrosystem. (The other two systems, mesosystem and exosystem, are less relevant to our argument and will not be discussed here.) The microsystem is important because proximal processes occur within microsystems, the settings within which individuals can have face-to-face interactions with others as they engage in the various types of activities made available within those settings. For most individuals, home is one such microsystem, as is childcare or school for many children and adolescents, and the workplace is another such system for adults who work outside the home.

The macrosystem is the other key system in this ecological model. Bronfenbrenner defined the macrosystem as a context encompassing any group ('culture, subculture, or other extended social structure') whose members share value or belief systems, 'resources, hazards, lifestyles, opportunity structures, life course options and patterns of social interchange' (Bronfenbrenner, 1993, p. 25). By this definition, different societies constitute different macrosystems but so too do different groups (socio-economic, regional, ethnic, racial) within society. This notion of a number of macrosystems within any society precludes societal homogeneity, making it difficult to accept that an entire society can be individualistic or collectivistic, or that all parents or all teachers in any society are equally interested in fostering autonomy or conformity.

The macrosystem is critically important because microsystems, where proximal processes (the everyday practices and interactions) occur, are profoundly influenced by the macrosystem within which they are situated. A group's values, beliefs and resources influence the types of settings that are made available to the young of the group, the way the young are treated, the nature of interactions, and so on. But note that the group's values, etc., only exert an influence; they do not determine settings, treatments, interactions, because proximal processes are as much determined by the individuals involved as by the context.

The final element of the PPCT model is time. Although the theory has consistently been concerned with human development (time therefore has to be a key factor) this became increasingly explicit in the last decade of Bronfenbrenner's life. From 1995 onwards T was added to what had until then been a PPC model, and Bronfenbrenner specified that an individual's proximal processes varied by aspects of the individual, the spatial context, and the temporal context, or 'the continuities and changes occurring in the environment over time, through the life course, and during the historical period in which the person has lived' (Bronfenbrenner, [2001] 2005, pp. 3–15). Bronfenbrenner drew on Elder's (1974, 1996) research to show how specific historical events could have varying effects depending on the ages of the individuals experiencing them. This idea, dealing with the impact of historical events, such as the collapse of the Soviet Union or a particular country experiencing a period of economic growth or entering a deep recession, is clearly relevant to this paper.

We have devoted so much attention to Bronfenbrenner's theory because, as with any good theory, it can help us to understand development. Typically, reading a sentence like this, one might think of developing individuals, but in this case the theory can help us to make sense of the development of a society, particularly one such as Russia that has been undergoing rapid change over the past two decades.

Western influences upon Russian schooling and society

It is impossible to consider schooling in contemporary Russia without considering what Bronfenbrenner termed macro-time. The immense changes that have taken place in that society since the early 1990s have had profound effects, as Bronfenbrenner would have predicted. A regular visitor to the major Russian cities in the mid-1990s could not fail to observe the rapidly increasing presence of western influences and iconography, perhaps reminiscent of the time of Peter the Great and the first major attempt to 'westernize' Russia. As the shops transmogrified from enterprises that almost sought to exclude potential customers, to become seductive purveyors of goods that had not hitherto been accessible to the majority of the people, the salience of western consumerism, from luxury cars to fast food, was heightened by a rapid and sustained embrace of advertising and marketing.

In the schools, a new-found infatuation with the west could similarly be observed. As the traditional school uniform was gradually phased out, youngsters sought to express their new found freedoms by wearing sweatshirts emblazoned with US sporting teams or iconic western products. On their feet, those profiting from economic transformation sported western training shoes, many costing more than their teachers would earn in a month.

Changes at the level of macro-time do not filter down to all microsystems at the same rate or with the same effects, mostly because old cultural patterns of activities (proximal processes) continue to exert an influence, particularly as the individuals involved (teachers, when thinking about schooling) for the most part stayed the same. Thus, despite this outward embrace of US culture, in the schools, teaching and learning continued very much as it had done throughout Soviet times. Students presented as hard-working, disciplined, compliant, and exhibited high educational standards. Despite the intense social, economic and ideological changes within wider society, there appeared to have been little impact upon everyday school practices (Alexander, 2000; Hufton & Elliott, 2000) and the majority of schools appeared essentially to be identifiable in the terms described by earlier writers (e.g. Bereday *et al.*, 1960; Grant, 1972). Rather than being disrupted by the social turbulence of the early 1990s, it appeared that schools were acting as a set of microsystems in which long-term continuity and stability of educational practice offered a degree of respite from external pressures at the macrosystem level.

However, the appropriation of physical symbols such as dress and material possessions served as only the advance party for the more pervasive influence of western ideas and practices. Despite a long history of high educational standards, largely superior to those in many Anglo-US contexts, it was not long before Russian schools and universities were playing host to teachers, academics and assorted education consultants from the US and Western Europe, all eagerly promulgating their theories and practices in respect of educational reform. In addition to small-scale partnerships, western-inspired reforms were also advocated by major international bodies such as the World Bank, the Soros Foundation, the British Council, the Carnegie Foundation and the United States International Agency (Polyzoi & Dneprov, 2003). Such initiatives, often presented by international aid agencies as value-free, technical approaches applicable to any context, in actuality reflect a particular political world-view in which democratic pedagogy, learner-centredness, and individual autonomy are seen as necessary prerequisites for full participation in a capitalist society (Tabulawa, 2003).

So what happens when one set of values and beliefs, related to a given macrosystem, is imported into another? As we pointed out earlier, the macrosystem influences the microsystem because group-wide values and beliefs are put into practice by individuals engaged in proximal processes. By the same token, as one should expect from a contextualist theory (i.e., one that does not deal in unidirectional flows), what occurs on an everyday basis within microsystems also influences the macrosystem. One should therefore not expect that the import of a new set of educational values and beliefs from the west would have any unidirectional or direct impact on what occurs in schools. Moreover, although it is undoubtedly the case that the prevailing ideology in the United States stresses autonomy and individualism (Hofstede, 1991, 2001) and Soviet ideology clearly stressed collectivism (Schwartz, 1994; Triandis, 1995; Realo & Allik, 1999) societies, as noted above, are not homogeneous. As scholars have increasingly come to recognize, values more commonly associated with collectivism are to be found in US society, related both to social class and ethnicity (Strauss, 2000; Gjerde, 2004). Even when children are of preschool age, many American parents are as likely to stress group values as those of the individual (Tobin *et al.*, 1989). And while American school ideology might well stress the importance of encouraging individualism and autonomy, the experiences of many children and adolescents might be far more suggestive of the opposite. Similarly, in the former Soviet Union the individual rewards for those associated with the *nomenklatura* [political elite], such as their more agreeable living conditions, access to goods and services that were next to impossible for ordinary Soviet citizens to receive, and relatively free ability to travel abroad, hardly fit well with an ideology of collectivism. In schools, too, although competition between groups was part of the collective ideal, there were also individual rewards for those who excelled scholastically, artistically, or in the world of sport.

Nonetheless, despite the lack of such clear-cut distinctions in practice, we will illustrate in the pages that follow a major difference between Soviet and western educational theory—the relative emphasis placed upon democratic classroom practice. We highlight ideas popular in the west that emphasize the role of personal agency and autonomy, the meeting of individual needs and the concomitant decline in emphasis upon subordinating one's own desires to the needs of the broader collective. How will such a set of values and beliefs fare when transplanted into a society in which the prevailing proximal processes are in accord with a different set of values and beliefs, those emphasizing far more individual conformity to the needs and wishes of the group?

Often in education, the success or failure of particular theories in impacting upon teacher practice is determined by the current zeitgeist that provides a context where it accords with other social and intellectual forces. Thus, for example, the immense popularity of Gardner's theory of multiple intelligences (Gardner, 1983) is, in part, attributable to the beliefs of many teachers that the standards movement, with its emphasis upon basic academic skills, has resulted in a neglect of the education of the whole person (Moseley *et al.*, 2005). Often, the adoption of theory is as much a consequence as a cause of changing social and educational circumstances and, for this reason, it seems likely that the embrace of western educational theory by Russian reformers may reflect more pervasive and global influences in which individualism, detachment from traditional ties and settings, and an emphasis upon personal choice and individual agency are key components of 'late modernity' or 'postmodern' society (Giddens, 1991; Inglehart & Welzel, 2005).

It is a truism that classroom learning cannot be maximized where there is disorder, indiscipline, and student behaviour that runs counter to the needs of the class group. To this end, Russian classrooms have historically been reported as typically being orderly and disciplined (Bronfenbrenner, 1967; Muckle, 1990; Alexander, 2000; O'Brien, 2000; Elliott *et al.*, 2005). Such a pattern, despite more recent concerns that we shall list below, appears to have persisted into the new millennium. In the Programme for International Student Assessment (PISA) study (OECD, 2003), for example, the views and performance of more than a quarter of a million students in 41 countries were examined, together with the perspectives of their teachers and principals. Russian informants were among those least likely to report that lessons were disrupted by noise and disorder, or that students were slow to become engaged in their lessons.

Since the end of the Soviet period, there has been much debate about the nature of teacher–student relations and the appropriateness of western democratic conceptions for Russian classrooms. One of the central canons of US values has been the importance of personal freedom and individualism, although the practice in American schools does not always accord with this prevailing ideology. Nonetheless, this has been represented in educational theorizing and practice by approaches that emphasize individual agency, choice, meeting individual student interests and preferences, and prioritizing student self-regulation over the exercise of adult authority (Deci & Ryan, 1985; Ryan & Deci, 2000).

Such ideas would appear alien in respect of Russian traditions that long pre-date the Soviet period and also that are largely at odds with socialization practices handed down from the Soviet period. From the age of three, most children were involved in group activities where, from within a supportive and caring environment (Markowitz, 2000), they were taught to cooperate, recognize and respect the interests of the group, and defer to the authority of adults (Tudge, 1991). In school, from the age of seven, Soviet children were taught clear codes of moral behaviour and respect for adult authority. However, in a way very different to that of the US, Soviet teachers also sought ultimately to develop children's capacity for self-regulation. Here, peer influences were crucial, as gradually a degree of behavioural regulation was transferred from the class teacher to the class group, and finally to the individual. Displaying a nice portrayal of the links between culture-wide values, the fostering of specific proximal processes, and a change in individual characteristics, a manual written for teachers and youth group leaders stated:

> The children not only try to do everything as well as possible themselves, but also take an evaluative attitude towards those who are undermining the achievement of the row. If similar measures arousing the spirit of competition in the children are systematically applied by experienced teachers in the primary classes, then gradually the children themselves begin to monitor the behavior of their comrades and remind those of them who forget about the rules set by the teacher, not to forget what needs to be done and what should not be done. The teacher soon has helpers. (Novikova, 1959, cited in Bronfenbrenner, 1970, p. 55)

Bronfenbrenner (2005) notes that not only did peers support behaviour consistent with the values of adult society, they were also encouraged to take personal initiative and responsibility for developing and retaining such behaviour in others. Thus, while pursuing the adult agenda, the process provided students with a sense of agency and control. Having employed monitors to help emphasize desirable standards of conduct, the teacher then encouraged children to provide their own self-evaluations with the aim of outlining areas for improvement. The teacher's ultimate aim was student self-regulation of behaviour, a goal that, superficially, might appear to be in concert with that of western theory. However, any freedom of choice and opportunity to operate in ways counter to the teacher's intention was largely illusory.

For many western educationists, such a picture might represent an Orwellian nightmare of oppression and mind control that runs counter to the major precepts of US motivation theory, where student engagement is seen to be increased by the presence of authenticity (i.e. activities have meaning for students' everyday experience and future goals), challenge, choice over content and learning approaches, and relate to student skills interests and abilities. Where such factors operate there is believed to be more likelihood of intrinsic motivation, a less passive orientation, increased feelings of control, and a greater sense of personal accomplishment (Yair, 2000; Seifert & O'Keefe, 2001).

While few would argue with the perceived value of the constructs listed above, the practicalities involved in creating effective educational contexts, underpinned by democratic principles, are sometimes understated. Indeed, not only are there dangers in assuming that individualism and self-determination will operate unproblematically in non-western classrooms, but there is often also insufficient recognition that there exist inherent difficulties in western contexts also. In his study of primary education in five countries, for example, Alexander (2000) describes the tensions that were evident in schools in Michigan where organizational complexity and an associated ideology of democratic pedagogy resulted in greater levels of student distraction, restlessness and challenge to teacher authority. As a result, monitoring, rather than instruction, formed a significant proportion of teacher–student interaction. Across the five countries studied, Alexander (2000) noted the sharpest contrasts between the Russian and the US lessons:

> In the one context the substantive messages about the nature of knowledge, teaching and learning and about behavioural norms and expectations were unambiguous yet also—bar the occasional brief reminder—tacit; in the other context they were the subject of frequent reminders by the teacher and often intense encounters ranging from negotiation to confrontation. (p. 318)

Such difficulties result from pedagogic practices that reflect very different underlying value systems:

> In an authoritarian teaching culture routines will not be negotiated or contested because teachers simply will not permit this to happen, while in a teaching culture that espouses democratic values routines not only will be negotiated and contested but by definition must be. The combination of complex classroom organisation, unpredictable lesson structure and avowedly democratic pedagogy, such as we found in Michigan, is a sure-fire recipe if not for conflict then certainly for the constant testing of regulatory boundaries. (Alexander, 2000, pp. 385–386)

While it is no doubt possible to create a democratic, collaborative classroom with high levels of self-regulation and discipline, the reality is such that it is often difficult for teachers, particularly those working in highly demanding socially disadvantaged contexts, to provide such environments and maintain high standards of student engagement and academic striving. In situations where motivation is not high, an 'implicit bargain' may be struck in which teachers and students come to an unspoken agreement that few heavy academic demands will be made in return for an acceptable level of compliance. Sedlak *et al.* (1986) argue that in such circumstances the result can be a diversion from an academic focus, informal banter, forms of pedagogy that, while meeting student preference, are lacking in rigour, and teacher–student negotiation about what should be taught, the standards that should be expected, and the nature of work assignments. What can be easily overlooked, therefore, is that increasing student academic freedoms, in a context where there are unclear understandings about adult authority, is likely to place great demands upon young people's capacity for self-discipline and self-regulation.

It is thus important to reiterate that not only are societies heterogeneous and that there are likely to be discrepancies between any society's ideology and the values and beliefs of any given macrosystem within that society, but also that there is no simple one-to-one correspondence between the values and beliefs of the macrosystem on the one hand and proximal processes on the other; values are not always put into practice, as one should expect from a contextualist theory that emphasizes that proximal processes (what happens on a regular basis in classrooms, for example) vary not only by the broader context but by the particular motivations, needs, demands, and so on of the individuals themselves. Rather than positing any unidirectional flow, Bronfenbrenner's theory is dialectical.

The need for change?

While visitors to Russian schools have largely praised their high standards of achievement and behaviour (Canning *et al.*, 1999; Alexander, 2000; Hufton & Elliott, 2000), it would be as misleading to provide an idealized picture of the earlier Soviet classroom in which all students were hard-working, highly motivated and shared the state's ideals and values as it would be to argue that all US schools, teachers, and students accept unconditionally that society's dominant ideology. While lauding the high academic and behavioural standards of the Soviet period, western commentators (e.g. Muckle, 1990; Westbrook, 1994) criticized the strong ideological component that minimized debate and controversy and often undermined students' individuality. Despite attesting to the high standards in mathematics, sciences and general level of erudition, Eklof (2005) raises concerns that Soviet students were less skilled in applying their knowledge. Polyzoi and Dneprov (2003) talk of authoritarian and inflexible teaching methods. Froumin (2005) refers to students in Soviet schools who were alienated by the emphasis upon control and conformity and whose behaviour was perceived by the authorities as 'disadaptation'. Markowitz (2000) is critical of the student passivity that resulted, whereby less motivated students tended to withdraw rather than disrupt. Others (e.g. Glowka, 1995) have countered this perspective by noting that Russia has a long tradition of authoritarianism (and therefore students might be more accepting of it), and Schweisfurth (2000) cites favourable adult reports of Soviet schooling. However, in an age when independence of thought and the need to adapt to high challenging times are seemingly universally emphasized (Giddens, 1991), such criticisms were widely recognized as meaningful by Russian progressives and by the end of the Soviet period many Russian educators had come to believe that the time for change had arrived.

Responding to calls for more democratic and individualistic emphases, the *1992 Law of Education in the Russian Federation* thus sought to increase opportunities for personal self-determination, democratic relations and 'humanization' (i.e. responding to students as unique individuals with differing goals and potentials). However, as one might expect from the simple importation of values without any corresponding means of changing proximal processes, teachers were largely unaware as to how to put these ideas into practice, particularly as their professional skills and knowledge were closely bound to long-established methods (Elliott *et al.*, 2005). Some paid lip-service (Eklof & Seregny, 2005) while others actively resisted calls to change believing that traditional methods were necessary for addressing Russia's difficulties (Belkanov, 2000; Mitter, 2003; Polyzoi & Dneprov, 2003). Given these uncertainties, it was not surprising that tensions soon emerged.

The positive and negative effects of change

> The individual's own developmental life course is seen as embedded in and powerfully shaped by conditions and events occurring during the historical period through which the person lives. (Bronfenbrenner, 1995, p. 641)

In Bronfenbrenner's theory, culture-wide values and beliefs are always undergoing change, simply by virtue of each new generation bringing their own perspectives, needs, drives, and interests to bear. In times of major historical shifts, as occurred with the break-up of the Soviet Union, this process of change is more rapidly seen.

It is possible to see the effects of the rapid and widespread changes that have taken place in the lives of everyone—young children, adolescents and their parents. Often, opinion is divided as to whether change has proven desirable. As part of the Cultural Ecology of Young Children project (see, e.g., Tudge *et al.*, 2000; Tudge, 2006), parents of children who had just entered school in a small city south of Moscow were interviewed about what was happening in their children's lives. The following two segments, both from single mothers (although from different social class groups) show clearly the range both of feelings about the changes and about the extent of changes that these women and their young children were experiencing. One woman, who worked as a cleaner and made barely enough to get by on, was not at all happy with the changes:

> I don't trust our government. I think they are highly incompetent...I am disappointed in the State; I had never dreamed my life would be so hard. So I tell [my son] all the time that he should learn and learn. I still hope things will turn for the better.

She also had this comment to make about her son's teacher: 'Their relationships are just wonderful. She is attentive and strict. She makes them work a lot, and the children learn well'. She noted, in fact, that her son's '...teacher is stricter than mine had been. His teacher uses play at the lessons, but the children stay quiet. They have freedom at break'. The teacher herself pointed out: 'When I was at school our teachers were more authoritarian than we are now'. However, she went on to say:

> At the age of 6–7 years democracy as such is not that important. The little ones are learning to be disciplined. If a child is not taught how to listen to the teacher and how to work, he will have a hard time learning later on. No talent will help. During the first two years at school the child is taught to be interested and attentive.

Such a perspective reflects findings from a parental survey undertaken by Froumin and colleagues in 1995 (see Froumin, 2005, p. 134) in which 45% of respondents regarded humanization as harmful, seeing strictness and high demands as the most desirable qualities in teachers. Similarly, parental desire to have their children study in experimental educational programmes fell from more than 70% in 1991 to 35% in 1996.

On the other hand, a middle-class mother, who at the time was making more than four times more money than the cleaner mentioned above, paid for her daughter to go to a new private school, and expressed her delight at the changes that had occurred in recent years:

> This school allows the parents a choice of programmes for their child. ... While with the usual kind of programme the teacher explains to the pupil all he needs to know, here the way to teach is to pose a problem before the child, and to do it in such a way that the child arrives at the solution himself or with the help of the teacher. The child goes all the way himself; he is not led by the hand.

The child's teacher also expressed her enthusiasm about the changes that had taken place: 'School has changed over the recent years, much changed, as a matter of fact. New programmes appeared...programmes of "developmental teaching" [i.e., teaching that is adapted to the pace of the child] as well as new methods of teaching'.

Debate has concerned not only the appropriateness of western pedagogic models and notions of teacher authority but also the desirability of differing cultural emphases upon the ultimate purpose of education. Many Russian commentators have expressed worry about the rise of materialism and, as a consequence, a perceived challenge to the esteem in which education has long been held. Growing instrumentalism has resulted in greater emphasis upon education as a means to an economic end rather than, as was found in the mid-1990s, a continuing belief in the power of education as a means to develop the cultured individual (Hufton et al., 2002; Elliott et al., 2005). Thus, during the period of the first author's investigations in St. Petersburg in the second half of the 1990s, it appeared that social changes had resulted in a relatively minor impact upon the behaviour and orientations of school students, although in the universities, recognition that some disciplines were key to economic well-being was being reflected by changing enrolment patterns (Rutkevich, 2000).

Young people in the 1990s were moving from a socio-economic context where differences in people's life standards had, for many generations, been relatively minimal—the old Soviet joke being that under capitalism, wealth was unevenly distributed, whereas under socialism, poverty was evenly distributed. Now, they were being confronted by increasingly wealthy individuals operating in a context where practical 'nous' appeared to be more important than analytical abilities (Grigorenko & Sternberg, 2001).

Students in schools and colleges became increasingly cognizant of their teachers' poor salaries, and the even worse position of many university academics. Observing their teachers' straitened circumstances, and believing that school curricula were failing to prepare young people for the new economic pressures that would mark their passage into adulthood (Iartsev, 2000), it was hardly surprising that teachers were gradually seen as less worthy of respect than had been the case hitherto (Bocharova & Lerner, 2000). White (2001) describes an encounter with a woman who tearfully recounted a conversation between her son and his teacher-father: 'You have two degrees, yet you come to me begging for cigarettes' (p. 11).

Recognizing that higher levels of scholarship did not appear to be reflected by an improved material position (Nikandrov, 1995; Zubok, 1999) increasing numbers of students came to consider that their schools were ill-preparing them for the new economic pressures that would mark their passage into adulthood (Iartsev, 2000).

A combination of western influences and the loss of adult influence appear to have resulted in the development of powerful, increasingly autonomous, youth subcultures (Sergeev, 1999). As Bronfenbrenner (1967) noted some four decades ago, where the peer group is highly autonomous, as is a feature of western but not of the former Soviet society, it is more likely that it will exert an influence that is oppositional to prevailing adult values. He noted that under the Soviets, the role of the peer group was not left mainly to chance, as it was in the US, but was the result of 'explicit policy and practice' (p. 206). The first author's work (Elliott *et al.*, 1999; 2001; Hufton *et al.*, 2002) suggested that peer influences in St. Petersburg were still operating in the 1990s in ways that supported teachers' messages. Ten years after the end of the Soviet period, there is growing concern that negative peer influence, similar to what we found in our studies in England, is increasing.

Alongside the growth in materialism, globalizing influences have led to a questioning of traditional ideals and values and a corresponding social and moral vacuum (Lisovskii, 1999). Shorn of the old ideals of country and collective, and dismissing the views of their elders as an irrelevance, increasing student anxiety and alienation has been ascribed to the loss of long-standing cultural and historical values (Karpukhin, 2000). Such tensions are reflected by intergenerational differences in terms of self-expression that are particularly substantial for countries formerly in the Soviet bloc (Inglehart & Welzel, 2005). Given the vacuum that resulted from the weakening of state and societal mechanisms of social regulation, young Russians' value systems have been seen as increasingly gleaned from intellectually undemanding mass culture (Zvonovskii & Lutseva, 2004). Erasov (1994) laments:

...the desanctification of attitudes toward the world and society, the decline of the ideal, exalted, romantic aspect of life, have been accompanied by its banalification, rendering it more bourgeois and susceptible to the laws of the market, converting it into a commodity. The old symbols and imagery, which expressed lofty and oftentimes unattainable ideals are being turned into products of mass spiritual assimilation—but an assimilation that is illusory, limited to audio-visual familiarity. Ideals are being turned into products of mass spiritual consumption rather than assimilation. (p. 217)

The breakdown of traditional values and codes of behaviour, together with the challenging economic climate, have resulted in widespread expression of fears about the erosion of young people's morality (Ol'shanskii *et al.*, 2000) with reports of a greatly increased incidence of drug use, violence and criminality. According to a recent World Health Organization report (Krug *et al.*, 2002), youth gangs are particularly strong in the Russian Federation, and youth homicide rates increased by 150% between 1985–1994 to 18.0 per 100,000, the seventh highest rate of the 75 countries surveyed. In a further comparative study of 35 countries (Pickett *et al.*, 2005) Russia was third highest in respect of boys' self-reports of the prevalence of physical fighting.

Bronfenbrenner's theory helps us to understand how educational reform and restructuring cannot exist in a vacuum from wider social change. Society-wide values and beliefs do not change simply with a change of regime or dominant ideology, and educational practices that are viewed (perhaps over-optimistically) as successful in one society cannot be easily imported into another society without creating tensions and unexpected side-effects. Growing emphases upon competitiveness and individualism were reflected in the Russian education system by a plethora of structural reforms, which have resulted in the development of socially divisive educational hierarchies and inequalities (Konstantinovskii & Khokhlushkina, 2000). The arrival of the market resulted in an inevitable mushrooming of selective schooling whereby the most able (or affluent) students and the most skilled teachers gravitated to well-resourced, specialist schools (Cherednichenko, 2000). In turn, economic incentives have led teachers to invest most energy in those with most academic promise. However, where there are winners, there must be losers, and many students appear increasingly alienated (Andriushina, 2000), particularly those for whom learning is a struggle and who find themselves in unfashionable schools. Interestingly, Froumin (2005) argues that the introduction of more democratic teacher–student relationships played out more effectively in the elite schools. The result of these divisive developments has been an increasing trend towards social exclusion that mirrors that more traditionally found in western society and the concomitant problems of increasing school drop-out rates (Grigorenko, 1998; Cherednichenko, 2000).

Looking to the future: striking a balance between resistance and accommodation

In times of dramatic social changes, it is particularly true that adolescents are the last children of the old system and the first adults of the new (Van Hoorn *et al.*, 2000, p. 4).

As we noted above, Bronfenbrenner highlighted the fact that historical events are likely to result in different developmental trajectories for those of different ages. Students appear to have generally embraced the 'modernizing' influences emanating from the west. Teachers, many of whom seemed initially to have found western pedagogic theory and practice beguiling, tied in as they are with a democratizing agenda, have now seemingly retreated and are widely perceived to be resistant to change. This should not come as any great surprise; the longer individuals engage in particular activities the more they come to be viewed as natural (hence the power of proximal processes). Having taken democratization and humanization training courses, many teachers return to their schools speaking the new language but quickly revert to their former modes of practice (Froumin, 2005). Interestingly, unlike many western reforms, the primary initiative for educational reform came from teachers whose focus, swept along by 'public euphoria over democracy' (Froumin, 2005, p. 131) was more upon student–teacher relations than school governance, as was the case in many western states (Froumin, op. cit).

Within the field of sociology, there has been considerable debate as to whether rapid value change, rather than that of social attitudes, is possible. Influenced by American cultural anthropology, many sociologists view individual value orientations as deriving from early socialization processes and, as such, as being deeply embedded within the individual personality structure (Klages, 2005). Klages (op. cit.), however, argues that rapid value change can be understood if considered as an aspect of rapid structural change occurring on an individual level, with the shift towards the 'individualistic' (which he believes to be a phenomenon of all highly developed nations) operating as a functional consequence of societal modernization (cf. also, Inglehart & Welzel, 2005).

Bronfenbrenner's theory, however, allows us to take a more subtle approach. What occurs at the level of everyday interactions (teacher practices, student–teacher and student–student interactions, etc.) is influenced both by what the individuals concerned bring to the situation and by the context, where context includes both the nature of the particular school classroom (microsystem), the specific macrosystem in which the school is situated (depending on social class, ethnicity, or region), and what is occurring in the society at large (overarching macrosystem). It is highly unlikely that changes at the level of macrosystem, particularly those as far-reaching at those experienced in Russia, can be translated speedily into changes in practices, especially those that have developed over many years. It is even more difficult to imagine that ideas about education that have developed in cultures with very different basic values can be easily imported. Teachers, who have participated in particular proximal processes for many years, should be expected to be more resistant to these types of change than are their students, particularly those who have the individual characteristics (resource and force characteristics) to take advantage of what the new system has to offer. On the other hand, any dialectical theory carries within it the notion that changes do not simply occur because of changes at the level of culture or society but in part because of the experiences of new generations; as today's Russian students grow up they will necessarily influence their culture's values and beliefs. Thus, calls for the return of the legacy of the Soviet school to ameliorate what is perceived to be excessive individualism resulting from the democratization of schooling (Likhachev, 1995) appear unrealistic. What will be particularly interesting to observe over the next few generations are the ways by which traditional Russian values and practices are reconciled with the seemingly inexorable drive towards 'modernization'.

Acknowledgements

The second author would like to thank Natasha Kulakova and Irina Snezhkova for interviewing the parents and teachers in Obninsk, Russia. For providing the time to finish writing this paper, the second author would also like to thank the University of North Carolina at Greensboro for the award of a year-long Research Assignment and the Psychology programme of the Universidade Federal do Rio Grande do Sul, Brazil, for the invitation to spend a year as Visiting Professor with financial support generously provided by CAPES (Coordenação de Aperfeiçoamento de Pessoal de Nível Superior).

Notes on contributors

Julian Elliott is Professor of Education at Durham University. His research interests include motivation theory, psychological assessment, children's memory and cognition, and clinical and educational responses to behavioural difficulties. Many of his projects involve cross-cultural comparison.

Jonathan Tudge is a professor in the Department of Human Development and Family Studies at the University of North Carolina at Greensboro, in the United States. His research examines cultural-ecological aspects of young children's development both within and across a number of different societies, including Russia, particularly focusing on the years prior to and immediately following the entry to school.

References

Alexander, R. (2000) *Culture and pedagogy: international comparisons in primary education* (Oxford, Blackwell).
Andriushina, E. V. (2000) The family and the adolescent's health, *Russian Education and Society*, 42(4), 61–87.
Belkanov, N. A. (2000) Pedagogicheskaya sovetologiya kak nauchny fenomen [Pedagogical sovietology as a scientific phenomenon], *Pedagogika*, 6(5), 81–87.
Bereday, G. Z. F., Brickman, W. W. & Read, G. E. (Eds) (1960) *The changing Soviet school* (London, Constable & Co.).
Bocharova, O. & Lerner, A. (2000) Characteristics of the way of life of adolescents, *Russian Education and Society*, 42(6), 37–48.
Bronfenbrenner, U. (1967) Response to pressure from peers versus adults among Soviet and American school children, *International Journal of Psychology*, 2(3), 199–207.
Bronfenbrenner, U. (1970) *Two worlds of childhood* (New York, Russell Sage Foundation).

Bronfenbrenner, U. (1979) *The ecology of human development: experiments by nature and design* (Cambridge, Harvard University Press).

Bronfenbrenner, U. (1993) The ecology of cognitive development: research models and fugitive findings, in: R. Wozniak & K. Fischer (Eds) *Development in context: acting and thinking in specific environments* (Hillsdale, NJ, Erlbaum), 3–44.

Bronfenbrenner, U. (1995) Developmental ecology through space and time: a future perspective, in P. Moen, G. H. Elder, Jr., & K. Luscher (Eds) *Examining lives in context: perspectives on the ecology of human development* (Washington, DC, American Psychological Association), 619–647.

Bronfenbrenner, U. (1999) Environments in developmental perspective: theoretical and operational models, in S. L. Friedman & T. D. Wachs (Eds) *Measuring environment across the life span: emerging methods and concepts* (Washington, DC, American Psychological Association Press), 3–28.

Bronfenbrenner, U. ([2001] 2005) The bioecological theory of human development, in: U. Bronfenbrenner (Ed.) *Making human beings human: bioecological perspectives on human development* (Thousand Oaks, CA, Sage), 3–15.

Bronfenbrenner, U. (2005) *Making human beings human: bioecological perspectives on human development* (London, Sage).

Bronfenbrenner, U., & Ceci, S. (1994) Nature-nurture reconceptualized in developmental perspective: a bioecological model, *Psychological Review,* 101, 568–586.

Bronfenbrenner, U. & Evans, G. W. (2000) Developmental science in the 21st century: emerging questions, theoretical models, research designs and empirical findings, *Social Development,* 9(1), 115–125.

Bronfenbrenner, U. & Morris, P. A. (1998) The ecology of developmental processes, in: W. Damon (Series Ed.) & R. M. Lerner (Vol. Ed.) *Handbook of child psychology: Vol. 1. Theoretical models of human development* (5th edn) (New York, John Wiley), 993–1028.

Canning, M., Moock, P. & Heleniak, T. (1999) *Reforming education in the regions of Russia, World Bank technical paper no. 457,* (Washington DC, The World Bank).

Cherednichenko, G. A. (2000) School reform in the 1990s, *Russian Education and Society,* 42(11), 6–32.

Deci, E. L. & Ryan, R. M. (1985) *Intrinsic motivation and self-determination in human behavior* (New York, Plenum).

Eklof, B. (2005) Introduction—Russian education: the past in the present, in: B. Eklof, L. Holmes & V. Kaplan (Eds) *Educational reform in post-Soviet Russia* (London, Cass), 1–20.

Eklof, B. & Seregny, S. (2005) Teachers in Russia: state, community and profession, in: B. Eklof, L. Holmes & V. Kaplan (Eds) *Educational reform in post-Soviet Russia* (London, Cass), 197–220.

Elder, G. H., Jr. (1974) *Children of the great depression* (Chicago, IL, University of Chicago Press).

Elder, G. H., Jr. (1996) Human lives in changing societies: life course and developmental insights, in: R. B. Cairns, G. H. Elder, Jr., & E. J. Costello (Eds) *Developmental science* (New York, Cambridge University Press), 31–62.

Elliott, J. G., Hufton, N., Hildreth, A. & Illushin, L. (1999) Factors influencing educational motivation: a study of attitudes, expectations and behaviour of children in Sunderland, Kentucky and St Petersburg, *British Educational Research Journal,* 25, 75–94.

Elliott, J. G., Hufton, N., Illushin, L. & Lauchlan, F. (2001) Motivation in the junior years: international perspectives on children's attitudes, expectations and behaviour and their relationship to educational achievement, *Oxford Review of Education,* 37–68

Elliott, J. G., Hufton, N., Illushin, L. & Willis, W. (2005) *Motivation, engagement and educational performance* (London, Palgrave Press).

Erasov, B. (1994) *Social culturology, Part 2* (Moscow, n.p.)

Froumin, I. D. (2005) Democratizing the Russian school: achievements and setbacks, in: B. Eklof, L. Holmes & V. Kaplan (Eds) *Educational reform in post-Soviet Russia* (London, Cass), 129–152.

Gardner. H. (1983) *Frames of mind: the theory of multiple intelligence* (New York, Basic Books).

Giddens, A. (1991) *Modernity and self-identity* (London, Polity Press).

Gjerde, P. F. (2004) Culture, power, and experience: toward a person-centered cultural psychology, *Human Development*, 47, 137–157.

Glowka, D. (1995) *Schulen und unterricht im vergleich. Rusland/Deutschland* [Schools and teaching in comparison: Russia and Germany] (New York, Waxmann Verlag).

Goldhaber, D. E. (2000) *Theories of human development: integrative perspectives* (Mountain View, CA, Mayfield Publishing).

Grant, N. (1972) *Soviet education* (3rd edn.) (Harmondsworth, Penguin).

Grigorenko, E. L. (1998) Russian 'defectology': anticipating perestroika in the field, *Journal of Learning Disabilities*, 31(2), 193–207

Grigorenko, E. L. & Sternberg, R. J. (2001) Analytical, creative and practical intelligence as predictors of self-reported adaptive functioning: a case study in Russia, *Intelligence*, 29, 57–73.

Guba, E. G. & Lincoln, Y. S. (1994) Competing paradigms in qualitative research, in: N. K. Denzin & Y. S. Lincoln (Eds) *Handbook of qualitative research* (Thousand Oaks, CA, Sage), 105–117.

Hofstede, G. (1991) *Cultures and organizations: software of the mind* (London, McGraw Hill).

Hofstede, G. (2001) *Culture's consequences: comparing values, behaviors, institutions, and organizations across nations* (2nd edn.) (Thousand Oaks, Ca, Sage).

Hufton, N. & Elliott, J. G. (2000) Motivation to learn: the pedagogical nexus in the Russian school: some implications for transnational research and policy borrowing, *Educational Studies*, 26, 115–136

Hufton, N., Elliott, J. G. & Illushin, L. (2002) Educational motivation and engagement: qualitative accounts from three countries, *British Educational Research Journal*, 28(2), 265–289.

Iartsev, D. V. (2000) Characteristics of the socialization of today's adolescent, *Russian Education and Society*, 42(11), 67–75

Inglehart, R. & Welzel, C. (2005) Modernization, cultural change and democracy: the human development sequence (Cambridge, Cambridge University Press).

Karpukhin, O. I. (2000) The young people of Russia: characteristics of their socialization and self-determination, *Russian Education and Society*, 42(11), 47–57.

Klages, H. (2005) Modernization and value change, in: W. Friedlmeier, P. Chakkarath & B. Schwarz (Eds) *Culture and human development: the importance of cross-cultural research to the social sciences* (New York, Psychology Press), 273–287.

Konstantinovskii, D. L. & Khokhlushkina, F. A. (2000) The formation of the social behaviour of young people in the sphere of education, *Russian Education and Society*, 42(2), 26–58.

Krug, E. G., Dahlberg, L. L., Mercy, J. A., Zwi, A. B. & Lozano, R. (Eds) (2002) *World report on violence and health* (Geneva, World Health Organization).

Kuczynski, L. & Daly, K. (2003) Qualitative methods as inductive (theory-generating) research: psychological and sociological approaches, in L. Kuczynski (Ed.) *Handbook of dynamics in parent-child relations* (Thousand Oaks, CA, Sage), 373–392.

Likhachev, B. T. (1995) Obrazovanie, ideologia i politika [Education, ideology and politics], *Pedagogika*, 4, 42–44.

Lisovskii, V. T. (1999) Young people talk about themselves and the times, *Russian Education and Society*, 41(12), 48–61.

Markowitz, F. (2000) *Coming of age in post-soviet Russia* (Chicago, University of Illinois Press).

Mitter, W. (2003) A decade of transformation; educational policies in central and eastern Europe, *International Review of Education*, 49(1–2), 75–96.

Moseley, D., Baumfield, V., Elliott, J. G., Gregson, M., Higgins, S., Miller, J. & Newton, D. (2005) *Frameworks for thinking* (London, Cambridge University Press).

Muckle, J. (1990) *Portrait of a soviet school under glasnost* (London, Macmillan).

Nikandrov, N. D. (1995) Russian education after perestroika: the search for new values, *International Review of Education*, 41(1–2), 47–57

O'Brien, D. (2000) *From Moscow: living and teaching among Russians in the 1990s* (Nottingham, Bramcote Press).

OECD (2003) *Literacy skills for the world of tomorrow: further results from PISA 2000* (Paris, OECD).

Ol'shanskii, V. B., Klimova, S. G. & Volzhkaia, N. (2000) School students in a changing society (1982–1997), *Russian Education and Society*, 42, 44–40

Overton, W. F. (1984) World-views and their influence on psychological theory and research: Kuhn—Lakatos—Laudan, in: H. W. Reese (Ed.) *Advances in child development and behaviour, Vol. 18* (New York, Academic Press), 191–226.

Overton, W. F. & Reese, H. W. (1973) Models of development: methodological implications, in: J. R. Nesselroade & H. W. Reese (Eds) *Lifespan developmental psychology: methodological issues* (New York, Academic Press), 65–86.

Pepper, S. C. (1942) *World hypotheses: a study in evidence* (Berkeley, University of California Press).

Pickett, W., Craig, W., Harel, Y., Cunningham, J., Simpson, K., Molcho, M., Mazur, J., Dostaler, S., Overpeck, M. & Currie, C. (2005) Cross-national study of fighting and weapon carrying as determinants of adolescent injury, *Pediatrics*, 116(6), 855–e863.

Polyzoi, E. & Dneprov, E. (2003) Harnessing the forces of change: educational transformation in Russia, in: E. Polyzoi, M. Fullan & J. P. Anchan (Eds) *Change forces in post-communist Eastern Europe* (London, RoutledgeFalmer), 13–33.

Realo, A. & Allik, J. (1999) A cross-cultural study of collectivism: a comparison of American, Estonian, and Russian students, *Journal of Social Psychology*, 139(2), 133–142.

Rutkevich, M. (2000) Change in the social role of the general education school in Russia, *Russian Education and Society*, 42(2), 5–25

Ryan, R. M. & Deci, E. L. (2000) Intrinsic and extrinsic motivations: classic definitions and new directions, *Contemporary Educational Psychology*, 25, 54–67.

Schwartz, S. H. (1994) Beyond individualism/collectivism: new cultural dimensions of values in: U. Kim, H. C. Triandis, C. Kagitcibasi, S.-C. Choi, & G. Yoon (Eds) *Individualism and collectivism: theory, methods, and applications* (Newbury Park, CA, Sage), 85–119.

Schweisfurth, M. (2000) Teachers and democratic change in Russia and South Africa, *Education in Russia, the Independent States and Eastern Europe*, 18(1), 2–8.

Sedlak, M., Wheeler, C. W., Pullin, D. C. & Cusick, P. A. (1986) *Selling students short: classroom bargains and academic reform in the American high school* (New York, Teachers College Press)

Seifert, T. L. & O'Keefe, B. A. (2001) The relationship of work avoidance and learning goals to perceived competence, externality and meaning, *British Journal of Educational Psychology*, 71, 81–92.

Sergeev, S. A. (1999) Youth subcultures in the republic, *Russian Education and Society*, 41(10), 74–91.

Strauss, C. (2000) The culture concept and the individualism–collectivism debate: dominant and alternative attributions for class in the United States, in: L. P. Nucci, G. B. Saxe, & E. Turiel (Eds) *Culture, thought, and development* (Mahwah, NJ, Lawrence Erlbaum Associates), 85–114.

Tabulawa, R. (2003) International aid agencies, learner-centred pedagogy and political democratization: a critique, *Comparative Education*, 39, 7–26.

Tobin, J. T., Wu, D. Y. H. & Davidson, D. H. (1989) *Preschool in 3 cultures* (New Haven, CT, Yale University Press).

Triandis, H. C. (1995) *Individualism and collectivism* (Boulder, CA, Westview Press).

Tudge, J. R .H. (1991) Education of young children in the Soviet Union: current practice in historical perspective, *Elementary School Journal*, 92(1), 121–133.

Tudge, J. R. H. (2006) The everyday lives of young children: culture, class, and child-rearing in diverse societies, Manuscript in preparation.

Tudge, J. R. H., Gray, J. & Hogan, D. (1997) Ecological perspectives in human development: a comparison of Gibson and Bronfenbrenner, in: J. Tudge, M. Shanahan, & J. Valsiner (Eds) *Comparisons in human development: understanding time and context* (New York, Cambridge University Press), 82–105.

Tudge, J. R. H. & Hogan, D. M. (2005) Accessing children's experiences: an ecological approach to observations of everyday life, in: S. M. Greene & D. M. Hogan (Eds) *Researching children's experiences: approaches and methods* (London, England: Sage), 102–122.

Tudge, J. R. H., Hogan, D., Snezhkova, I., Kulakova, N. & Etz, K. (2000) Parents' childrearing values and beliefs in the United States and Russia: the impact of culture and social class, *Infant and Child Development*, 9, 105–121.

Van Hoorn, J. L., Komlosi, A., Suchar, E. & Samelson, D. A. (2000) *Adolescent development and rapid social change: perspectives from Eastern Europe* (Albany, SUNY Press).

Westbrook, M. (1994) St. Petersburg's independent schools, in: A. Jones (Ed.) *Education and society in the new Russia* (Armonk, NY, M.E. Sharpe), 103–117.

White, A. (2001) Teachers in contemporary provincial Russia, *Education in Russia, the Independent States and Eastern Europe*, 19(1), 2–13.

Winegar, L. T. (1997) Developmental research and comparative perspectives: applications to developmental science, in: J. Tudge, M. Shanahan, & J. Valsiner (Eds) *Comparisons in human development: understanding time and context* (New York, Cambridge University Press), 13–33.

Yair, G. (2000) Reforming motivation: how the structure of instruction affects students' learning experiences, *British Educational Research Journal*, 26, 191–210.

Zubok, I. A. (1999) Exclusion in the study of the problems of young people, *Russian Education & Society*, 41(9), 39–53.

Zvonovskii, V. & Lutseva, S. (2004) Young people's favourite leisure activities, *Russian Education & Society*, 46(1), 76–96.

Teachers' ethnotheories of the 'ideal student' in five western cultures

Sara Harkness, Marjolijn Blom, Alfredo Oliva, Ughetta Moscardino, Piotr Olaf Zylicz, Moises Rios Bermudez, Xin Feng, Agnieszka Carrasco-Zylicz, Giovanna Axia and Charles M. Super

In almost all corners of today's world, children from about the age of six years onward are supposed to attend school. If one also takes into account the globalization of early childhood education, young children everywhere are leaving home each day to spend the majority of their most active time in settings designed to educate them—that is, to inculcate cognitive skills such as literacy and numeracy, considered essential for competency as members of their own societies. But that is not all—children may also attend school in order to learn to be members of a group (Lewis, 1995), to practise competing with peers (Whiting & Edwards, 1988), and to be inculcated with reliable work habits necessary for the maintenance of industrial and post-industrial societies (Perry, 2006). It is thus not surprising that although 'school' might appear to be a straightforward concept, there is in fact wide variation across cultures in what children are really supposed to be learning there, beyond a few basic skills.

Examination of the cross-cultural evidence suggests that even presumably universal concepts such as 'intelligence', which lie at the core of what schooling is all about, vary widely across different societies. On the one hand, anthropologists have long argued that in principle, people of all cultures have essentially the same repertoire of abilities and talents, despite their many different expressions. In contrast, some psychologists have argued for the cultural specificity of intelligence as demonstrated in the cross-cultural application of tasks or tests. As Wang *et al.*, (2004) state,

> We suggest that there are no such things as invariant, core competencies universal to every human child. Instead, cognitive competence is relevant to specific cultures, to the social and physical contexts in which the child participates in organized activities, and to the cultural and societal demands as perceived by the child him- or herself. (p. 227)

Strong contrasts have been found between the US emphasis on analytical intelligence and other (especially non-western) cultures' recognition that the intelligent child has more than just good cognitive skills. In general, studies in other cultures have identified social and interpersonal aspects of intelligence. For example, Serpell's research on children's development and schooling among the Chewa people of Zambia (Serpell, 1993) has highlighted the local importance of several culturally valued traits related to intelligence. He quotes a Chewa colleague:

> What leads us to call a person *wanzelu* [intelligent]? Among the A-Chewa a child with *nzelu* is a child who is clever (*-chenjela*), trustworthy (*-khulupilika*), who listens, understands, and obeys (*-mvela*), who is prompt (*-changu*), and who cooperates (*-mvana ndi anzake*) (Serpell, 1993, p. 32)

Harkness and Super (1992) found a similar pattern in a Kipsigis community of western Kenya. They asked adult members of the community to make similarity judgements on triads of 12 words and phrases that were locally judged to be common in describing children. When the results were subjected to multidimensional scaling, the terms for 'intelligent', 'talkative', 'clever', 'smart', and 'brave' were contrasted with 'polite', 'entertaining' (as in a child who can talk nicely with visitors), and a cluster of terms describing the culturally valued obedient, respectful, honest child who is good-hearted and responsible. This contrast indicates that the Kipsigis study participants differentiated between cognitive quickness on one hand and mature, responsible and cooperative behaviour on the other. Interestingly, the central term for 'intelligent', *ng' om*, is also a developmentally related concept, used only for children, who are recognized as *ng' om* when they are old enough to be relied on, for example to be sent on an errand and come back without getting distracted or forgetting the purpose on the way. The Kipsigis participants also recognized a special kind of intelligence described as being 'intelligent in school', with the clear implication that a child might be intelligent at school without being smart at home (a concept that may be familiar to some American parents!). Harkness and Super contrasted the Kipsigis ideas about children's qualities with American parents' free descriptions of their young children, which often centred round evidence of intelligence as a purely cognitive construct. These parents also mentioned other personal qualities that might support the child's rapid cognitive development—especially independence and self-reliance.

The largest amount of research on cultural concepts of intelligence has focused on comparisons between Asian societies and the US or Canada. As with the African research, social and interpersonal dimensions of intelligence emerge as important in Asian conceptualizations; but the actual content, and therefore the contrast, is distinctive. A core aspect of the Asian profile relates to an attitude towards learning— a 'heart and mind for wanting to learn' (Li, 2001, p. 122)—which is also part of an interpersonal relationship with the mother and, later, teachers. As Shapiro and Azuma describe this (2004):

> In children's early years, Japanese parents therefore tend to be oriented primarily toward instilling the socioemotional prerequisites of competence rather than on knowledge or skills as such. In particular, Japanese mothers tend to focus on cultivating interpersonal receptivity and an engaged, devoted attitude in the child. Such a mind-set is viewed as the foundation of later learning in that it encourages children to open up to the thinking of others, thereby enhancing their educability. (p. 193)

This cultural belief relates to Asian ideas about the importance of innate ability versus effort for success in school. Stevenson and Lee (1990) found that American parents believed school achievement had more to do with a child's ability than Asian parents did, whereas Asian parents tended to stress more the effort the child has put into school work. These differences are further related to parents' ideas about how best to foster children's motivation to succeed. Chao (1996) examined parents' beliefs about children's school success in Chinese–American and European–American mothers. Whereas the European–American mothers emphasized that learning should be fun and exciting, Chinese mothers stressed that learning and school involve great effort. As research by Parmar *et al.* (2004) has shown, Asian parents also emphasize the importance of academic learning in the pre-school years, and their patterns of participation in activities with their children reflect these ideas. The contrast between Asian and American ideas about qualities of an 'intelligent' person is further demonstrated by Azuma and Kashiwagi's (1987) study of Japanese college students and their mothers, replicating earlier work by Sternberg and his associates with American respondents (Sternberg *et al.*, 1981). When they asked the participants to rate an 'intelligent person' they knew using a previously elicited list of descriptors, the terms related to cognitive competence were rated most highly. However, factor analysis of the responses produced two groupings of interpersonal qualities which together accounted for 64% of the total variance. The first, Social Competence, included qualities such as sociability, humour, and leadership; the second, Receptive Social Competence, included sympathy, social modesty, and the ability to take other people's perspective. This picture presented a strong contrast to Sternberg's US sample, in which intellectual competence was the dominant construct. Okagaki and Sternberg (1993) demonstrated that parents' concepts of intelligence also differ across cultural groups within the US. They found that Anglo-American parents see cognitive attributes, including problem-solving skills, verbal skills, and creative ability as more important than non-cognitive attributes (such as motivation, social skills, and practical school skills) in defining intelligence. Conversely, parents from other cultural groups (such as Asian- and Hispanic-American) indicated that non-cognitive characteristics are as important or more important than cognitive characteristics, but differed among themselves on the level of importance of non-cognitive attributes.

Although cross-cultural differences in ideas about intelligence and competence have been widely observed, there is less recognition of cultural variability among western middle-class societies. The notion of the 'western mind', although popular, may hinder the perception of differences in ideas and practices in Europe and the US. Harkness *et al.* (2000), for example, found that American and Dutch parents differed in the ways that they described their young children, with the American parents much more frequently mentioning intelligence, in contrast to the Dutch parents' emphasis on social qualities. Even ideas about independence and dependence—equally mentioned by parents in both groups—were found to differ significantly between the two cultural groups. Whereas the Dutch parents described dependent behaviour by their young children as innate and normal for children that age, the American parents worried about their children's dependent behaviour and wondered whether it was caused by stress in the environment. Ironically, the Dutch parents also found independent behaviour non-problematic, in contrast to the American parents who viewed it as a struggle for both the child and themselves. Edwards and Gandini (1995) also found cultural differences in a comparative study of developmental expectations (or 'developmental timetables') of middle-class Italian and American parents and pre-school teachers. Using the Developmental Expectations Questionnaire (DEQ) developed by an international team of researchers (Hess *et al.*, 1980), they compared expectations in several domains: emotional maturity, compliance, politeness, independence, school-related skills, social skills with peers, and verbal assertiveness. The Italian parents had fairly early expectations for children's development, but the American parents had even earlier ones, especially with regard to social skills with peers and verbal assertiveness. Interestingly, the teachers were closer to each other than were the parents, which the authors suggest may be due to an international culture of education.

In summary, there is good evidence of cross-cultural variability in ideas about intelligence and competence, even within the western world. Understanding the nature of this variability is important not only for enhancing cross-cultural communication among education professionals from different western societies, but also for recognizing alternative perspectives on what constitutes successful development and how teachers can help children achieve it in the context of school. In this paper, we focus on teachers' cultural ideas, or ethnotheories, about the 'ideal student' in locations within five western societies: Italy, The Netherlands, Poland, Spain, and the US. The data are drawn from a larger study, the International Study of Parents, Children, and Schools (ISPCS), which also includes samples in Sweden and Australia. In all study sites, families participating in the study were broadly middle-class. Study samples were chosen in order to capture possible cultural or geographic dimensions of difference—for example, northern versus southern Europe, eastern versus western, and British heritage versus continental. The inclusion of Poland, from this perspective, makes sense given that country's Roman Catholic tradition and its historically close ties with western European societies.

Methods

Data presented in this study were drawn from a larger project, the International Study of Parents, Children, and Schools. Kindergarten and primary school teachers in each cultural community were interviewed about their beliefs and practices related to children's development and learning in school, including their concepts of the 'ideal student'. These semi-structured interviews were tape-recorded and transcribed in the original language, in order to capture important cultural concepts and preserve the richness of expression. Working collaboratively, the present authors then constructed a list of descriptive words and phrases that captured the range of distinct qualities or behaviours; in all but a few cases, these could be put in English for a common referent. Using text analysis software (generally NVivo), the descriptors were coded while preserving their context of occurrence in the interview texts. In the summer of 2001, the researchers met in Uppsala, Sweden, for the Tenth European Conference on Developmental Psychology to consider their own data in relation to the other sites. Through quantitative and qualitative analysis and discussion, the researchers arrived at thematic titles to capture the distinctive aspects of each cultural profile. As a final step, some descriptors were grouped into larger categories in order to facilitate both quantitative analysis and interpretability. This collaborative, iterative process has characterized many aspects of the ISPCS (Harkness *et al.*, 2006).

At all sites, teachers were initially contacted through school systems, referred either by school directors or by other teachers who participated in the study. Teachers' background varied within each group, with Spanish and US teachers being more homogeneous in educational attainment but having relatively larger variability in age and teaching experience compared to teachers in Italian and Dutch samples. Across sites, the average ages and teaching experiences were comparable. Whereas all Spanish and US teachers had completed a college education, the majority of teachers in the other groups had an educational level equivalent to high school or post-secondary teacher training institute. To help capture cultural ideas of students corresponding to the ages of the children in the larger study, we recruited teachers who taught at different grade levels in elementary school as well as in kindergarten/preschool.

The Italian sample consisted of 20 teachers, all of whom were employed in public schools in the city of Padua in northern Italy. Ten of the teachers taught at the preschool level and the other half taught in elementary schools. Fifteen percent of them had a college degree and the rest had a high school diploma. On average, these teachers were 42 years old (ranged 31–48 years) and had taught 20 years (ranged 10–26 years). Teachers were recruited through the council office for education in Padua. Those who were willing to participate at the initial contact were called later to schedule interviews either at their homes or schools.

In the Netherlands 12 (9 elementary school and 3 kindergarten) teachers were recruited from primary schools in the town of 'Bloemenheim', located in the eastern part of the country between Leiden and The Hague. Two (17%) of the teachers had received a college degree; the others had post-secondary teacher training degrees. These teachers had a mean age of 41 (range = 30–56) and had taught, on average, 19 years (range = 6–37) by the time of interview.

The 16 Polish teachers were recruited from public elementary schools in suburban areas of the city of Warsaw. Fifteen of the teachers were currently teaching first grade and three were teaching kindergarten-aged children. The majority of them were trained in special vocational schools for teachers. These teachers were on average 40-years-old and had 15 years of teaching experience.

In Spain, 20 teachers, 10 preschool and 10 elementary school teachers, participated in the study. Teachers were recruited from nine public and two private schools in the city of Seville (in southern Spain). Teachers' mean age was 45 years (range = 25–59 years). All teachers had a post-secondary teacher training or university education and an average of 20 years of teaching experience (range = 1–37 years). Interviews of Spanish teachers were all conducted at the schools.

In the US, teachers were recruited from two different states, Pennsylvania (n = 17) and Connecticut (n = 4). Among these 21 teachers, 19 taught grades 1–6 and three taught kindergarten. All teachers had a minimum of a college degree. These teachers had a mean age of 42 years (range = 24–57) and a teaching experience of 16 years (range = 2–35).

At all sites, locally appropriate procedures were followed in order to ensure informed and voluntary participation. Teachers were interviewed by researchers in the local teams, usually at their school but occasionally in their home. A typical interview lasted 30–40 minutes. All interviews were tape-recorded and later transcribed verbatim for analysis. Transcripts of interviews were then coded by researchers who were fluent in the language in which they were conducted.

Results

Both quantitative and qualitative analyses were used in order to examine similarities and differences in the ways that teachers from the five cultural samples described the 'ideal student'. First, the frequency of the inductively derived categories of descriptors was calculated as percentages of teachers who used each category (regardless of how extensively), and the results were compared. Second, using the table of descriptor frequencies as a guide, we examined the interviews to see how the indicated categories were used in discourse, and particularly how they related to other descriptors.

Table 1 presents the descriptors used by at least 24% of the teachers in each sample. In order to evaluate the degree of distinctiveness among the five cultural patterns of describing the ideal child, we computed a canonical discriminant analysis, using the 'nearest-neighbour' method of estimating non-parametric densities (SAS

Table 1. Qualities of the 'ideal student' mentioned by at least 24% of teachers

Italy (n=20)	Netherlands (n=12)	Poland (n=16)	Spain (n=20)	U.S. (N=21)
Vivace/lively (80%)	Social skills (67%)	Well-balanced (56%)	Social skills (45%)	Motivated (67%)
Creative (40%)	*Vivace*/lively (67%)	Curious (56%)	Motivated (30%)	Comfortable with self (38%)
Autonomous (35%)	Happy (67%)	Intelligent (56%)	Focused (25%)	Happy (38%)
Social skills (35%)	Focused (58%)	Motivated (50%)	Intelligent (25%)	Active learner (29%)
Reflective (30%)	Autonomous (42%)	Social skills (38%)		Cooperative (29%)
Attentive (30%)	Attentive (42%)	Well-behaved (38%)		Intelligent (29%)
Risk-taker (25%)	Motivated (33%)	Active learner (31%)		Autonomous (24%)
Active learner (25%)	Comfortable with self (25%)	Extrovert (31%)		Well-balanced (24%)
Persevering (25%)	Intelligent (25%)	Organized (31%)		
	Well-behaved (25%)	Persevering (31%)		
	Calm (25%)	Active (25%)		
		Comfortable with self (25%)		
		Focused (25%)		
		Cooperative (25%)		
		Good values (25%)		

Institute, 2002–2004). In this procedure, a mathematical algorithm is constructed to distinguish among the groups of teachers, based on their pattern of use of 21 descriptors (nearly identical to the Table 1 listing). Overall, this analysis was able to classify successfully 88% of the cases, a highly significant result (Lambda = 0.044, $F(84, 251.29) = 3.61$, $p < .0001$). All Spanish cases were correctly classified by the algorithm, as well as nearly all the Dutch and Italian cases. Over three quarters of the Polish and US teachers were correctly classified. One Polish teacher was misclassified as US, but all the other errors consisted of assigning a non-Spanish teacher to the Spanish profile. This result appears to be an artefact, due to the distinctive Spanish pattern of providing relatively few descriptors (discussed further below). The 11 teachers who were misclassified as Spanish provided a small number of descriptors (generally less than 4). In 9 of these 11 cases, the weighted figure for the correct assignment was a very close second to the Spanish result. Recalculation of the discriminant function using only those teachers offering a minimum of 4 descriptors increases the prediction rate to 94% (of 63 cases), and eliminates the Spanish bias in the errors.

Thus, it appears that there is a fairly consistent profile of descriptors for the 'ideal student' as described by teachers in each cultural sample. Examination of the individual interviews from each cultural sample, informed by the profiles of descriptor frequencies, suggests ways that the teachers thought about the importance of these qualities, how they related them to each other, and what practices they used to encourage the development of successful students. Table 1 presents the list of descriptors, in descending order, that were used by at least one quarter of the teachers in each sample.

Italy: the 'creative scientist'

Italian teachers' descriptions of the 'ideal student' were multifaceted and included qualities relating to a number of different domains. However, many teachers emphasized children's personal and social characteristics in terms of autonomy and independence, creativity, good social skills, and motivation for learning. A particularly valued aspect of children's personality was liveliness (*vivacità*) as related to both intellectual and behavioural dimensions; indeed, many teachers expressed their preference for those children with a curious and enthusiastic attitude towards learning:

> A child who is good at school should be intuitive, intellectually lively and interested in many things, but most of all very curious...a child who always asks 'why', but also gives her personal contributions to the others through an active participation in school activities...a child who may be more lively, exuberant, but also capable of involving and stimulating the other children.

For these teachers, having excellent grades was not essential to be considered a good student; rather, divergent thinking was viewed as a central characteristic because it allows children to cope successfully with all situations in life. Divergent thinking involves creativity, intuition, and critical thinking:

> A good student should be autonomous in thinking, be able to make connections between her own life experiences and the work done at school, to create links with many other aspects. And then a child should be smart, attentive, and alert...there is one boy in our class, he always understands things first, it's a sort of intuition.... He may seem a bit chaotic at times, but I must say he's definitely the best, he's just brilliant.

Although skills such as attention, persistence, and intelligence were seen as contributing to a child's success in school, for our participants the profile of the 'ideal student' is marked by a general positive attitude towards knowledge. Social skills are also part of this profile, since teachers highly appreciated those children who were able to engage their classmates, share ideas and collaborate during group activities:

> I think that a good student should be sociable, a positive leader...and be curious about life, about things, without complaining or annoying other children. A positive leader knows how to build relationships, how to collaborate and help other children, and therefore becomes a point of reference for the whole class. These children know when it is time to listen, to speak, or propose new ideas...They are tolerant, respectful, and aware of their own limits.

Italian teachers used several practices to encourage these qualities in their students. In general, the most frequently reported strategies included providing a secure base, establishing a supportive and nurturant relationship, stimulating children's curiosity through age-appropriate activities and/or materials, and teaching to become autonomous in personal agency as well as critical thinking. A teacher explained: 'Group activities are useful to engage children's attention and to foster their sense of responsibility with respect to a certain task because they learn to respect conversational turns, and everyone is treated the same way'; another said that 'a teacher should provide continuity, observe and listen to the children's needs, be affectionate and accepting...otherwise they don't develop a sense of trust and feel insecure'. Interestingly, many teachers thought that children have their own potential; hence, the teacher's major role is to help the child unfold their talents and abilities through providing an adequate learning environment, without putting any pressure on him/her:

> I think that each child has something special, and it's nice to see that children know each other's characteristics very well...in my everyday work I try to support these aptitudes by proposing a variety of activities, but at the same time I treat all children the same way because otherwise some will feel left out...and most of all it's important to respect their times and needs.

The Netherlands: the 'cheerful diplomat'

A remarkably consistent cultural model of the 'ideal student' emerges from the interviews of Dutch teachers from kindergarten through early and middle primary school. First and foremost, these teachers agreed that the ideal student is happy, stable, well-regulated, and 'comfortable in his skin'. Children with these qualities, as teachers commented, 'come to school with pleasure', get along well with others, and tend to have an easy time learning new things:

I'm thinking of a child who is balanced, stable, often joyful. She comes to school with pleasure, because school is also easy, so everything goes easily. She has good contact with the other students and with me – yes, everything goes well for that child. There's seldom any problem! Very positive.

Such children, according to the Dutch teachers, should not just be followers—they should be independent, even a bit naughty at times:

Very spontaneous, a child that is open to new things. A child that can nicely work independently. That's an ideal picture, a child who does what you say, but is also spontaneous. Also brings his own contribution. A happy child, who picks things up easily. Children who are not afraid of failing.

It comes back to a child who sits nicely in her skin. Who is spontaneous, natural, dares to try new things. From that base, a child is busy learning all day. Things to discover—it goes almost by itself.

Being independent (literally, self-reliant), a quality mentioned more by the Dutch teachers than by the teachers in any of the other samples, was considered important for individual development as well as being an asset in the classroom. Children who were independent, who could 'go their own way' or even occasionally 'say no', were also self-regulated in relation to learning. One teacher summed up these qualities as a seamless web of related characteristics:

Concentration, paying attention and working independently. And certainly cheerfulness, joyfulness. Sitting comfortably in one's skin. Getting along easily with people. Feeling at home in school. Respectful in dealing with others, adults as well as children.... The more they know their own place, the more successful it is. What I also find important, is that a child is creative, not in the sense of being artistic, but in doing new things. Knowing how to be daring, taking pleasure in making something one's own. Getting involved in new things. Those are children who aren't too dependent on you, who don't always ask directions to follow the familiar road, but go their own way.

Classroom practices used by the Dutch teachers were consistent with their focus on positive mood, self-regulation and being calm and focused. 'Circle time', a popular way to begin the morning, was described as an opportunity for children to unload whatever excitement or concerns they might have brought from home in order to re-focus their attention on school activities. Teachers also described using their own social skills to influence the emotional climate of the classroom, whether through the occasional joke to lighten a lesson or through individual attention to students. Individual help for a student who was having difficulty with a subject such as mathematics was seen as important for building self-confidence and thus motivation to learn more. Breaking down a task into parts that could more readily be mastered was a strategy described as part of a more general orientation to making learning easy and therefore enjoyable. Some teachers also commented that they felt they were working against the increasingly distracting influences of children's lives outside of school. As one teacher said:

I think that motivation is a very important aspect. If a child doesn't have the desire, then he may be ever so intelligent, but it still doesn't go well. Intellect is certainly very important, you have to be able to understand, but you also have to be motivated, to want to do something well, be diligent. That is very important. And being able to concentrate well. Many children can't do that any more. We have the impression that that is going backwards, concentration, that it is declining nowadays. So many distractions, and children have hectic lives. So many impressions, television, everything. Children belong to three clubs, watch television every day, lots of information, lots of impressions. I think that's why concentration is declining. Maybe children have more problems than they used to in earlier times. Life has become more complicated, I think.

Poland: the 'socialist entrepreneur'

For teachers in Poland and across Eastern Europe, the year 1989 was a turning point. The political collapse of the Soviet bloc entailed substantial changes in the educational context teachers had been involved in. Prior to that time, the social position of teachers was generally high, marked by hierarchy-based practices in dealing with students, who for their part were given little space to express their individuality and personal freedom. In Poland, the following decade of the 1990s was marked by several educational reforms—some of them uncompleted—often leaving teachers with misconceptions about new expectations. Moreover, they were authorized to choose among different curricula. For many, this was more a part of the problem than an answer to the challenges they were facing. Especially for teachers who had started their professional careers before 1989, the growing demands of parents often coupled with decreased subordination of many students discouraged some teachers from taking advantage of the new opportunities. Last but not least, remuneration of teachers in public schools fell consistently below the national average and was substantially lower than incomes of teachers of the proliferating private educational sector. As polls showed (Banach, 2002), almost half of all teachers were afraid of losing their jobs as a result of the reforms as well as the overall decline in Poland's student population.

Among the teachers who participated in our study in the late 1990s, two opposing models of expectations towards students can be distinguished. One is embedded in the previous collectivistic and strictly social hierarchy-based treatment of the children; the other, emerging model is oriented to encouraging independence, curiosity, and proactive learning. The latter approach perceives the ideal student—as stated by one of our interviewees—as a child who 'will be open-minded and courageous in his or her activities. Formerly it was emphasized that the student had to be well-behaved, concerned for others, and silent—which would make the child become a loser in the current world'. Another teacher representing the same general concept of the ideal student stated: 'She ought to be open to anything occurring around her'. In the most extreme version of this model, a third teacher identified behavioural compliance with external expectations as a substantial developmental barrier for the child.

The teachers who supported this newly emerging model dominate in the interviewed group, but they were working in relatively wealthy and liberal suburbs of the capital city of Warsaw. A small minority (three) of the teachers in the sample expressed views rooted in the collectivistic past—a model that is probably still more prevalent around the country. One such teacher described the ideal student as follows:

> [The ideal student] is a compliant child who reacts to my voice. He must know when to be focused and calm, and when he is allowed to play. Today, children do not have a sense respect in front of teachers—neither the teacher nor what she says is regarded as 'holy' any more.

To describe the most desirable student, these teachers tended to use descriptor categories related to good behaviour in the classroom, such as well-behaved, cooperative, and having good values. These teachers tended to complain more than others about 'bad times', and often cited official reports on the generally increasing misbehaviour of students in recent years.

Despite their differences in emphasis, both the more traditional and the more progressive teachers seemed to agree on the importance of harmony in behaviour and emotional functioning, represented by the term 'well-balanced' in the Polish teachers' descriptions. The idea of being 'balanced' was contrasted with over-reactiveness, which in their opinion underlay a range of social and academic problems the students faced at school. A first grade teacher expressed her concern:

> There are more and more over-reactive kids. It disturbs much. I have a boy in my class who is incredibly intelligent, just academically a good student. But he would achieve even much more if he could manage himself. He explodes even during quiet reading, he is unable keep himself under control. However there are also kids who are inhibited, calm, being afraid even to raise a hand.

This teacher explained how she tried to help them become more autonomous and self-regulated: 'You must mobilize them by diverse encouragements and praising'. Nevertheless, she and other teachers in the Polish sample seemed to believe that it is foremost the responsibility of the child's family to prepare it in terms of inner balance. Being balanced was perceived to produce proper self-confidence. On the other hand, *very* strongly self-assured students could show problematic behaviour in the classroom. As one teacher commented, 'Such exaggerated behaviour is a nuisance for the teacher and disturbs the relations with other children'. The same teacher thought one should gently moderate such behavioural tendencies without suppressing them too much. Most teachers thought they should not allow individual students' independence and strivings to undermine group cohesion.

Especially for the more progressive teachers, the idea of the active learner, who is not only intelligent but also curious and motivated, figured importantly in descriptions of the ideal student. As one teacher stated: 'The [ideal] child is engulfed by the subject matter. She wants to learn by herself, not because of pressure from her mother'. Being curious or open to learning spontaneously from the environment appeared more important than just intelligence alone: 'The child needs to be authentically curious about the world around, in order to independently strive for knowledge which will enable him to deal with future obstacles of various sorts as motivators'.

Often teachers tended to attribute motivational problems at school, and lack of curiosity, to TV watching and other passive activities while the children were at home.

'These terrible times' were mentioned frequently to account for much of the unwillingness of students to read school books. Thus, the Polish teachers differed among themselves in terms of their relative emphasis on the importance of intelligence or motivation for success in school, but they all agreed that inner balance was essential.

The teachers referred to experiential learning, based on the personal experience of the student, as a fundamental basis for lasting knowledge. Especially with first grade students, teachers tended in their classroom practices to organize experiences such as working with hands, touching or moving up and down the classroom. The new emphasis on experiential learning is probably best symbolized in Polish classrooms by the fairly common presence of a classroom carpet which serves as a space to be together and learn. This sitting and playing together with kids at the same physical level is a relatively new practice in this part of the world. Twenty years ago most of teachers would have felt feel denigrated by such 'childish' behaviour!

As regards social skills—a bit surprisingly—teachers tended to value group cooperativeness in their practices more than might have been predicted from their descriptions of ideal qualities in students. In particular, they strongly emphasized the need for team work, for example by splitting tasks and assigning them to smaller groups. Probably team work and social cooperation are so obvious nowadays that they are not so often mentioned when characteristics of desirable students are considered. The theme of parental responsibility also came up in teachers' talk about promoting such behaviour.

Spain: the 'sociable academic'

Spain, like Poland, has undergone a fundamental social transition resulting from the political change from the authoritarian regime of Franco to a democratic government. In parallel with this, there has been a reaction within the education profession against the more traditional model of school in which the focus was on obedience, effort, and memorization to a new focus on motivating the student, learning through discovery, play, and work in groups. In this new model, the role of the teacher is first and foremost to motivate the students by organizing activities for them, and facilitating the transition from home to school. At the present time in Spanish society, there is a debate between the two models, with some people feeling that certain traditional values should continue to be important: effort, discipline, and following rules.

These two models are both expressed in the ways that the Spanish teachers chose to describe the 'ideal student'. The traditional approach is well expressed by a second-grade teacher:

> Children should acquire good habits in school such as cleanliness, order, and spending time on both work and play. The best students in my class are calm, they don't get out of their chair every other minute, they are responsible and finish their work and pick up their materials. They like school and they are obedient. These are children who work very well, they like to work and they relate well to the other children.

The new focus on motivation and interest is captured by the frequency of 'motivated', along with related cognitive qualities of being 'focused' and 'intelligent' in teachers' descriptions. Interestingly, in contrast to the Italian emphasis on creative intelligence, none of the Spanish teachers described the ideal student as independent, a divergent thinker, or lively. The traditionally valued qualities are also in evidence here in the descriptions of the ideal student as organized, persevering, responsible, and well-behaved—important qualities as they reflect the child's ability to self-regulate. Teachers who favoured the newer, more student-centred approach also tended to mention some of the same qualities as their more traditional colleagues:

> They should be responsible, good workers, happy, intelligent, and express themselves well. Children who do well in school are well-balanced; they like school; they are alert, intelligent and interested in learning. I try to impress upon them that they come to work— just like your mother makes dinner, you have to work—I want them to have good study habits. It's a matter of creating habits in class that help them to study, with a teacher who guides them.

Qualities relating to sociability were the most frequently mentioned by the teachers, reflecting a shared cultural model which emphasizes the importance of the child's adaptation to school as an institution that represents society in general. In addition, however, the teachers placed great emphasis on the importance of the family as a determinant of the child s success in school, to the point that they sometimes talked more about the family than the child when asked to describe the 'ideal student'. The following response is typical:

> Motivation is fundamental. Many children are not motivated because the family does not take an interest in academic education, and this is noticeable. But we should try to change this and get parents involved in their children's education. When parents' interest fails, things go badly.

It seems likely that the Spanish teachers' tendency to shift the focus of their answers about the 'ideal student' from the child to the family's role—and their own role as teachers—accounts for the relatively low frequency of descriptors in *any* category, when compared with the other samples.

Within the classroom, the Spanish teachers' focus on the importance of motivation for learning is clearly instantiated in children's activities, especially at the kindergarten level. The kindergarten teachers tried to be affectionate with, and close to, their students, and they organized attractive, playful activities for the children in an effort to awaken interest in school. Songs, stories, and games were frequent in the kindergarten classroom. The classroom space itself also reflected this effort to motivate the children: walls were decorated with pictures in attractive colours, or with work by the children. Often there were also plants and a 'class mascot'. In addition to this effort to help children love school and learning, kindergarten teachers also tried to teach some basic habits: to remain seated and quiet during some activities, relate nicely to other children, express oneself correctly, and so forth. In the first years of primary school the situation is somewhat different, and the teaching style tends to be somewhat more formal, activities are less playful, and making an effort to learn becomes a requirement. As one second-grade teacher recounted:

> When they don't want to work, I say 'I'm so exhausted! Anyone who doesn't want to work can stand up for three minutes', or I go out of the classroom and say, 'I'm Señor Silence', and I come back into the classroom, and this affects them more than telling them to copy something one hundred times over.

US: the 'Wild West adventurer'

The American teachers' descriptions of an ideal child were similar to those of the European teachers in many ways. Like their European colleagues, the American teachers described children who came to school eager to learn, who got along well with other children as well as with the teacher, who were cooperative, helpful, well-balanced and happy. Regardless of their academic talents, such children were a pleasure to have in the classroom:

> I think the most important quality would be social skills. You know, being able to get along with their peers, be sensitive to differences, being an encouraging kind of friend and class-mate. Those qualities we just speak of as a child who's really comfortable with themselves. Any time that's present, even if they're not academically talented, they're going to be excellent learners. Or typically you would expect them to be excellent learners because all of those things are in place.

Despite these common themes, however, the American profile of the 'ideal child' in the classroom is distinctive in its emphasis on the importance of high motivation, the importance of effort, and a willingness to take risks. Motivation, as described by these teachers, often implied a sense of excitement, of engagement in a mutually satisfying process:

> I would rather have a student who likes to be engaged, who is enthusiastic... I like kids who like school and a lot of time that means they like to learn. And if they like to learn, we're going to get along great. We are going to have a ball.

As another teacher commented:

> They get excited about new information. One of the things as a teacher that really brings me pleasure is when we're learning things that Mike [a student] talked about. He's really gotten excited about after we finished the Wright Brothers. He's really all excited about hang gliding, he's bringing information about it and he's learning about it. That tells me that I've sparked a love of his. It's been a love of mine but this tells me that I'm doing something right and that this is exciting him.

The inculcation of a sense of excitement about new 'loves', was for this teacher a route to a more general motivation to make the effort to learn things that might not be as intrinsically interesting. As she continued:

> You see yourself as trying to expose them at this age to lots of different things and hope that you're able to make a spark. Just by reading aloud to them, showing them that you love that and getting excited. It may not be yours or what they're interested in, but at least it's an exposure. I think that if you show them you love books and that you love all these

wonderful things out in the world that they're out there to learn and need to get the basics, then it helps them to understand. Okay, it's worth working hard for. And it's worth sitting here sometimes doing things that aren't necessarily a lot of fun.

Ultimately, as this teacher explained, this kind of effort is important for establishing positive self-esteem:

They'd much rather be out playing. I don't blame them—I would too. But, we're here so let's use the time and let's develop the self-discipline that it would take to finish this paper and to do it well and say, 'I'm proud of myself, I did it well'. As best I could.

The importance of self-esteem is reflected in the relatively high frequency with which the US teachers referred to the ideal student as an individual who is 'comfortable' with him- or herself. 'Confident' was the first word that one teacher used in describing the ideal student. Another teacher recounts what a 'wonderful, wonderful thing' it was when a quiet child volunteered to read a story to the entire class:

… she'll come up with this voice that, you know, I didn't realize was in her because she was so quiet before, but now she's feeling comfortable being able to participate and she feels good about herself, and when she had volunteered to read a story to the class, I thought that was a wonderful, wonderful thing for her to feel comfortable enough to do.

Being comfortable with oneself, feeling good about oneself, was seen by the US teachers as essential for 'taking risks'. As one teacher expressed it:

There are children that are organized, but there are children who are not organized, but yet those children take risks more and they will try something that they normally wouldn't try. They are willing to try anything, actually. That organized person might be tentative and not delve into things too quickly. I tend to like the children who try even if they're wrong. If they don't have the right answer, if they're not sure of themselves, they still try… I like kids to be able to develop the confidence to speak in front of people and not be afraid…

Several US teachers attributed students' lack of self-confidence, and thus reluctance to take risks, to lack of support from parents or excessive pressure to excel. One teacher who described the ideal child as 'willing to take risks' explained:

There are a lot of children…They close right down and it is very difficult for them to learn new skills. They just won't do it. They won't try it. They're so insecure… Their whole self-confidence isn't there. So I think I'm stressing more that mistakes are okay.

She continued:

I think that comes from peer pressure and parent pressure, unfortunately. But I think parents have some unrealistic expectations as to what a seven-year-old or eight-year-old can do. You know, we forget that we have to learn everything. And, the first time we do something, it isn't right, but as we grow older we seem to forget that it took us a long time to be able to just walk up to someone and introduce ourselves… And I think that they [the children] don't want to leave [sic] the parent down. And I think sometimes we convey it to our children, even though we may not mean to. But they have a sense of that. Yeah, that they might make a mistake. 'Oh, Mom's going to be disappointed'.

It is noteworthy that 'taking risks' typically, as in these examples, involved public presentation of oneself, whether reading to the whole class or introducing oneself to an unfamiliar person. The ability to present oneself confidently in public, to 'speak in front of people' was seen as essential to future success, for example in college. The US teachers talked about giving children practice in developing this skill by calling on them in class to respond to a question or comment on the subject at hand. They also talked about reassuring children, both individually and as a group, that 'it's okay to make mistakes', in an effort to help the children achieve the desired sense of being comfortable with themselves. Parents, in the views of some of these teachers, were largely to blame for children's lack of self-confidence, either because they did not praise the children enough at home or simply because they were not present due to work commitments. On the positive side, teachers talked about their efforts to find just the right match for a child's interest, in order to nurture a sense of excitement and adventure in learning—a type of motivation, teachers believed, that would translate into a commitment of effort to learn other, less interesting material as well. In this view, the student was implicitly seen as a young pioneer, heading westward for adventures in learning, with some hard climbs along the way.

Discussion

The profiles of the 'ideal student', according to the teachers we interviewed in five different western countries, capture both cultural models specific to each sample and themes that are evoked, sometimes in different ways, across all the groups. The Italian model emphasizes the importance of a lively, *vivace* personality together with a cluster of cognitive-affective characteristics related to creativity and divergent thinking and, equally important, social and emotional intelligence. Children who have these qualities, according to the Italian teachers, help create a positive emotional climate in the classroom as they enliven and inspire other students to enjoy the process of learning. These findings are consistent with a study by Axia and Weisner (2002), who report that the *vivace* child is positively valued by Italian parents. Emotional closeness is also considered a central aspect of the child's development, and is defined by the importance of establishing significant affective relationships with others—both inside and outside the family (Axia *et al.*, 2003). In this cultural context, a shy child constitutes a source of concern for parents because of the difficulties he or she may encounter in the construction of social relationships (Axia, 1999).

The Dutch model is somewhat similar to the Italian model in its emphasis on positive mood, although in this northern European version, there seems to be more focus on calmness, on feeling 'comfortable in one's skin'. For the Dutch teachers, such qualities were important in enabling the child to focus on learning in an almost effortless way, while also enjoying good relationships with both the other children and the teacher. Consistent with this finding, the Dutch psychologist Paul Leseman emphasizes the importance of the social environment of kindergarten classrooms, especially encouraging intersubjectivity and cooperation in child-initiated activities (Leseman *et al.*, 2000). He relates this to a sociocultural perspective, according to which mutual understanding and shared thinking are the foundation of learning and development. Research on Dutch parents' ethnotheories of the child has also found a cultural focus on social qualities in parents' descriptions of their own children (Harkness *et al.*, 2000).

The Polish teachers' ideas were centred round changes in educational philosophy brought about by rapid socioeconomic and political change from an authoritarian communist regime to a new, more democratic society. This model can best be described as a dialectical struggle to find a balance between the traditional values of obedience and group cohesion, and the recognition that individual assertiveness is necessary for success in a capitalist society. Recent research in Poland suggests that this struggle is widely perceived. Slomczynski and Shabad (1997) studied attitudes and values related to social and economic changes in Poland, five years after the advent of systemic transformation. They found that among their sample of teachers, students, and parents, 'neither the cultural legacy of the past nor the emergent ideology of democratic capitalism holds sway' (p. 67), although the teachers tended to be most supportive of systemic change. However, a study by Czakon (2000) of teachers in the central region of Poland, away from large cities, found that they were often frustrated with their students, as expressed by the prevalence of negative over positive evaluations. These teachers strongly favoured obedience and industriousness; self-directedness, in contrast, was seen as of little value. These findings point to the importance of acknowledging intracultural differences when doing cross-cultural research.

Spanish teachers were facing a somewhat similar challenge in the context of the post-Franco era, followed by rapid economic development and greater integration with the rest of Europe. In the Spanish teachers' interviews, there seems to be the strongest expression of traditional values and practices of classroom management although there is also a new focus on helping students to become self-motivated. A previous study on a national sample of 800 parents and 800 teachers (Oliva & Palacios, 1997) found that both groups gave a great deal of importance to values related to social and personal development, whereas values related to autonomy were considered less important. We speculate that in the more collectivistic culture of Spain (see Kagitcibasi, 1996), autonomy is not highly valued in children or adolescents; on the contrary, the maintenance of close relationships with parents is strongly supported and is in fact considered essential for healthy development. Nevertheless, there are intergroup differences both between parents and teachers, and among teachers themselves. In both groups, several studies carried out in Spain (Hidalgo, 1999; Palacios & Moreno, 1996; Oliva & Palacios, 1997) have identified two cultural models of children's education and development: one more traditional, emphasizing obedience, order, and discipline, and the other, which we might consider more modern, that prioritizes creativity, initiative-taking, and individual development.

Finally, the US teachers' cultural model of the ideal student is also distinctive in the way that motivation, instigated by the teacher's efforts to create a state of excitement in learning, is related to self-esteem, effortful accomplishment, and future success on the public stage. These cultural images are widely portrayed in the media, as illustrated recently by films such as *Akeela and the Bee* in which a student or teacher attains fame and fortune through effortful pursuit of an apparently impossible goal.

The importance of stimulating interest and motivation is also widely recognized and implemented in teacher training. Joseph Renzulli, a leader in gifted and talented education, states that identification of gifted students can best be accomplished in the context of 'action behaviours', which he describes as

> the type of dynamic interactions that take place when a person becomes extremely interested in or excited about a particular topic, area of study, issue, idea, or event that takes place within the school or non-school environment. These interactions occur when students come into contact with or are influenced by persons, concepts, or particular pieces of knowledge. They create the powerful 'Aha's' that may become triggers for subsequent involvement. (Renzulli, 1999, p. 14)

Self-esteem is essential to sustaining this kind of goal-setting and sustained effort, and is widely assumed to be of central importance for children's successful development. Research by Harkness *et al.* (2000) found that American parents of young children, in comparison with Dutch parents, tended to describe their children more frequently as 'self-confident' and 'a leader' although the Dutch parents more often perceived their children as 'enterprising'. By a wide margin, the American parents also described their children more frequently as 'smart'—a condition of success in school and beyond.

Each of these cultural models of the ideal student, evidently, entails a unique set of connections among elements from a pool of ideas which are thereby transformed into local meaning systems. These ethnotheories are particularly evident in relation to four recurring themes:

Motivation was a theme mentioned by teachers in all five samples, but teachers differed in how they talked about creating motivation in students and why it was important. For the Italian teachers, motivation to learn was seen as an inherent quality of the child. Like their Italian counterparts, the Dutch teachers talked about motivation as an individual trait, but they also stressed the importance of creating a calm, comfortable environment in which children would naturally find it pleasant and easy to learn. For the Polish, Spanish, and US teachers, in contrast, motivation was seen as necessary in order to sustain the effort required for self-discipline and learning even when the process was not necessarily interesting in the immediate context.

Independence or autonomy was a quality mentioned by teachers in all samples except for the Spanish sample, but it seemed to mean slightly different things to teachers in each sample. For the Italian teachers, independence was mentioned as an aspect of creative, divergent thinking, whereas for the Dutch teachers, independence referred more to the ability to work on one's own without constantly turning to the teacher for help. The Polish teachers saw independence as a necessary quality for success in the new economy, although it needed to be limited in deference to the needs of the whole group in the classroom setting. Surprisingly, perhaps, the US teachers talked less about independence than did either the Italian or the Dutch teachers, and they were evidently concerned about maintaining an orderly classroom and dealing with disruptive students. The Spanish teachers did not mention independence at all, and instead talked specifically about the importance of obedience and respect as desirable qualities in students.

Self-regulation is perhaps the most general theme that pervades the interviews of teachers in all the samples. Teachers in all five cultural samples emphasized the importance of managing one's own behaviour and emotional state as a precondition for success in learning. There seemed to be a general consensus that intelligence is not enough to guarantee success in school, in the absence of self-regulation. This general theme, however, takes on a somewhat different character in each sample. For the Italian teachers, the *vivace* child is seen as the normative ideal, even if somewhat 'chaotic' as one teacher noted. Quite possibly, this same child might be seen as a bit out of control in the Dutch context, with its greater emphasis on being well-balanced and calm. For the Spanish and Polish teachers, regulation of the child's behaviour was presented more as a classroom management issue, even for young children. The US teachers' emphasis on the importance of positive self-evaluation, 'feeling comfortable' with oneself, was described as necessary for taking risks in trying new things and, particularly, for self-presentation in front of a group—a scenario barely mentioned by teachers in the other groups. Nevertheless, the US teachers were acutely aware of issues in classroom management.

Related to these differences in cultural themes, teachers also gave somewhat differing accounts of their classroom practices, with the Italian and Dutch teachers emphasizing the creation of a positive, even intimate emotional climate while the Spanish teachers emphasized learning good manners in the classroom. The US teachers talked about directly confronting students' fears and encouraging students to challenge themselves; in contrast, the Dutch teachers were more inclined to adapt their own demands to the comfort level of the child (e.g. a child who was afraid to go to the blackboard could show the teacher his answer at his desk). The Polish teachers, as we have noted, seemed to maintain classroom practices more expressive of traditional group cohesion, even while espousing the new individualistic qualities as developmental goals for children.

An unanticipated finding was the importance of family for teachers in all the samples. This was most evident in the Spanish sample, where teachers made it clear that support for academics by the child's family is the foundation for success in school. Teachers in the other samples talked critically about families too, however. The Dutch and Polish teachers typically worried that children were overloaded with too many distractions in their daily lives, while the US teachers were concerned about parents' overbearing expectations of their children or, on the other hand, lack of time to spend helping their children to develop the self-confidence to succeed.

Conclusions

As we noted at the beginning of this paper, children around the world go to school to learn much more than just the academic skills that occupy the formal curriculum. In post-industrial countries, school is the main site for learning how to be a competent member of society, and it is therefore a particularly valuable place in which to learn about the beliefs and values that shape the larger culture. The teachers in the present study all described ideas that are familiar in western theories of education, yet the divergence among them suggests that even within this framework, there is plenty of room for the expression of particular cultural ideas and practices. One example of this was presented with startling simplicity when a Dutch teacher explained to the first author that 'circle time' is important because it helps children to learn how to listen to each other—in contrast to the familiar American idea that circle time's main function is to teach children to 'share' their own stories with others.

The teachers in the present study probably differed from their own formal theories of education, however, in the extent to which they talked about social, emotional, and self-regulatory skills. It is clear that such skills are what make a classroom 'work' for the teacher as well as the children, even though little attention is given to them in most teacher training programmes. In this sense, the formal curriculum of children's class-rooms can be seen as a scaffold upon which to build related areas of competence rather than being an end in and of itself. The teachers in all our western samples talked about the importance of various kinds of competence such as responsibility, caring, social skills, and emotional intelligence in ways that evoke non-western ideas of intelligence. In particular, the teachers' attention to the importance of interper-sonal relationships in the classroom seems consistent with non-western conceptual-izations. Teachers in all five of our samples specifically stated that cognitive qualities are not enough for success in school. Thus, it appears that western educational theories of intelligence and education may be somewhat disconnected from actual ethnotheories and practices in the classroom, even in mainstream schools of the western world. Unfortunately, the current political emphasis on developing cognitive skills may undermine teachers' efforts to help students learn other kinds of competence that may be just as important in the wider world.

Acknowledgement

This research was funded in part by generous grants from the Spencer Foundation. All statements made and opinions expressed are the sole responsibility of the authors.

Notes on contributors

Sara Harkness, Ph.D., M.P.H., is Professor of Human Development and Anthropol-ogy, and Director of the Center for the Study of Culture, Health and Human Development at the University of Connecticut.

Marjolijn Blom, Ph.D., is Instructor at the Roosevelt Academy, an honors college in Middelburg, the Netherlands. Her research interests include the political, social, and cultural contexts of child health and development.

Alfredo Oliva, Ph.D., is Associate Professor in the Department of Developmental and Educational Psychology at the University of Seville, Spain.

Ughetta Moscardino, Ph.D., is an Assistant Professor of cultural developmental psychology at the University of Padua, Italy. Her research interests include the role of culture in human development, parents' childrearing beliefs and practices, and mixed-methods approaches to parenting in ethnically diverse populations.

Piotr Olaf Zylicz, Ph.D., is Senior Lecturer in psychology at Warsaw School of Social Psychology, Warsaw Poland.

Moisés Ríos Bermúdez is Assistant Professor in the Department of Developmental and Educational Psychology at the University of Seville, Spain.

Xin Feng, Ph.D., is a postdoctoral fellow in the Department of Psychology at the University of Pittsburg.

Agnieszka Carrasco-Zylicz, M.A., is Psychologist at the Didasko Preschool in Warsaw, Poland.

Giovanna Axia, Ph.D., is Professor in the Department of Developmental and Social Psychology, University of Padua, Italy.

Charles M. Super, Ph.D., is Professor in the Department of Human Development and Family Studies and Co-Director of the Center for the Study of Culture, Health and Human Development at the University of Connecticut.

References

Axia, G. (1999) *La timidezza* [Shyness] (Bologna, Il Mulino).

Axia, G., Bonichini, S. & Moscardino, U. (2003) Dalle narrative parentali ai dati quantitativi. Etnoteorie parentali in famiglie italiane e nigeriane immigrate in Italia [From parental narratives to quantitative data. Parental ethnotheories in Italian and Nigerian immigrant families in Italy], in: C. Poderico, P Venuti, & R. Marcone (Eds) *Diverse culture, bambini diversi? [Different cultures, different children?]* (Unicopli, Milan), 119–140.

Axia, G. & Weisner, T. S. (2002) Infant stress reactivity and home cultural ecology of Italian infants and families, *Infant Behavior and Development*, 140, 1–14.

Azuma, H. & Kashiwagi, K. (1987) Descriptors of an intelligent person: a Japanese study, *Japanese Psychological Research*, 28, 17–26.

Banach, C. (2002) Skarb ukryty w edukacji. Strategia rozwoju edukacji do roku 2020 (Hidden treasure of education. Strategy of educational development until 2020) *Konspekt*. Available online at: http://www.wsp.krakow.pl/konspekt/12/strategia.html (accessed January 2007).

Chao, R. K. (1996) Chinese and European-American mothers' beliefs about the role of parenting in children's school success, *Journal of Cross-Cultural Psychology*, 272(4), 403–423.

Czakon, D. (2000) Wzajemne oczekiwania [Mutual expectations], *Edukacja i Dialog*, 121(8), 23–30.

Edwards, C. P. & Gandini, L. (1995) The contrasting developmental timetables of parents and preschool teachers in two cultural communities, in: S. Harkness & C. M. Super (Eds) *Parents' cultural belief systems: their origins, expressions, and consequences* (New York, Guilford Press) 270–288.

Harkness, S. & Super, C. M. (1992) Parental ethnotheories in action, in I. Sigel, A. V. McGillicuddy-DeLisi & J. Goodnow (Eds) *Parental belief systems: the psychological consequences for children* (2nd edn) (Hillsdale, NJ, Erlbaum), 373–392.

Harkness, S., Super, C. M. & van Tijn, N. (2000) Individualism and the 'western mind' reconsidered: American and Dutch parents' ethnotheories of children and family, in: S. Harkness, C. Raeff & C. M. Super (Eds) *The social construction of the child: understanding variability within and across contexts (Vol. 87) New Directions in Child Development* (San Francisco, Jossey-Bass), 23–39.

Harkness, S., Moscardino, U., Rios Bermudez, M., Zylicz, P. O., Welles-Nyström, B., Parmar, P., Axia, G. & Super, C. M. (2006) Mixed methods in international collaborative research: the experiences of the International Study of Parents, Children, and Schools, *Cross-Cultural Research*, 40(1), 65–82.

Hess, R. D., Kashiwagi, K., Azuma, H., Price, G. G. & Dickson, W. P. (1980) Maternal expectations for mastery of developmental tasks in Japan and the United States, *International Journal of Psychology*, 15, 259–271.

Hidalgo, M. V. (1999) Parents' ideas about child development and education: their change and continuity during the transition to parenthood, *Infancia y Aprendizaje*, 85, 75–94.

Kagitcibasi, C. (1996) The autonomous-relational self: a new synthesis, *European Psychologist*, 1(3), 180–186.

Kitayama, S. & Duffy, S. (2004) Cultural competence—tacit, yet fundamental: self, social relations, and cognition in the United States and Japan, in: R. J. Sternberg & E. L. Grigorenko (Eds) *Culture and competence: contexts of life success* (Washington, DC, American Psychological Association), 55–87.

Leseman, P. P. M., Rollenberg, L. & Gebhardt, E. (2000) Co-construction in kindergartners' free play: effects of social, individual and didactic factors, in: H. Cowie & G. Van der Aalsvoort (Eds) *Social interaction in learning and instruction: the meaning of discourse for the construction of knowledge* (Amsterdam, Pergamon/Elsevier Science), 104–128.

Lewis, C. (1995) *Educating hearts and minds: reflections on Japanese preschool and early elementary education* (New York, Cambridge University Press).

Li, J. (2001) Chinese conceptualization of learning, *Ethos*, 29(2), 111–137.

Okagaki, L. & Sternberg, R. J. (1993) Parental beliefs and children's school performance, *Child Development*, 64(1), 36–56.

Oliva, A. & Palacios, J. (1997) Differences in the expectations and values of Spanish preschool children's mothers and teachers, *Infancia y Aprendizaje*, 77, 61–67.

Palacios, J. & Moreno, M. C. (1996) Parents' and adolescents' ideas on children: origins and transmission of intracultural diversity, in: S. Harkness & C. M. Super (Eds) *Parents' cultural belief systems* (New York, Guilford), 215–253.

Parmar, P. Harkness, S. & Super, C. M. (2004) Asian and Euro-American parents' ethnotheories of play and learning: effects on pre-school children's home routines and school behavior, *International Journal of Behavioral Development*, 28(2), 97–104.

Perry, C. (2006) *Young America: childhood in nineteenth-century art and culture* (New Haven, Yale University Press).

Renzulli, J. S. (1999) What is this thing called giftedness, and how do we develop it? A twenty-five year perspective, *Journal for the Education of the Gifted*, 23(1), 3–54.

SAS Institute (2002–2004) *SAS 9.1.3 Help and documentation* (Cary, NC, SAS Institute).

Serpell, R. (1993) *The significance of schooling: life-journeys in an African society* (Cambridge, Cambridge University Press).

Shapiro, L. J., & Azuma, H. (2004) Intellectual, attitudinal, and interpersonal aspects of competence in the United States and Japan, in: R. J. Sternberg & E. L. Grigorenko (Eds) *Culture and competence: contexts of life success* (Washington, DC, American Psychological Association), 187–206.

Slomczynski, K. M. & Shabad, G. (1997) Continuity and change in political socialization in Poland, *Comparative Education Review*, 41(1), 44–70.

Sternberg, R., J., Conway, B. E., Ketron, J. L. & Berstein, M. (1981) People's conceptions of intelligence, *Journal of Personality and Social Psychology*, 41, 37–55.

Stevenson, H. W. & Lee, S. Y. (1990) Context of achievement. *Monographs of the Society for Research in Child Development*, 55 (Serial No. 221) (Oxford, England, Blackwell Publishing).

Wang, W., Ceci, S. J., Williams, W. M. & Kopko, K. A. (2004) Culturally situated cognitive competence: a functional framework, in: R. J. Sternberg & E. L. Grigorenko (Eds) *Culture and competence: contexts of life success* (Washington, DC, American Psychological Association), 225–250.

Whiting, B. B. & Edwards, C. P. (1988) *Children of different worlds: the formation of social behavior* (Cambridge, MA, Harvard University Press).

Schooling's contribution to social capital: study from a native Amazonian society in Bolivia

Ricardo Godoy, Craig Seyfried, Victoria Reyes-García, Tomás Huanca, William R. Leonard, Thomas McDade, Susan Tanner and Vincent Vadez

Introduction

At the core of cultural anthropology lies the belief that culture—norms, technology, and social organization—evolved through generations to help people adapt to their environment (Steward, 1955; Alland, 1973; Durham, 1992; Richerson & Boyd, 2004). Throughout our evolutionary history, humans have survived by relying on non-biological cultural means, such as local knowledge of the environment (Reyes-García *et al.*, 2005) and local forms of social capital or generosity, including gift giving, sharing, and reciprocity (Sahlins, 1972; Mauss, 1990). Besides helping people adapt to their environment, culture bestows a sense of time, place, and belonging that contributes to the well-being of individuals (Brumann, 1999; Kuper, 1999; Steedly, 1999).

Understanding why traditional cultures weaken matters because cultures have allowed humans to adapt to their environment and because they embody humanity's heritage (Sutherland, 2003). By traditional culture we mean a culture with only recent continuous exposure to the market economy or westerners. Among abraders of traditional cultures, schooling has received much attention. Researchers have noted that schooling and academic skills learned in school undermine aspects of traditional culture, such as knowledge of the local environment (Sternberg, 1997; Benz *et al.*, 2000; Sternberg *et al.*, 2001; Zent, 2001), social organization (Chavajay & Rogoff, 2002), ethos (Middleton, 2005), and the local language(Akinnaso, 1992).

Clearly the effect of formal schooling on traditional cultures will depend on the type of schooling and on the number of years of school exposure. Schooling may not help people in all communities in the same ways. Schooling that infuses traditional knowledge with the acquisition of academic skills likely enhances learning outcomes (Lipka *et al.*, 2001; Grigorenko *et al.*, 2002), but others argue that simple school exposure, independent of its content or quality, influences outcomes such as health and fertility, particularly among females (LeVine *et al.*, 2001), and behaviours valued in the market, such as obedience and punctuality (Bowles & Gintis, 1975).

Here we assess whether schooling weakens a core dimension of traditional culture: social capital. Social capital stands for norms and behaviours that enable people to act collectively. In industrial nations, proxy variables for social capital have included trust, safety nets, social networks, membership of local organizations, and political and civic engagement (Portes, 1998; Ostrom, 2000; Durlauf & Fafchamps, 2005). In pre-industrial societies, proxy variables for social capital have included expressions of generosity, such as gifts (Hill, 2002) or labour help given to other households, or participation in communal chores (Erasmus, 1956; Leatherman, 2005). In pre-industrial societies social capital matters because it contributes to group cohesion and because it helps protect household consumption against mishaps (Godoy, 2001; Carter & Maluccio, 2003).

Table 1 contains a summary of 14 quantitative studies about the effect of schooling on social capital in industrial and developing nations, and in small-scale, pre-industrial rural societies. Six findings stand out.

First, except for two studies, researchers have found positive associations between schooling and social capital. The finding held up across studies that varied in sample size, from a low of only 470–716 people to a high of 76,156 people. Glaeser *et al.*, (2002) note that the relation between social capital and schooling is 'one of the most robust empirical regularities in the social capital literature' (p. 455) and Putnam

Table 1. Review of quantitative studies of the effects of schooling on social capital

Author and year of publication A	Name, country and year(s) of survey B	Sample population and age C	Method D	Definition of social capital (in italics) and controls E	Question and social capital outcome F	Statistically significant support G
			I. INDUSTRIAL NATIONS:			
1. (Brehm & Rahn, 1997)	General Social Survey USA 1972–1994	9118 residents of the continental USA 18 years of age and over	IVs for social capital=early childhood experiences, parental divorce, being a victim of crime, ethnic membership	*- Interpersonal, trust* *- Confidence in government* *- Partisanship* *- Days reading newspaper* - Income - TV hours - Size of city - Race - Gender - Divorce - Life satisfaction	Does education affect civic engagement? Does education increase interpersonal trust?	Each additional year of schooling increases civic engagement by .11 (t=27.5) Each additional year of schooling increases trust by .10 ($t = 5$)
2. (Bynner & Ashford, 1994)	UK Economic and Social Research Council's 16–19 Initiative 1987–1989	5000 British citizens from Swindon, Sheffield, Liverpool and Kirkcaldy 16–19 years of age	Multiple regressions	*- Voting* - Mother/father's social class - Age at which father left school - Age at which mother left school - City of residency - Income	Does education affect the likelihood of a person voting?	Not being enrolled in school decreased the likelihood of an individual voting by .14 R=.47 (t cannot be determined from data provided)
3. (Egerton, 2002)	British Household Panel Study UK 1991–1999	470 British citizens 17–23 years of age from a study of 5,000 British households	Logistic regression	*- Social groups* - Gender - SES - Father's occupation - Level of education	Does a college education make a citizen more likely to join social groups?	The odds ratio for between membership in civic groups and completing a 4-year degree programme is 3.21 (p<.05)
4. (Glaeser et al., 2002)	General Social Survey USA 1972–1998	19,245 Americans in the continental USA 18–59 years of age	OLS	*- Average sociability of occupation* *- Average membership in peer groups* - Age - Gender - Race - Education - Income	Does education make people more likely to join groups?	An additional year of school raises the total number of membership in groups by .21 (t= 42.4)

Table 1.   (continued)

A	B	C	D	E	F	G
Author and year of publication	Name, country and year(s) of survey	Sample population and age	Method	Definition of social capital (in italics) and controls	Question and social capital outcome	Statistically significant support
5. (Mettler & Welch, 2004)	World War II Veterans Survey USA 1950–1998	716 members of WW II military units	OLS	- *Political participation defined by* ★ *contacting political officials* ★ *working on campaigns* ★ *serving on government boards/council* ★ *contributing money to an individual or party* ★ *participating in a protest, march or demonstration* - Standard of living - Parents' political activity - Use of GI Bill - High school diploma - 2-year college degree - 4-year college degree - Unfinished college experience	What is schooling's effect on political participation?	Being a graduate of a 4-year college programme increased the likelihood of political participation by .37 (p<.001)
6. (McVeigh & Smith, 1999)	Evangelical Influence Survey USA 1996	2591 American citizens Over 17 years of age	Multinomial logistic regression	- *Participation in institutional politics and political protests* - Income - Education - Financial situation - Ascriptive identities - Organizational activities - Religious affiliation	Does completion of 4-year degree programme encourage participation in : a) institutional politics b) political protests	Having a 4-year degree increases: a) participation in institutional politics by .582 ($p < .01$) b) participation in political protests by .559 ($p < .05$)
7. (Nie, Junn, & Stehlik-Barry, 1996)	General Social Survey 1976–1994 National Election Study	15,887 USA citizens, 25 and older, residing in the continental USA	OLS	- *Political engagement and tolerance* - Age - Education - Race - Gender	Does individual educational achievement correlate with	Each additional year of school increases an individual's: Knowledge of principles of democracy by .17 (t=5.53) Tolerance by .23 (t = 7.04)

Table 1. *(continued)*

Author and year of publication	Name, country and year(s) of survey	Sample population and age	Method	Definition of social capital (in italics) and controls	Question and social capital outcome	Statistically significant support
A	**B**	**C**	**D**	**E**	**F**	**G**
	1972–1994; USA			- Family income - Occupational prominence	higher levels of political engagement? Does a higher level of average education reduce a community's level of political engagement?	Knowledge of political leaders by .09 (t=2.92) Participation in difficult political activities by .08 (t=2.95) Voting by .07 (t= 2.28) Political attentiveness by .20 (t=6.39) Knowledge of other current political facts by .26 (t=7.69) Each additional year added to a community's average years of schooling reduces political engagement by –3.69 (t=–16.4)
8. (Helliwell & Putnam, 1999)	US General Social Survey (GSS) USA (1974–1994)	19,214 participants throughout USA (24 years and older)	OLS	*Social trust, political engagement* - TV Generation - TV Era - Lifecycle - Gender	Does individual education encourage social trust and engagement?	Each additional year of schooling increased: GSS social trust by .04 (t=40.3) DDB social trust by .02 (t=3.2) Each additional year of schooling increased: the GSS number of social engagements by .22 (t=51.7)
	DDB-Needham Life Style USA (1975–1997)	76,156 participants throughout USA (age not given)		- Average education in region - Divorce - Geographic region	Does average education encourage social trust and engagement?	The results for average education on both social trust and social engagement are statistically insignificant, except for GSS social trust, where the region's average years of schooling raises social trust by .02 (t=3.2)

Table 1. (continued)

II. DEVELOPING NATIONS:

Author and year of publication	Name, country and year(s) of survey	Sample population and age	Method	Definition of social capital (in italics) and controls	Question and social capital outcome	Statistically significant support
A	B	C	D	E	F	G
9. (Seligson, 1999)	Survey of metropolitan areas in capital cities of six Central American countries in 1991, 1995 for Costa Rica	4181 residents of San José Guatemala City Managua Tegucigalpa Panama City San Salvador (age not given)	OLS	- *Citizen's demand on government* [not defined] - Age - Gender - Education [not defined] - Democratic values - Trust - Wealth	Does education increase the likelihood that citizens will make demands of government officials?	Each year of school schooling increases the number of political demands made by: Costa Rica .0037 (t=.37) El Salvador .0099 (t=.99) Guatemala .016 (t=1.6) Honduras .034 (t=3.4) Nicaragua .0019 (t=.19) Panama .0009 (t=.09)
10. (Henrich et al., 2004)	Experimental games played in 6 pre-industrial societies 1996–2004	Mapuche: 62 participants Tsimane': 134 participants Orma: 262 participants Sangu: 80 participants Au: 60 participants Gnau: 50 participants Age not given	Ultimatum game and Public goods game. OLS, bivariate, multivariate Analysis	- Results of experimental games - Age, sex, village, language, trips to town, wage labour	Does formal schooling affect pro-social behaviour as revealed through experimental games?	Generally no effect, except among Tsimane' (more schooling, less offer in Ultimatum game, but no effect in Public goods game)
11. (Gregson et al., 2003)	People in Manicaland, a rural province in eastern Zimbabwe 1998–2000	9843 participants 15–54 years of age	Logit	- *Social groups* - Groups that meet during school hours - Age - SES	Does education affect an individual's participation in community and social groups that meet outside of school hours	Women with secondary education more likely to report membership in a community group (OR=1.34, p=.023)

Table 1. *(continued)*

Author and year of publication	Name, country and year(s) of survey	Sample population and age	Method	Definition of social capital (in italics) and controls	Question and social capital outcome	Statistically significant support
A	B	C	D	E	F	G
12. (Grootaert & Narayan, 2004)	Local Level Institutions Study Bolivia; study in following provinces: Tiahuanacu Mizque Charagua, Villa Serrano. 1996	A study of 1432 families, conducted by asking only the leader of the household over the age of 15	Bivariate associations	- *Social groups* - Province - Head of household - Religion - Income (divided into quin-tiles)	Does education increase a household's number of group memberships?	No clear pattern; education associated with increasing participation in some groups and decreased participation in other groups
13. (Krishna, 2002)	Study of 69 Rajasthan villages India 1998–2000	2232 Indians from rural villages Over 18 years of age	OLS	- *Political activity measured in 100-point index* - Gender - Age - Religion - Education - Independent political educa-tion - Wealth - Caste - Distance to nearest town - Infrastructure	Does an individual's years of schooling influence his or her decision to become politically active?	An additional year of schooling increases an individual's score of political activity by .61 (t=2.77)
14. (Maluccio, Haddad, & May, 2000)	KwaZulu-Natal Income Dynamics Survey and individual survey to check against the KNID survey South Africa 1993–1998	The heads of 1,393 households in KwaZulu-Natal Ages 20 and over	OLS	- *Social groups* - Location - Race - Household size - Gender - Age	Does education increase the number of group memberships in a household?	Each additional year of schooling increases the number of group memberships by .08 (t=10.6)

Notes. IV: Instrumental variable
OLS: Ordinary least square
OR: Odds ratio

(2000) echoes the observation by noting that schooling is 'the most powerful predictor of virtually all forms of altruistic behaviour' (p. 18).

Only Seligson (1999), in her study of six Central American cities, and Henrich *et al.* (2004) in his study of 15 pre-industrial societies using field laboratory experiments found no strong association between schooling and social capital. An example of a field laboratory experiment is a game with two participants who cannot see each other in which one participant makes an offer (often of money) to the other participant, who can either refuse or accept. If the second participant refuses, neither player receives a reward, but if the second participant agrees to the amount, then the sum is split along the lines indicated by the first participant. Seligson found strong relations in Guatemala and Honduras, but her studies in Panama, Nicaragua, Costa Rica, and El Salvador failed to demonstrate such a relation. Of the six pre-industrial societies studied by Henrich *et al.* for which they had information on schooling and social capital, only among the Tsimane' of Bolivia did researchers find evidence of an association between schooling and pro-social behaviour. Tsimane' with more schooling offered less in some types of field laboratory experiments than Tsimane' with less schooling, but schooling bore no association with the amount offered in other studies. The weak results among the Tsimane' might reflect both a small sample size of observations (n=134) and participants' lack of understanding of the task in the field experiment.

Second, except for the study by Brehm and Rahn (1997), none of the other studies listed in Table 1 corrects for the endogeneity of schooling. An endogenous variable is an explanatory variable whose use produces a biased estimate owing to the role of omitted variables in the model, random error in the measure of the endogenous variable, or two-way causality between the endogenous variable and another explanatory variable. For example, the studies of Table 1 suggest that schooling contributes to social capital, but studies from industrial nations also suggest that social capital expressed through such things as participation in parent-teacher associations lowers the likelihood that children will drop out of school, thereby improving children's school performance (Coleman, 1988; Furstenberg & Hughes, 1995; Teachman *et al.*, 1997; McNeal, 1999; Morgan & Sorenson, 1999). Furthermore, social capital and schooling might both reflect the role of third, unmeasured variables. For instance, people of some ethnic groups might invest more in schooling and also engage in more pro-social behaviour than people of other ethnic groups. The possible two-way causality between social capital and schooling and the role of unmeasured variables (e.g., ethnicity) suggests that the estimates of schooling's effect on social capital in Table 1 may contain biases of an unknown direction and magnitude.

Third, the association between schooling and social capital is stronger in industrial nations than in developing nations, or than in small-scale, pre-industrial societies. All the studies from industrial nations in Table 1 found strong positive associations between schooling and social capital, but only four of the six studies from developing nations found such an association. This may result from higher schooling levels in industrial nations, but may also suggest that social capital is stronger in some societies than in others.

Fourth, all but two of the studies in industrial nations used some form of political participation to measure social capital. Political participation can benefit an entire society because it increases one's trust in one's society. While a person's political goals may not be reached, political participation promises that an individual's opinions can be heard. This is why researchers have chosen to quantify political participation to measure the kind of social capital that produces more democratic and tolerant societies. Therefore, in societies where the measurement is applicable researchers have used various forms of political participation to measure social capital.

Fifth, the studies from industrial nations summarized in Table 1 may contain a bias from self-selection into the sample used in the study. In those studies researchers used surveys to identify levels of participation, but completion of the survey itself requires civic mindedness (Hauser, 2005). Therefore, there may be an upward bias in some of the estimates shown in Table 1 because people who valued participation may have been more likely to answer the survey. As a result, people with low levels of social capital may be underrepresented in the studies.

With the exception of the study by Bynner and Ashford (1994), all the other studies listed in Table 1 examined data from nationwide surveys. As a result, the findings imply that the relation between schooling and social capital applies to the entire nation. In fact, the finding may gloss over diversity within a nation. For example, studies in the USA suggest higher levels of social capital in the mid-west and lower levels in most urban areas (Goldin & Katz, 1999).

Sixth, except for the study by Henrich *et al.* (2004) none of the other studies has focused on pre-industrial societies. Many quantitative studies in anthropology focus on gift giving in pre-industrial societies (Reyes-García *et al.*, 2006), but few of them contain estimates of schooling's effect on social capital.

In this paper we have three aims. *First,* we want to improve on previous estimates of the effects of schooling on social capital by correcting for the endogeneity of schooling, and do so by using instrumental variables for schooling (Durlauf, 2002; Durlauf & Fafchamps, 2005). An instrumental variable is a variable that correlates highly with the endogenous explanatory variable but does not correlate with the outcome, except through the endogenous variable. For example, in estimating the effects of schooling on earnings, researchers are faced with the endogeneity of schooling; schooling could increase earnings, but earnings could affect schooling, and both could reflect the role of a third variable (e.g., motivation). Researchers have used variables such as parental schooling as an instrumental variable for own schooling because parental schooling is likely highly correlated with own schooling, but uncorrelated with earnings (except through own schooling) (Wooldridge, 2003). Valid instrumental variables allow one to reduce biases from endogeneity (Angrist & Krueger, 2001).

Second, we want to test whether the positive association between schooling and social capital found in industrial nations holds in a small-scale pre-industrial society. Unlike industrial societies, in pre-industrial societies we expect schooling to have ambiguous effects on social capital.

Third, we want to test three hypotheses about the effects of a person's own schooling on social capital. We focus on a person's own schooling rather than on parental schooling or on the average level of schooling of the household because we use parental schooling as an instrumental variable to reduce endogeneity biases. The studies summarized in Table 1 focus on a person's own schooling, so our use of own schooling facilitates comparison with other studies. The three hypotheses are detailed below.

Hypothesis #1

Own schooling will lower a person's social capital expressed through labour help offered to people of other households or through participation in communal work. Research in developing nations suggests that schooling contributes to higher earnings if people acquire more than 4–6 years of schooling (Mingat & Bruns, 2002). Beyond a minimum threshold of schooling, schooling opens employment opportunities outside the village economy. As the economic value of their time rises, more schooled people will reduce the amount of labour they allocate to help others or to do communal work because it will become more expensive to show generosity in this way.

Hypothesis #2

Own schooling will increase individual social capital expressed through gifts given to people of other households. Greater income from more schooling should induce the better off to flaunt their riches by giving it to the rest of the community. As long as the social capital of a community does not collapse, the rest of the community should be able to pressure the better off to give away some of their resources. Anthropologists have shown how the fear of envy, gossip, mistrust, and false reports bruited through a community can end in accusations of witchcraft, sickness, and death (Briggs, 1970; Haviland, 1977). The fear of odium should push those with more resources to share their riches.

Hypothesis #3

Own schooling will increase the probability of displaying generosity to people unrelated by blood or marriage. Schooling should change not only how people express social capital, but also whom they give it to. People in traditional societies rely on kin to organize production and social relations. When one's village of residence contains a wide network of kin related to one by marriage and by blood, generosity to what at first sight may appear a stranger is, in actuality, generosity to one's relative. If we take our cues from research findings based on observational studies of industrial nations (Abramson & Inglehart, 1995; Inglehart & Norris, 2003) we would expect schooling to increase the likelihood of displaying social capital to strangers. For example, Abramson and Inglehart (1995) used a nationally-representative panel (or longitudinal) and repeated cross-sectional surveys from industrial nations and found that schooling helped internalize concerns with equity, quality of life, and the environment rather than with survival and immediate kin.

Methodology

To test the three hypotheses we use data from a highly autarkic society of farmers and foragers in the Bolivian Amazon, the Tsimane', who are in the early stages of continuous exposure to the market economy and the western world.

Sample, data, and measure of variables

(see also, Appendix 1 for further technical details). Information comes from a survey undertaken in 2004 in 13 Tsimane' villages straddling the Maniqui river, province of Beni. Participants in the study included people in all 236 households of the 13 villages, but we only use information from people over 16 years of age (n = 574) because we did not collect information on social capital for people under 16 years of age. Sixteen years is a cut-off age for adulthood; after that age, people start to clear their own plots for farming and set up unions. The 2004 survey formed part of a panel study in progress that started in 1999 (Godoy *et al.*, 2005a, b). A panel study is a longitudinal study in which researchers track the same people and households over time. Experienced translators and interviewers who had been part of the panel study from the start carried out the 2004 survey. Translators included Tsimane' whom we had trained in the implementation of the survey. They have deep knowledge of the questions since they have pilot tested the questions, used them on themselves in practice runs, and applied them to other Tsimane' in different survey waves. The surveyors included people who wrote down answers and included several researchers who had done their Ph.D. with the Tsimane', understood the local language (though they still needed a translator to understand answers to some of the more complex questions), and had helped develop the survey instrument.

Social capital.   For reasons discussed earlier, we equate social capital with gifts given to people of other households, work done for people of other households, and with participation in communal work. We constructed three dependent variables for social capital for each adult. The dependent variables captured different expressions of social capital, but only during the seven days before the day of the interview. We did not increase the recall period farther back into the past to avoid measurement errors from faulty recall.

We followed three steps to collect information on social capital and create the variables for social capital used in the statistical analysis. First, we asked people to list all the gifts they had given. Gifts included items such as fish, game meat, rice, manioc, plantains, maize, cooked food, and medicines. Second, we asked people about unpaid work done for people of other households, and about participation in communal work. Unpaid work for others included things such as help in farm work, running errands, or helping ill people. Third, we added answers to the two questions to arrive at a measure of total expressions of social capital. We also asked who received the gift or help. We grouped recipients of generous acts into the following categories: immediate family, Tsimane' of other households in the village, Tsimane' of other villages, and napos, or Bolivians who are not native Amazonians. To test hypotheses 1–2 we excluded expressions of social capital to immediate family and *napos*.

Own schooling and instrumental variables for own schooling. We asked people about the maximum school grade they had attained. We did not ask about the quality of schooling received, though later we comment on changes in school quality.

To obtain information about instrumental variables for own schooling, we asked them about the maximum school grade attained by their mother and by their father, the ability of their mother and their father to write and speak Spanish, and whether their same-sex parent was taller, of the same physical stature, or shorter than they. We coded answers to questions about parental ability to speak Spanish as follows: 0 = unable, 1 = with difficulty, and 2 = fluent. We coded answers to questions about parental writing ability as follows: 0 = cannot, 1 = some, and 2 = well. We coded people's answers to questions about physical stature relative to their same-sex parent as follows: −1= taller than parent, 0 = same physical stature as parent, and +1= shorter than parent. We asked about parental physical stature as a possible instrumental variable for own schooling because studies have shown positive associations between adult physical stature and indicators of individual well-being, such as income, longevity, and occupation (Fogel, 2005).

Besides the variables just described, we coded for the respondent's sex (female=0; male=1) and asked participants to report their age. Table 2 contains definition and summary statistics of the dependent, explanatory, and instrumental variables used in the regression analyses.

Table 2. Definition and summary statistics of variables for Tsimane' over 16 years of age used in regression analysis

Variable	Definition	N	Mean	Std Dev
Dependent variables (social capital expressed during 7 days before interview):				
Gifts	Number of gifts given to people of other households	574	0.109	0.602
Labour	Number of times person helped people of other households with labour or did communal work	574	0.207	0.808
Total	Sum of the two variables: Gifts and Labour	574	0.317	1.202
Explanatory variables:				
Schooling	Maximum school grade achieved by respondent	574	1.993	2.411
Age	Age of respondent in years	574	36.538	17.602
Male	Sex of respondent; male=1; female=0	574	0.49	0.50
Instrumental variables:				
Father writing	Respondent's father's writing ability (0 = cannot; 1 = some; 2 = well)	565	0.152	0.401
Village	Respondent's childhood village of residence	569	48.311	42.751

The people

In recent publications we discuss general aspects of Tsimane' ethnography and history (Godoy *et al.*, 2005b, c), so below we provide a synopsis of the Tsimane' and a description of the dependent variable, social capital, and schooling, the explanatory variable of main interest.

Ethnographic synopsis. The Tsimane' number 8,000 people and live in 100+ villages scattered along river banks and logging roads, mostly in the department of Beni at the foothills of the Andes, in the Bolivian Amazon. Villages in our sample are small and contain an average of 24 households (S.D. = 10.8); each household has 7.3 people (S.D. = 2.6) made up of 1.1 adult females (S.D. = 0.4) and 1.1 adult males (S.D. = 0.4).

The Tsimane' practise hunting, gathering, fishing, and slash-and-burn farming. Though they had sporadically taken part in the market in the past during the boom of selected forest goods (e.g., pelts), they started to take part in the market economy more continuously only since the 1970s. It is still not clear whether increasing participation in the market economy and the western world reflects a shortage of natural resources, a desire to acquire western goods, or both (Godoy *et al.*, 2005c). The opening of a motorized dirt road that linked much of the Tsimane' territory with the highlands brought an onslaught of highland colonist farmers, cattle ranchers, and logging and oil firms. The Tsimane' take part in the market economy by selling farm crops (principally rice) and forest goods (principally logs and thatch palm), and by working as unskilled labourers in cattle ranches, logging firms, or in the farms of colonist farmers.

Like other native Amazonian societies, Tsimane' practise cross-cousin marriage (Daillant, 1994); a man marries his mother's brother's daughter. Residence is with the wife's kin group shortly after marriage, followed by a neolocal or independent post-marital living arrangement, neither with the husband's nor with the wife's relatives. Polygamous in the past, the Tsimane' today practise monogamy and live in nuclear households, run jointly by a wife and a husband. Only 10% of the households were run by a single parent (8% headed by a single female and 2% headed by a single male).

Neolocal or independent residence after marriage, plus preferential cross-cousin marriage creates a wide and thick web of relatives linked by blood and marriage potentially available for social support. Thirty-six percent of wives and 39% of husbands lived in their village of birth, suggesting that wives and husbands each likely benefit from the social support of people known since childhood. Village composition is fluid because people move constantly in and out of settlements in search of better places to farm, hunt, and fish (Ellis, 1996).

Social capital. The Tsimane' share goods, give gifts, help each other, and do communal work, but also have a stingy side. The Tsimane' routinely share the ubiquitous *chicha*, a beverage made by fermenting crops such as manioc or plantains. The alcoholic content of *chicha* varies by the duration of fermentation. *Chicha* generally has less than 5% alcoholic content by volume (1%–12%) (Jennings *et al.*, 2005). Tsimane' give freshly made *chicha* to children and infants because it does not contain alcohol, sufficient time not having elapsed for fermentation to take place, but *chicha* several days old is strong and is reserved for adults. Any Tsimane' can walk into a household serving *chicha* and expect to be served. Tsimane' stigmatize as misers and hold in contempt people who do not prepare and share *chicha*. People drink *chicha* sitting in a circle with people of the same sex. They take a few sips from a gourd, then pass it to the person next to them until all is consumed, at which point the host refills the gourd, and the drinking round starts again. As they pass time drinking *chicha*, they tell stories and make commentaries about a wide range of subjects. Unlike the drinking of commercial alcohol, which is done alone or in small groups, mostly by men, the drinking of *chicha* takes place in groups with the participation of all adult Tsimane' present. Many legends and myths of the Tsimane' centre on the drinking of *chicha* (Huanca, 2005). In part because the drinking of *chicha* links with the religious beliefs of Tsimane', Protestant missionaries and Tsimane' who have converted to the Protestant faith abjure and inveigh against drinking *chicha*.

Besides sharing *chicha*, Tsimane' also share food. In the smaller villages, people cook in open courtyards and shout when the meal is ready so all can join in communal eating. In those villages people literally eat from a common pot. Successful hunters share game with others. In an earlier panel study undertaken during five consecutive quarters in 1999–2000 in two villages, we found that 11% of all goods entering households from morning until dusk came as gifts from friends or relatives.

Communal work prevails in the construction and in the maintenance of schools, in hunting expeditions far from villages, in the cleaning of public places, in preparations for village festivities, and in some types of fishing. In remote villages, people work together in the more arduous farm tasks, such as felling large trees before planting. During the dry season, Tsimane' work in groups to set up fish traps and prepare plant poison (Pérez, 2001). In the 1999–2000 study we found that group fishing accounted for a quarter of all fishing events.

Nevertheless, offsetting public displays of generosity one also finds evidence of stinginess. The presence or lure of public schools, the territorial circumscription from the expansion into the Tsimane' territory of loggers, cattle ranchers, and migrant farmers, and the indebtedness into which some Tsimane' have fallen with outside merchants— all create incentives to accumulate more material possessions and to share less.

Even without the presence of markets, one finds a strong ethos of economic independence among households because most food comes from farm and forest goods procured by each household, rather than from goods produced by the village working in unison. For example, during communal fishing people cooperate to set up the traps and to prepare the plant poison, but they keep the fish they catch with their own nets; they do not redistribute the catch among all the people who fished, or among all the people in the village. People in villages closer to towns build walls to enclose their homes and put fences around their courtyards. To guard their material possessions, some Tsimane' put locks on their doors when they leave the village (Byron, 2003). People even hold back on food. People in larger villages do not go out of their way to invite others to share meals, and prefer to eat from dishes rather than from a common pot. Tsimane' often turn their backs to others when they eat (Ellis, 1996). Social capital might permeate daily life, but it does not get activated after a neighbour suffers a misfortune. In the study of 1999–2000 we probed into how households had coped with unforeseen misfortunes (e.g., crop loss), and found that only 5% of the sample received help from kin or neighbours after a misfortune.

Schooling.   The first recorded contact of Tsimane' with westerners dates back to the seventeenth century, but continual exposure to westerners dates back only to the 1940s when Protestant missionaries from the USA entered the department of Beni for the first time (Chicchón, 1992). The work of missionaries took off during the 1950s when the Bolivian Government gave them the responsibility for schooling remote lowland native Amazonian populations such as the Tsimane' (Castro Mantilla, 1997). The agreement lasted from 1954 until 1985. As part of the agreement, missionaries in 1955 set up a centre in the town of Tumichuco, several days away from the Tsimane' territory, with the purpose of training Tsimane' to become bilingual school teachers and to translate the Bible into the Tsimane' language. Protestant missionaries offered scholarships to promising Tsimane' young men so they could attend Tumichuco for three months a year to work as informants for missionary linguists. In Tumichuco missionaries taught Tsimane' academic and practical skills (e.g., modern hygiene) and the Scriptures so Tsimane' could proselytize in the Tsimane' language when they returned to their villages. After 27 years of operating in Tumichuco, missionaries transferred their training centre to the town of San Borja (population ~19,000), closer to the Tsimane' territory. After receiving training, schooled Tsimane' returned to their villages, where they worked as lay missionaries and teachers using instructional materials in the Tsimane' language prepared by missionaries. In 1985, when the agreement with the Government of Bolivia ended, the State took over the responsibility for educating the Tsimane', which meant keeping Tsimane' as school teachers and paying their salaries. To this day, missionaries produce the textbooks used in Tsimane' classrooms, run training seminars for Tsimane' teachers, and offer courses in reading and writing twice a year for Tsimane' adults. Most of today's top Tsimane' political leaders received their training from Protestant missionaries.

At present about 40% of Tsimane' villages have a primary school covering the first five grades. No village has a middle school or a high school. Four villages close to the town of San Borja have an education programme for adults where Tsimane' with primary schooling can earn a high-school diploma by attending classes one week a month.

Despite nearly five decades of exposure to schools, Tsimane' adults have little modern human capital, with males having more than females. The average adult had completed only 1.99 years of schooling (S.D. = 2.41) (Table 2). The average female had completed 1.25 years of schooling (S.D. = 1.51), but 44.14% of females had no schooling. In contrast, the average male had more than twice as many years of schooling (2.72 years; S.D. = 2.88) as the average female. Only 28.52% of males had no schooling. Ninety-one percent of males but only 51% of females knew some Spanish, and 49.82% of males but only 12.11% of females spoke fluent Spanish.

A striking feature of Tsimane' schooling is that it was developed *in situ* by missionaries using the Tsimane' language to prepare instructional material. Instruction has always taken place in village schools with Tsimane' teachers, who receive refresher courses in the Tsimane' language. We say 'striking' because indigenous children in the rest of Bolivia have generally been taught in Spanish. Only with the advent of Bolivia's educational reform during the mid-1980s has the school curriculum for some of the largest indigenous groups, such as the Quechua, Aymara, and Guaraní, started to change so teachers at present instruct using the local language. To support this work, instructional materials in the local language are prepared by Bolivia's Ministry of Education (Contreras & Talavera, 2003). We have been unable to assess the current quality of Tsimane' schooling, but Tsimane' often refer to the years when Tumichuco operated as the golden age of schooling, perhaps because missionaries had direct oversight over the curriculum and its implementation.

Results

Selection of instrumental variables

We followed two steps to select instrumental variables for the maximum school level achieved by the person interviewed. First, we ran a regression with own schooling as a dependent variable and the following explanatory variables: village of residence during childhood, age, sex, and mother's and father's maximum school grade attained, mother's and father's writing ability, and the perceived physical stature of the same-sex parent relative to physical stature of the respondent. In column [a], Table 3, we show the results of the regression. Second, we regressed each of the three measures of social capital (dependent variables) against the instrumental variables that had borne a statistically significant relation with own schooling in column [a], Table 3. We show those results in columns [b]–[d] of Table 3.

The results of column [a], Table 3, suggest that two instrumental variables—village of residence during childhood and father's writing ability—bore a strong statistical association with measures of own schooling, but not with the three measures of social capital. Each of the two instrumental variables was associated with own schooling at the 95% confidence level or higher in the regression of column [a]; combined, the two instrumental variables also bore a statistically significant association with own schooling (F=5.36, p=0.005). The last three columns ([b]–[d]) of Table 3 contain regression results with the three measures of social capital as separate dependent variables; as explanatory variables we include own schooling, the significant instrumental variables of own schooling from column [a] of Table 3, and the two control variables, age and sex. Those results suggest that neither of the two instrumental variables alone or together bore a statistically significant relation with social capital. The results suggest that the writing ability of the respondent's father and the respondent's village of residence during childhood provide reasonable, valid instrumental variables when using

Table 3.   Testing the adequacy of instrumental variables for own schooling for Tsimane' adults (16+ years of age) in Bolivia, 2004

Explanatory Variables:	Schooling: [a]	Dependent variables: Social capital: Gifts [b]	Labour [c]	Gifts + labour [d]
Subject:				
Schooling	∧	0.036 (0.151)	0.147 (0.91)*	0.187 (0.138)
Age	−0.108 (.009)***	0.008 (0.022)	0.006 (0.014)	0.008 (0.022)
Male	2.133 (0.275)***	3.768 (1.064)***	3.384 (0.651)***	5.150 (0.981)***
Instrumental variables:				
A. Subject's mother:				
Schooling	0.091 (0.203)	∧	∧	∧
Writing	0.453 (0.979)	∧	∧	∧
Spanish	0.087 (0.254)	∧	∧	∧
B. Subject's father:				
Schooling	−0.010 (0.082)	∧	∧	∧
Writing	1.048 (0.439)**	−1.083 (1.178)	−0.799 (0.705)	−1.335 (1.077)
Spanish	0.052 (0.223)	∧	∧	∧
C. Same-sex parental height relative to subject's height	−0.137 (0.155)	∧	∧	∧
D. Village	−0.007 (0.003)**	0.0005 (0.008)	−0.004 (0.005)	−0.006 (0.008)
Observations:				
Total	493	560	560	560
Left censored	192	527	491	491
Left censored as % of total	38	94	87	87
Pseudo R2	0.117	0.066	0.087	0.079
Joint: F and p>F	5.36 (0.005)	0.43 (0.653)	0.90 (0.407)	1.01 (0.365)

Notes. Regressions are left-censored Tobits with constant (not shown). In cells we show coefficients and, in parenthesis, standard errors. *, **, and *** significant at the 10%, 5%, and 1% level. Joint is F test of joint significance for father's writing ability and respondent's childhood village of residence. ∧ = variable intentionally left out. Instrumental variables refer to the attributes of the respondent's parents and the respondent's childhood village of residence. Village = village of childhood residence. Schooling under instrumental variables = maximum school grade attained by parent. Spanish refers to parental ability to speak Spanish: 0 = unable, 1 = with difficulty, and 2 = fluent. Writing = parental writing ability: 0 = cannot, 1 = some, and 2 = well. Physical stature relative to their same-sex parent (row C): −1= taller than parent, 0 = same physical stature as parent, and +1= shorter than parent.

own schooling as an endogenous variable to explain variation in personal expressions of social capital.

The effect of own schooling on own social capital

Table 4 contains the main regression results. The first three columns contain the regression results without instrumental variables, and the next three columns contain the regression results with instrumental variables. Table 4 contains four noteworthy findings. First, the variable for own schooling did not bear a significant statistical

Table 4.   Results of Tobit regressions: effect of schooling on social capital among Tsimane' adults (16+ years of age) in Bolivia, 2004

	Dependent variables – social capital expressed through:					
	Gifts	*Labour*	*Total*	*Gifts*	*Labour*	*Total*
Explanatory variables:	*[a]*	*[b]*	*[c]*	*[d]*	*[e]*	*[f]*
Schooling	0.009	0.127	0.156	−1.494	−0.957	−1.677
	(0.150)	(0.089)	(0.136)	(1.606)	(1.268)	(1.920)
Age	0.011	0.009	0.013	−0.068	−0.049	−0.084
	(0.022)	(0.014)	(0.022)	(0.088)	(0.068)	(0.103)
Male	3.822**	3.428***	5.225***	6.079**	5.040**	7.949***
	(1.067)	(0.652)	(0.983)	(2.720)	(2.025)	(3.040)
Observations						
Total	574	574	574	560	560	560
Left censored	541	505	505	527	491	491
Left censored as % of total	94	88	88	94	88	88
Over-identification	Not applicable			0.939	0.938	0.939
Regression type:	Tobit			Tobit with instrumental variables		

Notes. Cells contain coefficients and, in parenthesis, standard errors. *, **, and *** significant at the 10%, 5%, and 1% level. Instrumental variables = respondent's father's ability to write and respondent's childhood village of birth. Over-identification test is p-value from a chi2 distribution (Wooldridge, 2003).

association with any of the three measures of social capital. The conclusion applies whether or not we use instrumental variables.

Second, coefficients from the regressions with instrumental variables differed in size and in magnitude from the coefficients of the regressions without instrumental variables. The regression results of the first three columns without instrumental variables suggest that schooling contributes to social capital. For example, in column [a] an additional year of schooling was associated with 0.009 more gifts given and with 0.12 more episodes of helping and doing communal work in a week (column [b]). Since the average respondent in one week gave 0.10 gifts and helped others or did communal work 0.20 times (Table 2), an additional year of schooling would be associated with an 8.20% *increase* in gifts given and with a 61.30% *increase* in episodes of labour help and communal work in a week. Though not statistically significant at the 95% confidence level or higher, the amounts are large and have economic significance. Once we use instrumental variables for schooling, an additional year of schooling was associated with a *decrease* of 1.49 gifts given and with a *decrease* of 0.95 in the number of times a respondent helped people of other households or took part in communal work during a week. Using the mean values of gifts and labour help just mentioned, the estimates with instrumental variables imply that schooling would be associated with a 13-fold *decrease* in gifts given and with an almost five-fold *decrease* in the number of times a respondent helped people of other households or did communal work.

Third, the information in columns [d]–[e] of Table 4 do not confirm the first two hypotheses. We had hypothesized that schooling would reduce labour help offered and participation in communal work, and that it would be associated with an increase in the amount of gifts given to people of other households. Results in columns [d]–[e] suggest that schooling bore no significant statistical association with gifts given, labour help offered, or with participation in communal work. If we leave aside statistical significance and focus only on the sign and on the size of coefficients, then the information in columns [d]–[e] of Table 4 would support hypothesis 1 (more schooling, less labour help offered), but not hypothesis 2 (more schooling, more gifts given).

To test hypothesis 3 (more schooling, more generosity to non-kin) we restricted the analysis to people who had made gifts, offered help, or done communal work (n=66) and ran a probit regression (not shown); we excluded people who had not displayed social capital. The dependent variable took the value of one if respondents had directed their social capital to people of their household, and zero if they had directed their social capital to people outside their household. Probit regressions are appropriate when the dependent variable only takes two values, as in this case. As an explanatory variable we used a binary variable that took the value of one if the person had any schooling and zero otherwise. We did not use instrumental variables nor did we control for other explanatory variables besides schooling because of the small sample size. As hypothesized, we found that schooling was associated with a 16.52% *lower* probability of directing one's generosity toward one's household, but results were statistically insignificant (z=1.22; p=0.22).

Robustness

To test the robustness of the main results (columns [d]–[f], Table 4), we undertook further analysis, which included the following: (a) dropping the variable for schooling and replacing it with a summary variable for the modern human capital of the respondent, (b) using probit and ordinary least squares regressions instead of using Tobit regressions, and (c) using another definition of social capital.

During the survey we collected information on many dimensions of modern human capital besides the maximum school grade attained by the respondent. Other dimensions of modern human capital included academic skills (measured through objective tests) and competence speaking Spanish (assessed by the interviewer). We found that respondent's maximum school grade attained, fluency in spoken Spanish, and maths, reading, and writing skills correlated highly (Cronbach's alpha = 0.92), so we used principal component factor analysis to create a summary measure for modern human capital and re-estimated regressions [d]–[f] of Table 4 with the new measure of modern human capital instead of using the maximum school grade attained. For the new estimation we used Tobit regressions with instrumental variables and the controls of Table 4. The results of the analysis (not shown) confirmed the results discussed so far. The coefficients for the summary measure of modern human capital bore a negative sign but were statistically insignificant. The coefficients for modern human capital in the three regressions were as follow: −2.87 (p=0.35) for gifts given,

−1.42 (p=0.53) for labour help offered and communal work, and −2.62 (p=0.45) for total social capital (gifts plus labour).

Since dependent variables had a large share of zero values, we transformed them into binary variables and ran probit regressions. We also ran ordinary least squares regressions with the values of social capital used in Table 4. The use of probit regressions with instrumental variables or the use of two-stage ordinary least squares regressions did not alter the main findings of column [d]–[f] in Table 4.

Finally, we dropped the three variables of social capital and used a new variable for social capital. During the survey we asked peoples how often they had consumed *chicha* during the seven days before the day of the interview. This variable had many zero values; 65.26 % of respondents had not consumed *chicha* during the seven days before the day of the interview. We used a Tobit regression with instrumental variables and found that an additional year of schooling lowered by 0.80 the number of times a person drank *chicha* (p=0.15) in a week, so the results mesh with the earlier results. That is, as own schooling increases, social capital expressed through *chicha* drinking declined.

Discussion and conclusion

We end by discussing three topics: (a) the importance of correcting for the endogeneity of schooling when estimating the effects of schooling on traditional cultures, (b) comparison with the results of other studies, and (c) possible reasons for the weak statistical results.

Our results suggest that treating the endogeneity of schooling in a cavalier fashion might produce flawed conclusions about how schooling affects traditional cultures. We saw in columns [a]–[c] of Table 4 that parameter estimates of schooling uncorrected for endogeneity biases yield the impression that schooling contributes to the formation of social capital, consistent with most of the results of Table 1 that schooling and social capital move in the same direction. Nevertheless, parameter estimates corrected for the endogeneity of schooling lead one to the opposite conclusion; as schooling increases, personal expressions of social capital decrease.

How do our results compare with the results of previous studies? The answer depends on how one reads the coefficients of schooling in columns [d]–[e] of Table 4. If we rely chiefly on levels of statistical significance, then we would conclude that once we instrument schooling, schooling produces no significant effect on social capital, and our results would mesh with the results of Seligson (1999) and Henrich *et al.* (2004) in Table 1. If we focus instead on the magnitude and on the sign of the coefficients and leave aside levels of statistical significance, then our results would mesh with the writings of researchers discussed earlier who have found consistent evidence that schooling undermines traditional cultures.

Why did schooling bear such a weak effect on social capital? The answer likely has to do with methods and with substance. First, neither schooling nor social capital had much variance. Recall that the typical Tsimane' had only about two years of schooling and that all variables for social capital contained a large share of zero values. Furthermore, we had a small sample size of observations (574 and 560) for the regressions of Table 4. In fact, our sample size falls toward the lower end of the sample size of studies in Table 1; only the study by Egerton (2002) had fewer observations than our study. The lack of variance in schooling and in social capital, and the small sample size of observations would weaken results. Second, possible random measurement errors in social capital from faulty recall about acts of generosity during the seven days before the day of the interview would have inflated standard errors and further weakened statistical results. Third, and in a more substantive note, Tsimane' are still in the early stages of continual exposure to the market economy so perhaps not enough time has elapsed for schooling to erode social capital if, in fact, schooling has such an effect. Fourth, unlike other rural areas of developing nations, in the Tsimane' territory all schooling takes place in the Tsimane' language, in traditional villages, by Tsimane' teachers, using a curriculum in the Tsimane' language developed by Protestant missionaries *in situ*. So far, Tsimane' have managed to adapt schooling to their needs and way of life.

What are the likely links between schooling and Tsimane' culture in the future? Tsimane' value schooling and many have started attending night courses in the region, joined the army as a way to gain more schooling and skills in Spanish, or sought further opportunities for education by moving to some of the larger towns in the department of Beni. The increasing demand for schooling by Tsimane' has been matched by an increase in the supply of schools. Several non-government organizations and institutions in the area have started to strengthen or expand schooling opportunities for the Tsimane'. But formal education is not equally accessible to all; people in more remote communities are likely to be worse served than people in communities closer to roads, so one should see increasing disparities in schooling levels and academic skills over the years.

When they return to their territory after studying outside the region, Tsimane' gravitate to the larger towns and seek to emulate the lifestyle of people in towns, or else take up employment with the logging firms. They dress, speak, and behave like townspeople. Until now, schooled Tsimane' have limited themselves to living and working around their territory, but over time they will likely start to migrate to other regions of Bolivia in search of better employment opportunities. We do not know what increasing disparity in school achievement and migration will do to Tsimane' society.

Acknowledgements

Research was funded by grants from the programmes of Biological and Cultural Anthropology of the National Science Foundation (0134225, 0200767, and 0322380) and the Wenner-Gren Foundation (Gr 7250). Thanks go to Esther Conde, Bernabé Nate, Paulino Pache, Evaristo Tayo, Santiago Cari, José Cari, Manuel Roca, Daniel Pache, Javier Pache, and Vicente Cuata for help collecting the information and for logistical support. We also thank the Gran Consejo Tsimane' for their continuous support and Julian Elliott and Elena Grigorenko for having commented on several earlier versions. Thanks also to Brigid M. Walker for providing careful editorial assistance.

Notes on contributors

Ricardo Godoy is a professor of cultural anthropology at the Heller School for Social Policy and Management, Brandeis University, Massachusetts, USA and has worked as a member of the Amazonian Panel Study (TAPS) team in Bolivia since 1999. His research interests include economic development, the use of experimental research design for causal identification, and tropical rain forest conservation. Theoretical interests include the evolution of private time preference, intra-household discrimination, the private and social returns to modern and traditional human capital, and the effect of market economies on well-being and conservation.

Craig Seyfried is a policy analyst and has recently moved from the Heller School for Social Policy and Management at Brandeis University to Georgetown University, Washington DC, USA.

Victoria Reyes-García is a cognitive anthropologist working at the Heller School for Social Policy and Management, Brandeis University and is a member of the Amazonian Panel Study (TAPS) team in Bolivia.

Tomás Huanca is a research associate at the Heller School for Social Policy and Management at Brandeis University, USA. A cultural anthropologist, he has worked on Aymara healers and, more recently on how the Tsimane' use ethnobotanical knowledge to increase the productivity of forests. He has worked continuously with the Tsimane' since 1997. He recently completed a book on Tsimane' history, oral traditions, and myths.

William R. Leonard is a physical anthropologist and professor in the Department of Anthropology and Director of the Laboratory for Human Biology Research at Northwestern University, Illinois, USA. His main research interests are biological anthropology, adaptability and growth and development, particularly in the South American context.

Thomas McDade is a physical anthropologist and an associate professor at the Department of Anthropology at Northwestern University, Illinois, USA. His research interests include culture change and health in the Bolivian Amazon.

Susan Tanner is a physical anthropologist and has recently moved from the Department of Anthropology at Northwestern University, Illinois, to the University of Goergia. She has focused on the importance of economic and cultural change on patterns of infectious disease. She conducted her dissertation research among the Tsimane' on parasite infections and their links to anthropometric indices of nutritional status. She is currently exploring further the causes and consequences of high parasite loads among Tsimane' children.

Vincent Vadez is an agronomist and his research centres on how market exposure affects subsistence farming and the conservation of natural resources among indigenous peoples. He has worked on the complementarities between modern and indigenous farming among Bolivian Amerindians and the effect of market openness on agricultural diversity. He introduced a new cover crop among the Tsimane' and used an experimental research design to assess its impact on well-being and conservation. The second phase started in January 2006 and will last three years.

References

Abramson, P. & Inglehart, R. (1995) *Value change in global perspective* (Ann Arbor, Michigan, University of Michigan Press).

Akinnaso, F. N. (1992) Schooling, language, and knowledge in literate and nonliterate societies, *Comparative Studies in Society and History*, 34, 68–109.

Alland, A. (1973) *Evolution and human behaviour: an introduction to Darwinian anthropology* (New York, Doubleday).

Angrist, J. D. & Krueger, A. B. (2001) Instrumental variables and the search for identification: from supply and demand to natural experiments, *Journal of Economic Perspectives*, 15, 69–85.

Benz, B. F., Cevallos, J., Santana, F., Rosales, J. & Graf, S. (2000) Losing knowledge about plant use in the Sierra de Manantlan Biosphere Reserve, Mexico, *Economic Botany*, 54, 183–191.

Bowles, S. & Gintis, H. (1975) *Schooling in capitalist America: educational reform and the contradictions of economic life* (New York, Basic Books).

Brehm, J. & Rahn, W. (1997) Individual-level evidence for the causes and consequences of social capital, *American Journal of Political Science*, 41, 999–1023.

Briggs, J. L. (1970) *Never in anger: portrait of an Eskimo family* (Cambridge, MA, Harvard University Press).

Brumann, C. (1999) Writing for culture: why a successful concept should not be discarded, *Current Anthropology*, 40, 1–27.

Bynner, J. & Ashford, S. (1994) Politics and participation: some antecedents of young people's attitudes to the political system and political activity, *European Journal of Social Psychology*, 24, 223–236.

Byron, E. (2003) *Markets and health: the impact of markets on the nutritional status, morbidity, and diet of the Tsimane' Amerindians of Lowland Bolivia* (Department of Anthropology, University of Florida).

Carter, M. R. & Maluccio, J. (2003) Social capital and coping with economic shock: an analysis of stunting of South African children, *World Development*, 31, 1147–1163.

Castro Mantilla, M. D. (1997) *La viva voz de las tribus: El trabajo del ILV en Bolivia, 1954–1980* [The live voice of the tribes: the work of the Ilv in Bolivia, 1954–1980] (La Paz, Bolivia, Ministerio de Desarrollo Sostenible y Planificacion, Vice Ministerio de Asuntos Indigenas y Pueblos Originarios).

Chavajay, P. & Rogoff, B. (2002) Schooling and traditional collaborative social organization of problem solving by Mayan mothers and children, *Developmental Psychology*, 38, 55–66.

Chicchón, A. (1992) *Chimane resource use and market involvement in the Beni Biosphere Reserve, Bolivia* (Ph.D. thesis, Department of Anthropology, University of Florida, Gainesville).

Coleman, J. S. (1988) Social capital in the creation of human capital, *American Journal Of Sociology*, 94, S95–S121.

Contreras, M. E. & Talavera, M. L. (2003) *The Bolivian education reform: 1992–2002. Case studies in large scale education reform* (Washington DC, The World Bank).

Daillant, I. (1994) *Sens dessus-dissous. Organisation sociale et spatial des Chimanes d' Amazonie boliviene* [Social and spatial organization of the Chimanes of the Bolivian Amazon] (Unpublished Ph.D. thesis, Laboratoire d' ethnologie et de Sociologie Comparative, Université de Paris).

Durham, W. H. (1992) *Co-evolution: genes, culture and human diversity* (Palo Alto, Stanford University Press).

Durlauf, S. N. (2002) On the empirics of social capital, *The Economic Journal*, 112, F459–F479.

Durlauf, S. N. & Fafchamps, M. (2005) Social capital, in: P. Aghion & S. N. Durlauf (Eds.), *Handbook of Economic Growth* (In press), (Amsterdam, North Holland).

Egerton, M. (2002) Higher education and civic engagement, *British Journal of Sociology*, 53, 603–620.

Ellis, R. (1996) *A taste for movement: an exploration of the social ethics of the Tsimanes of lowland Bolivia* (Ph.D. thesis, St. Andrews University, Scotland).

Erasmus, C. J. (1956) Culture, structure, and process: the occurrence and disappearance of reciprocal farm labor, *Southwestern Journal of Anthropology*, 12, 444–469.

Fogel, R. W. (2005) *The escape from hunger and a premature death, 1700–2100* (New York, Cambridge University Press).

Furstenberg, F. & Hughes, M. (1995) Social capital and successful development among at-risk youth, *Journal of Marriage and the Family*, 57, 580–592.

Glaeser, E. L., Laibson, D. & Sacerdote, B. (2002) An economic approach to social capital, *The Economic Journal*, 112, F437–F458.

Godoy, R. A. (2001) *Indians, markets, and rain forests: theory, methods, analysis* (New York, Columbia University Press).

Godoy, R., Reyes-García, V., Vadez, V., Leonard, W. R., Huanca, T. L. & Bauchet, J. (2005a) Human capital, wealth, and nutrition in the Bolivian Amazon, *Economics and Human Biology*, 3, 139–162.

Godoy, R. A., Byron, E., Reyes-García, V., Vadez, V., Leonard, W. R., Apaza, L. *et al.* (2005b) Income inequality and adult nutritional status: Anthropometric evidence from a pre-industrial society in the Bolivian Amazon, *Social Science & Medicine*, 61, 907–919.

Godoy, R. A., Reyes-García, V., Huanca, T., Leonard, W. R., Vadez, V., Valdés-Galicia, C. *et al.* (2005c) Why do subsistence-level people join the market economy? Testing hypotheses of push and pull determinants in Bolivian Amazonia, *Journal of Anthropological Research*, 61, 157–178.

Goldin, C. & Katz, L. (1999) Human capital and social capital: the rise of secondary schooling in America, 1910–1940, *Journal of Interdisciplinary History*, 29, 683–723.

Gregson, S., Terceira, N., Mushati, P., Nyamukapa, C. & Campbell, C. (2003) Community group participation: can it help young women to avoid HIV? An exploratory study of social capital and school education in rural Zimbabwe, *Social Science & Medicine*, 58, 2119–2132.

Grigorenko, E. L., Meier, E., Lipka, J., Mohatt, G., Yanez, E. & Sternberg, R. J. (2002) *Academic and practical intelligence: a case study of the Yup' ik in Alaska* (New Haven, CT, Department of Psychology, Yale University).

Grootaert, C. & Narayan, D. (2004) Local institutions, poverty and household welfare in Bolivia, *World Development*, 32, 1179–1198.

Hauser, R. M. (2005) Survey response in the long run: the Wisconsin longitudinal study, *Field Methods*, 17, 1–26.

Haviland, J. B. (1977) *Gossip, reputation, and knowledge in Zinacantan* (Chicago, The University of Chicago Press).

Helliwell, J. F. & Putnam, R. D. (1999) *Education and social capital [7121] Working Paper* (Cambridge, Massachusetts, National Bureau of Economic Research).

Henrich, J., Boyd, R., Bowles, S., Camerer, C., Fehr, E. & Gintis, H. (2004) *Foundations of human sociality: economic experiments and ethnographic evidence from fifteen small-scale societies* (New York, Oxford University Press).

Hill, K. (2002) Altruistic cooperation during foraging by the ache, and the evolved human predisposition to cooperate, *Human Nature*, 13, 105–128.

Huanca, T. (2005) Tsimane' oral tradition, landscape, and identity in tropical forest (Waltham, MA, Brandeis University). Unpublished Work

Inglehart, R. & Norris, P. (2003) *Rising tide. Gender equality and culture change around the world* (New York, Cambridge University Press).

Jennings, J., Antrobus, K. L., Atencio, S. J., Glavich, E., Johnson, R., Loffler, G. *et al.* (2005) 'Drinking beer in a blissful mood'. Alcohol production, operational chains, and feasting in the ancient world, *Current Anthropology*, 46, 275–294.

Krishna, A. (2002) Enhancing political participation in democracies: what is the role of social capital? *Comparative Political Studies,* 35, 437–460.

Kuper, A. (1999) *Culture, the anthropologists' account* (Cambridge, MA, Harvard University Press).

Leatherman, T. (2005) A space of vulnerability in poverty and health: political-ecology and bio-cultural analysis, *Ethos,* 33, 46–70.

LeVine, R. A., LeVine, S. E. & Schnell, B. (2001) 'Improve the women': mass schooling, female literacy, and worldwide social change, *Harvard Education Review,* 71, 1–50.

Lipka, J., Wildfeuer, S., Wahlberg, N., George, M. & Ezran, D. R. (2001) Elastic geometry and storyknifing: a Yup' ik Eskimo example, *Teaching Children Mathematics,* 7, 337–343.

Maluccio, J., Haddad, L. & May, J. (2000) Social capital and household welfare in South Africa 1993–1998, *Journal Of Development Studies,* 36, 54–81.

Mauss, M. (1990) *The gift: the forms and reason for exchange in archaic societies* [orig. 1927] (New York, W. W. Norton).

McNeal, R. (1999) Parental involvement as social capital: differential effectiveness on science achievement, truancy, and dropping out, *Social Forces,* 78, 117–144.

McVeigh, R. & Smith, C. (1999) Who protests in America: an analysis of three political alternatives—inaction, institutionalized politics, or protest, *Sociological Forum,* 14, 685–702.

Mettler, S. & Welch, E. (2004) Civic generation: policy feedback effects of the GI Bill on political involvement over the life course, *British Journal of Political Science,* 34, 497–518.

Middleton, J. (2005) *From child to adult: studies in the anthropology of education* (New York, The Natural History Press).

Mingat, A. & Bruns, B. (2002) *Achieving Education for All by 2015: simulation results for 47 low-income countries* (Washington, DC, World Bank).

Morgan, S. & Sorenson, A. (1999) Parental networks, social closure, and mathematics learning: a test of Coleman's social capital explanation of school effects, *American Sociological Review,* 64, 661–681.

Nie, N., Junn, J. & Stehlik-Barry, K. (1996) *Education and democratic citizenship in America* (Chicago, The University of Chicago Press).

Ostrom, E. (2000) Social capital: a fad or a fundamental concept? in: P. Dasgupta & I. Serageldin (Eds) *Social capital: a multifaceted perspective* (Washington, DC, The World Bank), 172–214.

Pérez, E. (2001) *Uso de la ictiofauna entre los Tsimane'* [Use of fish resources among the Tsimane'] (Bachelor of science La Paz, Bolivia: Department of biology, Universidad Mayor de San Andrés, La Paz, Bolivia).

Portes, A. (1998) Social capital: its origins and applications in modern sociology, *Annual Review of Sociology,* 24, 1–24.

Putnam, R. (2000) *'Bowling alone': the collapse and revival of American community* (New York, Simon and Schuster).

Reyes-García, V., Godoy, R., Vadez, V., Huanca, T. & Leonard, W. R. (2006) Individual and group incentives to invest in pro-social behavior: an empirical study in the Bolivian Amazon, *Journal of Anthropological Research,* 62, 81–101

Reyes-García, V., Vadez, V., Byron, E., Apaza, L., Leonard, W. R., Perez, E. *et al.* (2005) Market economy and the loss of folk knowledge of plant uses: estimates from the Tsimane' of the Bolivian Amazon, *Current Anthropology,* 46, 651–656.

Richerson, P. J. & Boyd, R. (2004) *Not by genes alone: how culture transformed human evolution* (Chicago, The University of Chicago Press).

Sahlins, M. (1972) Stone age economics, *Aldine,* Chicago.

Seligson, A. L. (1999) Civic association and democratic participation in Central America: a test of the Putnam thesis, *Comparative Political Studies,* 32, 342–362.

Steedly, M. M. (1999) The state of culture theory in the anthropology of Southeast Asia, *Annual Review of Anthropology,* 28, 431–454.

Sternberg, R. J. (1997) *Successful intelligence* (New York, Plume).

Sternberg, R. J., Nokes, C., Geissler, P. W., Prince, R., Okatcha, F., Bunda, D. A. *et al.* (2001) The relationship between academic and practical intelligence: a case study in Kenya, *Intelligence*, 29, 401–418.

Steward, J. H. (1955) *The theory of cultural change: the methodology of multilinear evolution* (Urbana, University of Illinois Press).

Sutherland, W. J. (2003) Parallel extinction risk and global distribution of languages and species, *Nature*, 423, 276–279.

Teachman, J., Paasch, K. & Carver, K. (1997) Social capital and the generation of human capital, *Social Forces*, 75, 1–17.

Wooldridge, J. M. (2003) *Econometric analysis of cross section and panel data* (Cambridge, MA, MIT).

Zent, S. (2001) Acculturation and ethnobotanical knowledge loss among the Piaroa of Venezuela: demonstration of a quantitative method for the empirical study of traditional ecological knowledge change, in: L. Maffi (Ed.) *On biocultural diversity: linking language, knowledge, and the environment* (Washington, DC, Smithsonian Institution Press), 190–211.

Appendix 1. Technical details

Estimation strategy. We use multivariate regressions to estimate the effect of schooling on social capital, but we cannot use a standard approach because of the endogeneity biases discussed earlier. We care about the bias from endogeneity because it can affect the sign and size of the coefficient of schooling, and its level of statistical significance. As a result, we proceed in two steps. First, we identify suitable instrumental variables for schooling and, second, we use the instrumental variables to obtain more accurate estimates of schooling's effect on social capital.

For the first step we use the following expression:

$$[1] \; \widehat{E}_{ihv} = \alpha' + \beta' FW_{ihv} + \pi CVR_{ihv} + \theta C_{ihv} + \varepsilon'_{ihv}$$

In expression [1] $\widehat{E}_{ihv}$ is the predicted schooling level of person i, in household h, and village (or community) v. FW and CVR are the two instrumental variables that enter directly into expression [1] but not into expression [2]. FW stands for father's writing ability and CVR stands for childhood village of residence. C stands for two control variables, age and sex. ε' is an error term with standard properties.

For the second step, we use the predicted value of schooling, $\widehat{E}_{ihv}$, from expression [1] to assess the effect of schooling on social capital, SC:

$$[2] \; SC_{jihv} = \alpha + \beta E_{ihv} + \theta C_{ihv} + \varepsilon_{ihv}$$

In expression [2] SC stands for social capital, $\widehat{E}$ stands for predicted own schooling from expression [1], and the subscripts j, i, and v stand for the type of social capital (j = labour help or participation in communal work, and gifts given to people of other households), person (i), household (h), and village (v) or community. ε is an error term with standard properties.

We next explain the rationale for selecting the two instrumental variables. Researchers have used parental schooling as an instrumental variable for own schooling when estimating the effects of schooling on the earnings of workers in the USA (Wooldridge, 2003). As we can see, parental modern human capital (measured through the writing ability of the respondent's father) also works reasonably well as an instrumental variable in our sample because it overlaps with a respondent's schooling level, but not with the expressions of social capital of the respondent. The respondent's village of residence during childhood is not endogenous because children do not have much choice of where to live during their childhood when they attend school. Villages far from market towns would have been more likely to lack schools, so people growing up in those villages would have been less likely to attend school.

It is possible that the two instrumental variables might bear a strong association with a person's social capital; if so, one would question the validity of the instrumental variables because, by definition, instrumental variables should not be linked (or only weakly linked) to the outcome of substantive interest (in this case, social capital). For example, parents with more schooling might have discouraged their children from displaying traditional forms of social capital; thus, expressions of social capital of adults would reflect their parents' schooling. It is also possible that role models in the childhood village of residence influenced the displays of social capital of children as adults. Though possible, it is not likely; the associations between the instrumental variables and social capital were weak; and we later present regression results showing that the two instrumental variables bore significant statistical associations with a person's own maximum schooling level, but not with a person's display of social capital.

A large share (88–94%) of the observations for the dependent variable, social capital, had values of zero, as the row 'Left censored as % of total' in Table 4 shows. When the dependent variable has a large share of zero values we speak of censoring or left or lower censoring. Because the outcome variable had a large share of zero values, we used Tobit regressions to estimate expression [2]. Tobit regressions are more appropriate than Ordinary Least Squares regressions when the dependent variable is censored. Since own schooling is endogenous, we also use instrumental variables with the Tobit regressions.

Hitting, missing, and in between: a typology of the impact of western education on the non-western world

Elena L. Grigorenko

The western educational system is fairly young, relatively speaking, when compared with, for example, such ancient approaches to education as the Chinese one (see Niu, this volume). Yet, a look at the distribution of educational systems on the global map registers the overwhelming dominance of western educational practices throughout the world. In fact, according to 1998 UNESCO data (UNESCO, 1998), ~80% of the world's children were enrolled in public school, had a structured school day, used textbooks (when available), and followed some curriculum. Thus, the world's chief educational practices are western, as initially conceptualized in ancient Greece, adapted by ancient Romans, limited by the European Middle Ages, expanded by the Renaissance, and rationalized by the Industrial and Scientific Revolutions. Needless to say, there are endless variations on the theme and differences in interpretation. Yet, today, it is difficult to find a widespread educational practice that is radically different from the dominant secular educational paradigm of the west.

So, when there is no large-scale variation (i.e., there are no real grounds for comparison between the western and eastern educational systems, because the western educational paradigm has successfully spread to Asian and Middle Eastern countries and was adapted by them to meet their specific cultural needs), small-scale variation becomes very important. Thus, as all modern secular paradigms in education can be defined as western, the next question to ask is whether there are differences (cultural, geographic, religious, and so forth) in the ways the western educational paradigm operates. And it is quite obvious that there are many differences! Putting aside the variation between educational systems in countries that are conventionally defined as 'western' (i.e., the societies of Europe and their genealogical, colonial, and philosophical descendants, (Wikipedia, n.d.), here I am interested in exploring ways that non-western cultures have adopted and adapted western educational approaches.

In this essay, the definition of the western educational approach is borrowed from the writings of Cole (2005) and Serpell and Hatano (1997). In that definition, there are six main characteristics of the western educational approach. First, it is a prerogative of a secular state whose population is large enough to differentiate childhood and adulthood and separate schooling and labour. Second, it relies on a certain level of economic development. Third, its existence both capitalizes on and necessitates the presence of bureaucracy, whose role is to standardize and centralize education. Fourth, it employs and develops mental (rather than physical) capacities of both students and teachers. Fifth, it is supported by the use of symbolic systems (e.g., an alphabet) and their products (e.g., books). Finally, its nature is public and inclusive (rather than private and exclusive), although it is never socially neutral. Western schooling is a pervasive circumstance of today's life, irrespective of geography, culture, and religion.

In unfolding the discussion, I proceed along the following lines. I begin with a description of ways in which non-western cultures adopted and used western educational approaches. Then I provide an illustration(s) of each category in the typology. In doing so, I briefly present the history of the category (based primarily on information from Goetz, 1989), detail its modern state, and discuss selected aspects of the effectiveness of a particular educational system. Efficacy is discussed along the following indicators for the country(ies) exemplified in a given category: (1) literacy rates in the general population, (2) standing of the country's students as exemplified by results of international comparison studies, and (3) perceived standing of higher-education graduates of a given educational system as judged by the international labour market or commented on by the international community. Although limited, these criteria provide a basis for the context in which this discussion unfolds.

Typology

In broad strokes, the degree of penetration of western approaches to non-western cultural, societal, and educational systems can be subdivided into four different classes in a simplified 2 × 2 table (see Table 1) with two dimensions: (1) triggered

Table 1.   Typology of interactions among western educational systems and non-western societies

Triggered	Reinforced	
	By the west	Internally
By the west	Africa	India
Internally	None to date	Arab States

from/by the west or internally (by the society) and (2) reinforced by the west or internally (by the society). By 'triggering', I mean an introduction of an educational platform in the context of an 'absence' of formal education (as was the case, for example, in Africa) or in the context of the presence of another educational system (as was the case in modern Russia). By 'reinforcing', I mean strengthening and supporting the introduced system by means of developing it further and establishing a structure for the system to self-perpetuate (as was, for example, the case with the British educational system in India). In the text below, I further detail these terms and explore Table 1, providing examples for all its cells.

Triggered by the west and reinforced by the west

The first cell in the typology describes a category of educational systems in which the western educational approach was introduced and reinforced by the west. Arguably, nearly all African systems of public education fit into this category. Serpell's contribution to this volume provides an excellent discussion of the struggles in which African systems of higher education (in his particular example, the Zambian system of higher education) are currently engaged in an attempt to redefine and strengthen themselves. Here, I briefly present the history of the infiltration of the western educational system into Africa and discuss the three points of comparison drawn throughout this article: national literacy rates, the results of international comparison studies, and the standing of graduates of African educational systems in the international markets for higher education and high-skilled jobs.

In Africa, early accounts of the first direct educational influences from outside can be traced back to religious missionaries (Portuguese, French, Dutch, English, and German, from the fifteenth to the nineteenth centuries, roughly in the order above). Various religious missions were the first to establish and support schools and initiate and promote studies of indigenous languages.

The colonial partitioning of Africa in the nineteenth and twentieth centuries initially resulted in the development and promotion of existing missionary schools and then the establishment of so-called lay (official or public) schools. These general trends, of course, varied depending on the European colonizer (e.g., the colonial governments of England, Portugal, Germany, and Belgium all had their own 'peculiarities' in the way they ran lay schools), and the social, cultural, religious, and linguistics specifics of the country. Yet, the general idea behind western-type colonial education in Africa was common to all these 'variants'; it was to train indigenous people to fill the administrative positions supporting the administrative structure. In short, these systems did not pretend to aim to educate all 'locals'; the agenda was to educate enough of them to 'extend the language and policies of the colonizer' (Goetz, 1989, p. 89). Of interest here is that, unlike in India, no colonial educational system in Africa ever rose to the heights and standards of those in the 'mother' country (e.g., England). And, correspondingly, throughout the years of colonialism, there was no development of local languages, unless the local governments permitted education to take place in the local vernacular; religious missions used these permissions both for purposes of education and dissemination of a particular religion in a particular African tongue.

The end of the Second World War brought many progressive changes to the western educational system in Africa, primarily related to the use of international African languages (e.g., Swahili), use of the mother tongue in primary education, and establishment of higher education institutions (late 1940s and 1950s). After a set of events across the continent that resulted in independence of African countries, a review of the educational system in Africa indicated that in British colonies, for example, which were in fact substantially better off than other colonies, only ~40% of the general population had primary education. Secondary education was scarce; Ghana had the highest rate, with 10% (Goetz, 1989).

Thus, newly formed independent African states had numerous problems to face in the domain of education. Their success in dealing with them has been variable and has depended partly on whose particular system (e.g., German, French, Belgian, or British) the nation inherited. For example, the Francophone model contributed to lower mean enrolment levels, a slower expansion of enrolments from 1970–1985, and a more rapid expansion of enrolments from 1985–2000 (Garnier & Schafer, 2006). Yet, the variation among various African nations is overridden by their common problems: poverty, political instability, lack of qualified educators, and the dominant presence of the 'old' educational models—revised and expanded, perhaps, but not reflective of the actual needs of the countries. In addition, as a typical African nation has dozens of mother tongues, the question of which language should be the medium of instruction at what stage of education is central to educational reforms across the continent. The inherent dilemma is how to promote African languages across all domains of African life so that education in these languages can be supportable, justifiable, and market-relevant (Owino, 2002). Despite the strategic realization of the importance of African languages, African governments often explicitly support tactics using the colonial language as the medium of instruction at all levels of education (e.g., English in Kenya).

Today, education in many African countries is carried out under the Declaration on Education for All (EFA). The EFA is a programmatic document first formulated in 1990 (as the Jomtien [Thailand] Declaration) with the goal of improving the equity and quality of educational systems worldwide and the promise of all nations having universal basic education by 2000. When it became clear in 2000 that the Jomtien Declaration was overambitious, it was reformulated as the Dakar Framework for

Action (UNESCO, 2001), which established a new target of 2015 as the year in which all children, particularly girls and children in difficult circumstances and of ethnic minorities, will have access to and complete good quality primary education (UNESCO, 2002b). Today, in 2007, we are presumably almost 50% of the way into this process. So, a quick review of available, although limited, statistics on selected countries in Africa might provide some insight into how realistic the target of 2015 really is.

I start with an examination of the 2006 estimates of literacy rates (UNESCO, 2002c), presenting only selected (all currently available) statistics for adult literacy rates for a number of African countries: Namibia—85.0%, South Africa—82.4%, Lesotho—82.2%, Swaziland—79.6%, Kenya—73.6%, Tanzania—69.4%, Zambia—68.0%, Uganda—66.8%, Rwanda—64.9%, Malawi—64.1%, Sudan—60.9%, Burundi—59.3%, Ghana—57.9%, Togo—53.2%, Senegal—39.3%, Sierra Leone—35.1%, Benin—34.7%, Niger—28.7; Burkina Faso—21.8%, and Mali—19.0%. Clearly, even today, the rates are variable, with some (e.g., Burkina Faso and Mali) being devastatingly low.

In the context of such low literacy rates, it seems that the first priority must be an attempt to get as many children as possible into schools. An estimated 42.2 million school-aged children in Africa do not attend school, representing ~40% of the world's out-of-school children; 60% of these children are girls (UNESCO, 2002b). An important push for quantitative expansion of education (e.g., in Uganda, enrolment went from 2.5 million in 1996 to 6.5 million in 1999), however, created multiple 'ripple' effects—less-qualified teachers, large classes, deteriorating facilities, and a shortage of textbooks (Chapman & Mählck, 1993), all of which resulted in drastically poorer-quality education. The quality has dropped (and is still dropping!) so low that education, which used to be viewed as a way to improve life, became viewed by parents as a waste of family resources and their children's, especially girls', time (Davidson & Kanyuka, 1992; Lloyd & Blanc, 1996; Logan & Beoku-Betts, 1996). What brings returns is quality of education, not years of schooling (Hanushek, 1995); and the quality of African education is poor. Thus, in its attempt to bring more children to school, the system has actually decreased its own value. It is no surprise, then, that in econometric models of economic growth the education variable, defined as the literacy rate, shows no effect on economic growth in Africa (Tiruneh, 2006). In other words, in Africa, a country's education capital does not have an impact on its economic growth. Finally, there is a growing concern that the skills and knowledge learned in African schools are unrelated to the skills and knowledge required to make a living in African societies (Levin & Kelly, 1994).

Multiple international gatherings of education officials from African countries, international development agencies, and representatives of African societies have noted the continent's poor quality of education, stressing that only a small portion of children are reaching grade-specific standards, that curricula appear irrelevant to the needs of learners and societies, and that educational systems do not perform at the expected standards. Exemplifying these comments, Greaney and Kellaghan (2004) present data from various African countries (Ethiopia, Mozambique, Senegal,

Guinea, Ghana) indicating a high (40%–70%) failure rate in these countries' own benchmark examinations (i.e., transition from primary to secondary schools) and very low (e.g., 0%–6%) rates of 'mastery' of a particular domain (e.g., French or maths).

For a number of reasons that are outside the scope of this article, the participation of African countries in international comparison studies is low. However, when African countries do participate in international comparisons, the level of student performance is substantially lower than the international average (Martin *et al.*, 2000; Mullis *et al.*, 2000). Although typically, and justifiably, these low results are attributed to poverty and other financial difficulties faced by African schools, key contributing factors are outdated curricula based on traditional content and its memorization (Valverde, 2005). Thus, it is not only how children in Africa are taught, it is also what they are taught that holds them behind their international peers.

International studies also indicate the presence of a growing knowledge gap between school students in the majority of African countries and the rest of the world. Thus, it has been estimated that, given the current state of educational systems in Africa and at the current rate of enrolment, it would take approximately 150 years to reach the 'simple' goal of enrolling all children in Africa in school (Honawar, 2006a).

Another dimension of comparison is the standing of higher-education graduates from Africa both in African and international markets. A few remarks are in order here.

As is common in many developing counties, the drop-out rates of African students at higher education institutions are high, as they often have no other means of financial support for their studies and are forced by life circumstances to concentrate their efforts on supporting themselves and their families rather than on their educational aspirations (Lindow, 2006). An additional negative factor is the lack of job opportunities, driven by the fact that Africa's economies appear to be too weak to incorporate and benefit from the skills of educated citizens (Tiruneh, 2006). Degree holders are often forced to accept employment outside their chosen professions simply because of the unavailability of jobs in the fields they selected (Minnis, 2006).

A noticeable new trend is for universities around the world (e.g., in the US and Europe especially, but also South Africa) to 'woo' African natives from their troubled countries for an education abroad (MacGregor, 2006). Although these universities often 'score' for admitting these students and showing their international diversity, very few of these students return to their countries (O'Leary, 2006). In addition, local academic and industrial markets cannot sufficiently interest their highly skilled graduates. A report from the World Bank indicates that ~50,000 African-trained Ph.D. holders are currently employed on other continents, with the brain drain being particularly noticeable in Central, Eastern, and Western Africa, where up to 30% of Ph.D.s are employed by international labour markets rather than their home labour markets (Kigotho, 2006).

In sum, it appears that, as it stands now, the primary beneficiaries of western education in Africa are a few select individuals who are able to continue their education and either leave the country for further education or upon completion of their studies, or use the education-based cultural commodity as a competitive advantage in the pursuit of social success within their societies. This trend has been discussed in alarming terms since the early 1990s, when the first data on the effectiveness of western educational systems in Africa after independence were reviewed (Psacharopoulos, 1994). Such data are, if anything, even more evident now (Minnis, 2006). Some argue that African '...formal education has become a vast public subsidy for private consumption and ambition' (Minnis, 2006, p. 122).

Thus, it is clear that today's interpretation of the western approach to education in Africa is failing. The need for change is obvious, but there is no clarity on what needs to happen. A substantial part of the problem is the lack of presence and influence of education research and policy structures in Africa; policy decisions are typically not evidence-based or premeditated, they are simply made. It has also been pointed out that the literature on African education contains few meaningful ideas on what to do and how to proceed (Akala, 2006).

However, a number of possibilities are currently being pursued. First, there is an idea that the western education approach might work but needs to be restructured and reorganized in Africa. There are currently a number of specific applied projects linking educational systems in the developed world to those in Africa (e.g., Portugal and Mali, Benin, Mauritius, and Niger) in an attempt to 'get the western system right' and develop public education adequately ('Policy Dialogue and Education: African and Portuguese Experiences', 2006).

Second, there are a growing number of innovative ideas and programmes from various non-governmental organizations being developed and executed in Africa. One such example is the Molteno Project (2005). The project, which originated in South Africa through a grant from the Molteno Brothers' Trust to the Institute of the Study of English in Africa (ISEA) at Rhodes University, aims to reduce the failure by South African pupils to master English as a second language. The thrust of the Molteno Project is first to build reading skills in the mother tongue and then, capitalizing on these skills and the mother tongue enliteration process, develop speaking, reading, and writing competencies in English using the British programme *Breakthrough to Literacy*. Since its establishment in 1974, Molteno has worked in more than 40 languages[1] (all official South African languages, 8 Namibian languages, 5 Ugandan languages, 7 Zambian languages, 4 Ghanaian languages, 1 Malawian language, and the national languages of Botswana and Lesotho) and is currently operating in a number of African countries (South Africa, Botswana, Namibia, Botswana, Ghana, Uganda, Zambia, Malawi, and Lesotho). Thus, the work of the Molteno Project exceeds the boundary of a single nation and demonstrates the importance for children of working with native languages prior to acquisition of literacy in an essentially foreign language. In terms of the inspirational and cultural connotation of its work, the Molteno Project is extremely powerful. Its ideology matches well the thought that 'Languages are not mere media but rather stand at the very core of major cultural and political questions. We must seek to understand the complex totalities of these relations' (Pennycook, 2000), p. 56). Empirically, however, the Molteno Project cannot be referred to as an 'evidence-based' pedagogical practice. It has been stated that 20+

iterations of the project have been conducted and all commented positively on the impact of this strategy for the acquisition of English (Dikotla, 2006). Yet, outcomes from the Molteno Project have not been published, to my knowledge, as empirical articles; thus, it is impossible to validate these observations.

Finally, it is important to acknowledge initiatives to promote alternative (nonformal and informal) education in African countries (Minnis, 2006). This type of education is aimed at adults and out-of-school children and is assumed to develop and strengthen basic skills in arithmetic, reading, and writing. In Africa, these types of educational approaches have had a long history (Fordham, 1993), but their importance has decreased under pressure to bring the majority of students into formal educational structures. The importance of nonformal education cannot be overstated in rural areas, where the agricultural sector is extremely important. In Africa, the agricultural sector accounts for ~45% of GDP and employs ~70% of its labour force. In addition, the majority of African societies are driven by informal economies (i.e., loosely regulated or unregulated private sectors); the International Labour Organization's projections indicate that 70% of all future jobs created in sub-Saharan Africa will be in the informal sector[2] (cited in Minnis, 2006) and will require the most basic literacy and numeracy skills. Thus, there is a clear appraisal from economic profiles of the development in African countries that most jobs available now, and future jobs, are not those that require several years of schooling (Daun, 2000). And there is evidence suggesting that limited, targeted, informal education provides the required skills and correlates with the ability to mobilize societal capital more effectively (Reardon & Crawford, 1994).

Thus, by all three parameters used in this paper for the comparison of education systems, the current African interpretation of the western approach is failing miserably. Literacy rates are low, the social capital linked to education is of abysmal value, and African formal education has no standing in the global job or education markets.

Triggered by the west and reinforced internally

The second illustration is of an educational system that was imposed by the west, but was then supported and reinforced internally. One of the most interesting examples in this category is the Indian system of education. Today, in the early 2000s, India is home to approximately one fifth of the world's population. Its primary education system, teaching approximately 108 million children aged 6–10, is the second largest in the world after China's (UNESCO, 2005a). In 2004, according to the most recent available data, India spent ~3.3% of its GDP on education (World Bank, n.d.).[3]

The penetration of the west into Indian culture is typically attributed to the establishment and development of the British East India Company in 1600. Although the company's main agenda was commerce, it slowly expanded its objectives to influencing administrative and political structures and raising its status to a colonial ruling structure in the mid- to late eighteenth century. Yet, in spite of its power, the company did not invest any money or political consideration in the education of Indians until the mid-nineteenth century. Only then, and gradually, were consistent investments made in the translation of English textbooks into Sanskrit and Arabic, production of English textbooks in India, and establishment of English schools and colleges. This early work unfolded in parallel with the educational work of Christian missionaries, begun in the sixteenth century, who used the term 'English education' to refer to the teaching of western subjects through the medium of English.

The critical moment in the trajectory of the Indian education system came in the 1830s, when two different approaches to education were advocated to the Governor General, Lord William Bentinck: one, promoted by orientalists, stated the necessity of teaching in Indian languages and promoting oriental learning, and the other, promoted by Anglicists, stressed the importance of English education. Bentinck decided that the government of India would adopt English education. The decision resulted in a number of fundamental changes not only in the educational, but also legal and civic domains of the society. Over the next 10 years, Persian was abolished as the language of record and was replaced by English and local Indian languages, and the government made clear political moves to indicate the preference of using English in all governmental transactions and appointments. As for the language of instruction, English soon became almost wholly predominant. Although local governments, especially that of Bengal, did not prohibit or give up vernacular education, they were not able to compete, in terms of promotion and financial support, with English-based education. In fact, one of the most successful steps in the development of the Indian education system was the establishment of vernacular primary schools in remote areas with assumed transition to English at higher levels of education. These first attempts at 'dissemination' of education resulted in the establishment of a body of (predominantly male) candidates eligible for university-level education; as a result, the first Indian universities (in Calcutta, Bombay, and Madras) were created in the mid-1850s. Needless to say, education (or rather 'accreditation', because the universities were primarily examination and diploma-giving rather than teaching institutions) at the university level, as well as in preparatory schools, was in English.

Only in the late nineteenth century, in pre-independence years, did the significance of paying attention to Indian languages and culture strongly surface in Indian education. The threshold between the two centuries is marked by a colourful tapestry of attempts to develop indigenous institutions and yet centralize and standardize the quality of the nation's education. The growing tension between local Indian structures and the central British government found its reflection in education. Indians became more and more critical of the dominant 'English education' model, which had remained almost unchanged since the sixteenth century, although the term was substituted with the term 'British system of education'. The lack of cohesive leadership in education in the latter part of the nineteenth century resulted in the mushrooming of private schools of various types and forms and the decline of free public elementary education. Understandably, the quality of education was extremely variable. Moreover, the overwhelming majority of the population, especially girls and women, remained illiterate.

Aware of these difficulties, the British government tried yet again to bring order to education using English as a vehicle and the British educational system as the means.

This resulted in the development, in 1910–1920, of standards, curricula, and the institution of accreditation for educational outlets. Formally, the publication of the new Indian constitution in 1921 transferred education and all education-related issues from British to Indian control. The primary responsibility for education was given to the state or provincial governments. The years between the 1921 constitution and the 1947 constitution that followed independence were characterized primarily by (1) the introduction of systematic educational platforms where Hindi was taught instead of or alongside English as an all-India language; (2) the passing of compulsory-education acts by provincial governments and the development of Gandhi's 'basic education', where teaching traditional subjects was joined by teaching crafts; (3) the expansion of the number of schools, especially secondary schools; (4) the expansion of schools for girls; and (5) the broadening and improvement of academic profiles of higher-education institutions.

After independence, the Indian education system remained mostly along the lines specified above, with the primary task of dissemination and reaching the masses. For example, in the first 20 years of post-independence education, enrolment in recognized educational institutions rose 4.7 times (from 18 million to 70 million). Whereas there were only 30 universities and 600 colleges with about 170,000 students in the 1950s, there are now approximately 300 universities and 13,000 colleges educating some 9.5 million students or approximately 7% of India's 18- to 24-year-old population (Neelakantan, 2005).

Today, both primary[4] (6–11 years of age, grades 1–5) and upper primary (11–14 years of age, grades 6–8) education is a fundamental right of all Indian children. And yet, not every child in India goes to school and far from every high school graduate goes to college. The estimated population of India today is 1,095,351,995, but the estimated literacy rate (defined as mastering skills of reading and writing at the age of 15 and up) is only ~61% (~73% for males and ~48% for females). It is estimated that about 30% of children aged 6–14 (i.e., ~59 million children) are out of school, some 59% of whom (~35 million) are girls (Honawar, 2005b). In fact, India 'has the highest absolute number of out-of-school children' (UNESCO, 2005b). Only ~7% of Indians go to college. This is explained, primarily, by the huge size of the Indian population, its linguistic and cultural diversity, a lack of resources, and profound poverty in many regions of India. Here I explore only one aspect of the diversity of the Indian education system, the linguistic one. One of the reasons to concentrate on this issue is that linguistic diversity is common to many non-western cultures.

Hindi is the national language and primary tongue of 30% of Indians. India has 14 other official languages: Bengali, Telugu, Marathi, Tamil, Urdu, Gujarati, Malayalam, Kannada, Oriya, Punjabi, Assamese, Kashmiri, Sindhi, and Sanskrit; Hindustani is a popular variant of Hindi/Urdu spoken widely throughout northern India, but it is not an official language. Newspapers and magazines are published in more than 90 languages; radio is broadcast in 70 and TV in 13 languages. Thus, although Hindi is spoken by the largest majority group, the majority of people in India have mother tongues other than Hindi. In addition, given the cultural and political complexities of multiethnic and multireligious India, in reality, English remains the unifying language.

In fact, English is used in ALL aspects of Indian life (but not by all people, of course!). Similarly, given the natural distribution of linguistic preferences in India, the educational system often defaults to the old, established structures dominated by English. Therefore, although English enjoys associate status, it is the most important language for national, political, commercial and educational transactions.

Education-related language-policy issues in India have generated considerable controversy regarding 'appropriate' media of instruction throughout the school years and for further and higher education (Jayaram, 1993). The dominant approach is referred to as the 'three-language formula', which assumes the importance of three languages in the educational context—Hindi[5], a vernacular language, and English. The implications of this formula are rather complex; it is viewed as a mandate to teach a combination of three languages 'to achieve national unity by creating multilingual citizens, specifically, ones equipped with languages of other regions in the nation' (Chaise, 2005, p. 461). Because Hindi is a required language taught in all Indian schools, the question is what to do about the other two languages. It has been pointed out that, despite many issues regarding language policy in education, '...one area of general consensus has been that students opting to be educated in English take the vernacular language as a foreign language requirement, while students opting to be educated in the vernacular have English as a foreign language' (Ramanathan, 2005, p. 56). Thirty-nine vernacular languages are eligible to be taught as first, second, or third languages. The first language in most cases is either the mother tongue or the regional language. The mother tongue may be a majority or a minority language. The regional language is the majority language of the state and often the official language of the state (for the majority of the schools, it is Hindi). The second language is typically English; sometimes, however, English is taught as the third language. The third language is typically Hindi, unless the education takes place in the states where Hindi is the majority language (again, learning Hindi is compulsory). Thus, English can be taught as a first language if English is the medium of instruction and as a second or third language if instruction is in Hindi or another mother tongue. English is taught in the majority of Indian schools (Annamalai, 2004).

Typically, Hindi- and vernacular language-medium schools are less expensive and under government administration. English-medium schools tend to charge higher fees and are typically affiliated with some private structures. Correspondingly, there is a form of differentiation in respect of who goes where to get their education. Typically, better educated and financially well-off middle-class parents send their children to English-medium private schools. This decision is based on the belief that English-medium schools provide better education and higher likelihoods of college and university acceptance, guaranteeing employment and better quality of life (Dhesi, 2001). Thus, as Chaise eloquently pointed out, 'Although Hindi represents the nation, English provides spatial and economic mobility within it' (Chaise, 2005, p. 470).

Having briefly characterized the Indian system of education (for more detail, see Chopra & Jeffery, 2005), what relevant issues can be discussed with regard to our three comparative points?

The overall literacy rate in India is one of the lowest in the world. Yet, there is extreme variation in these rates across the country. Interestingly, for example, in Kerala, where per-capita income is extremely low, the adult literacy rate is ~91%. This high literacy rate allowed many more youngsters to enter colleges and universities, but may actually be backfiring now. Of the nation's 5.3 million currently unemployed university graduates, approximately half a million are from Kerala, (a disproportionate number compared with the rest of India) (Neelakantan, 2005). Thus, by ensuring and promoting higher education, unlike other states in India, Kerala ends up with bus drivers who have multiple masters' degrees.

Ironically, the problem of unemployment for university graduates coexists in India with a shortage of skilled workers in technology, knowledge, and services. Although India produces ~290,000 engineers a year in a very competitive environment[6], it is estimated that a large number of engineers emigrate to other countries[7] (Grose, 2006; Honawar, 2005b). In general, Indian engineers are viewed as highly qualified and a major source of concern for Europe and the United States, who have lost and are still losing technology jobs to India. In addition, many Indian scientists and engineers are employed by the US.

Even with this successful engineering push, these 290,000 per year are only ~13% of the nation's university graduates, and only ~20% of engineering graduates are 'top-notch' (Honawar, 2005b). With India's rapid increase in GDP (e.g., 8.4% in 2006) and its rise in the information technology sector (e.g., ~30% per year), the nation has a shortage of engineers. It is estimated that India needs to graduate ~65,000 more engineers annually than it does now (Grose, 2006). In addition, other growing sectors of the Indian economy (media, entertainment, fashion, advertising, banking, and tourism) have difficulty filling vacancies.

Thus, a multidimensional tension is present in India. India produces top-notch engineers, many of whom live and work abroad because of high-level international demand for them, while there is a substantial shortage of engineers within the country; yet there is huge competition for slots in engineering programmes and the system is unable to educate all who wish to enter. In addition, there are many vacancies in India in developing industries, yet graduates of higher education and professional schools are not able to fill these vacancies because they are found to be under-qualified. Yet, there are many college, university, and professional school graduates who are unable to find jobs. It has been argued that part of the problem here is that the major portion of the Indian higher education system has not kept up with the needs of its rapidly growing economy and has not revised its books and syllabi in years (Neelakantan, 2005). But, of course, changes are on the way in a number of universities (e.g., University of Mumbai, University of Madras).

Finally, according to international opinion, based on comparative results on standardized tests e.g., SAT and GRE) and the admission rates of international students to higher education institutions around the world, India, among other Asian countries, is often at the top of the list, creating high levels of concern in US leaders about their own students' competencies (Honawar, 2005c, 2006b; Klein, 2006). Indeed, it has been stated that India has successfully positioned itself as one of the leading producers of high school, college/university, and professional school graduates desired by leading higher education institutions and science- and technology-oriented companies within India and abroad (Honawar, 2005a, b).

A few remarks are in order in closing this section. First, as stated earlier, the current Indian educational system was initiated during British colonization, and, although diversified substantially both pre- and post-independence by introducing linguistic diversity, fundamentally remained a western-like education system. Second, as a system fitting into the second category ('triggered by the west and internally reinforced'), the Indian educational system is a quilt of inconsistencies: it is seriously deficient in terms of delivering on the promise of 'education for all' and yet it is astonishingly successful in terms of meeting the high standards of international education, especially in maths and sciences. In these domains, its graduates are among the strongest candidates for highly skill-demanding jobs in challenging markets.

Triggered internally and reinforced externally

The next cell of Table 1 to be discussed is an educational system in which western influences were triggered internally, but were/are supported externally. I cannot find an example of such a system; this 'empty cell', however, is of interest on its own. The lesson here, from my point of view, is that, in the non-western world, the presence of the western educational system is typically related to pressure from the west that existed at some point, unless there is some degree of readiness in the society to change and sustain the western educational system internally, without a 'push' from the west. After the system is introduced, the question is whether or not it will be supported internally. It appears that if the system is ready internally, it can self-sustain (see the following section). It also appears that the internal adoption of the western approach to education in the absence of the system's potential to self-sustain this adoption, although possible in theory, has not happened in reality. Thus, this cell remains empty.

Triggered internally and reinforced internally

To illustrate the final typology, I briefly describe the history of education in the Arab world, exemplifying several common aspects of this system with a number of observations from selected Arab countries.

The modern system of education in Arabic speaking countries was influenced, pre-independence, by three major traditions. The first one was associated with the Ottoman Empire, which between the fifteenth and early twentieth centuries influenced vast amounts of what are now Arab nations. The second one was related to European, primarily British and French, influences, which became quite important at the decline of the Ottoman Empire. Finally, and most importantly, the third tradition is the Arabic custom and language, which were conscientiously promoted by the independent Arab states in their efforts to distance themselves from Ottoman and European political, economic, and educational dominance.

In the latter part of the twentieth century, as independent states, almost all Arab countries have demonstrated remarkable accomplishments in the establishment, development, and further enhancement of their national systems of education. Common to their educational systems prior to independence was (1) an almost exclusive dominance of Koranic schools all the way up to the mid-nineteenth century, when European influence strengthened; (2) an establishment of the European system of education on a limited scale, which promoted teaching of the language of the country that controlled a given territory (i.e., English, French, or Italian); (3) an expansion of the number of schools and their homogenization; (4) an aggressive expansion in enrolment among school-aged children; (5) creation of universities, colleges, and vocational schools; and (6) a systematic and controlled transformation of a pre-independence school system into a system that used Arabic[8] as the medium of instruction and 'Arabinized' curricula at all levels of education.

Arab countries have made considerable investments in education since gaining their independence. In 1997, for example, their spending on education was estimated, on average, at 5.4% of their GNP. Of note is that there is substantial variation in education indices across the Arab countries. The first source of variation comes from financial support extended by the government for education. Education expenditures are highest in Saudi Arabia (9.5% of GDP) and Tunisia (7.5% of GDP). The United Arab Emirates, Lebanon, and Mauritania commit the lowest proportions of their income to education, ~2% to 3%.

In 2001–2002, the UNESCO Institute for Statistics conducted a survey of major educational indicators in the 'Arab States', a collective that refers to 20 different Arab countries belonging geographically to sub-Saharan Africa, North Africa, and Asia (Algeria, Bahrain, Djibouti, Egypt, Iraq, Jordan, Kuwait, Lebanon, the Libyan Arab Jamahiriya, Mauritania, Morocco, Oman, the Palestinian Autonomous Territories, Qatar, Saudi Arabia, Sudan, the Syrian Arab Republic, Tunisia, the United Arab Emirates, and Yemen). The report quantified the enrolment rates at different levels of education (pre-school, primary, secondary, and tertiary), and stratified this enrolment by gender. Specifically, of 15 million pre-school-aged children living in the region, ~15% (~14% of girls and ~17% of boys) were enrolled in educational institutions. The enrolment ratios vary dramatically, from 0.4% in Djibouti to 78.4% in the United Arab Emirates. The United Arab Emirates, Morocco, and Lebanon are clearly ahead of the rest with enrolment rates of over 55%, whereas at the other extreme are the ratios for Djibouti, Algeria, Yemen, Saudi Arabia, Oman, and Iraq, with enrolment rates at ~6%.

With regard to primary education, in the 1999/2000 academic year, just over 5 million children entered primary school for the first time in the surveyed nations. Given the population estimates of age-appropriate children, broadly defined (e.g., 5–7), this figure corresponds to an apparent intake rate of 91%, with the rate being 94% for boys and 88% for girls. When this figure was corrected by limiting the counted children only to those who should be enrolled at the official age of enrolment (e.g., age 6 in the United States), it decreased to a little under two-thirds of all children of official primary entrance age. In other words, only 67% of 6-year-olds eligible for enrolment entered primary school in 1999/2000. Thus, this figure suggests that access to primary education at the official age is still insufficient in the region. When all years of primary schooling were considered together, it was reported that nearly one child in five of official primary school age was still not enrolled in primary school; this was more so for girls than boys, with one girl in four not being enrolled in school. Enrolment rates varied tremendously through the region, ranging from 99% (the Palestinian Autonomous Territories) to 30% (Djibouti). It was estimated that the Arab States region had some 8 million children out of school during 1999/2000, almost 60% of whom were girls.

With regard to secondary education, enrolment was at ~60% of the population of the official age for this level, with ~47% of the enrolled being girls.

Similarly, the region is characterized by relatively low post-secondary participation, ranging from 0.3% to 29% for different countries. The countries with the highest post-secondary enrolment rates were Bahrain (29%), Kuwait (19%), Oman (17%), and the Palestinian Autonomous Territories (12%), with other countries at ~5%. Not unexpectedly, there were high gender parity ratios, with females involved less in tertiary education than were males.

Thus, Arab states have made enormous strides in education since gaining independence. There are, of course, challenges. One of these is the unprecedented increase in population [ranging from 1.5% in Tunisia to 4.8% in Yemen, (UNESCO, 2002a)], which has resulted in the constant demand for more facilities and more educators. This issue is something that the Arab leadership is aware of, and to which it pays attention by lobbying for increased government funding for education (Lipsett, 2006b). The expanding population is linked to the literacy rate in the Arab world, which is still quite lower than that of the developed world and varies substantially, disadvantaging women across all Arab states (i.e., for males and females, respectively, the rates are 75% and 55% in Algeria, 91% and 82% Bahrain, 75% and 53% in Djibouti, 66% and 43% in Egypt, 55% and 23% in Iraq, 95% and 83% in Jordan, 84% and 79% in Kuwait, 92% and 80% in Lebanon, 90% and 67% in the Libyan Arab Jamahiriya, 50% and 30% in Mauritania, 61% and 35% in Morocco, 79% and 59% in Oman, no data are available for the Palestinian Autonomous Territories, 80% and 82% in Qatar, 82% and 65% in Saudi Arabia, 68% and 45% in Sudan, 88% and 59% in the Syrian Arab Republic, 80% and 59% in Tunisia, 74% and 78% in the United Arab Emirates, and 66% and 24% in Yemen). In general, ~30% of men and ~50% of women in the Arab States are illiterate, with female literacy being lowest in Iraq, Morocco, Mauritania, and in Yemen. The issue of disadvantaging women is particularly important because in many Arab countries education is segregated by gender. Thus, it is essential to ensure that both quality and quantity of education for boys and girls are comparable.

A special issue for the Arab system of education is related to the aftermath of September 11, 2001 (Barazangi, 2004; Karmani & Makoni, 2005). One result of that event was the triggering of a process of reforms in education. There has been an unprecedented call from Arab leaders for urgent educational reforms to help eradicate Islamic extremism and the threat of fundamentalism (Morgan, 2005). Specifically, a number of documents [e.g., *Political and economic reform in the Kingdom of Saudi Arabia* (2005) and the *Tunis Declaration of sixteenth Arab summit* (2004)] highlight the importance of the democratization and enhancement of the educational system and the reinforcement of women's rights. The following is an excerpt from one of these documents that exemplifies the nature of planned and ongoing changes:

> In Saudi Arabia today, there are eight public universities, more than 100 colleges and more than 26,000 schools. Some five million students are enrolled in the education system, which boasts a student to teacher ratio of 12.5 to 1—one of the lowest in the world. Of the 5.2 million students enrolled in Saudi schools, half are female, and of the 200,000 students at Saudi universities and colleges, women comprise more than half of the student body. The government allocates about 25% of the annual state budget to education. Recent initiatives include:
>
> Saudi Arabia is in the middle of a multi-year program to update textbooks and curricula, introduce new teaching methods and provide better training for our teachers.
>
> Student councils are being set up in public schools to begin educating young Saudis about civic responsibilities and participatory governance.
>
> In August 2002, the Department of Statistics reported that 93.2% of Saudi women and 89.2% of Saudi men are literate.
>
> In October 2003, Dr. Maha Abdullah Orkubi was appointed Dean of the Jeddah branch of the Arab Open University (AOU), the first time for a Saudi woman to be appointed to such a senior academic position.
>
> Saudi Arabia has introduced English language classes to the Sixth Grade for the 2004–2005 academic year in order to improve English teaching at intermediate and secondary schools'. (*Political and economic reform in the Kingdom of Saudi Arabia*, 2005, pp. 4–5)

At this point, there are only case-based illustrations of such changes. For example, the admission of one female student to a male-only Higher College of Technology in the United Arab Emirates (UAE) illustrates ongoing changes in the UAE's resolutely single-sex education system (Lipsett, 2006a). In addition, education for females is viewed less and less as a stepping-stone for finding a male life partner, and more and more as a career stepping-stone. With these changes, women can add to their options professions other than teaching, which previously had been their only realistic professional career option (Clarke, 2006). Now, for example, 80% of graduates at the UAE's all-female Zayed University can easily find jobs after graduation (Wojtas, 2006), and their choices are not limited to teaching (Al Karam & Ashencaen, 2006).

Along the lines of developing women as professionals who contribute to the economy of the country, another change being implemented is the development of a new private college for women, in which the medium of instruction is English and whose explicit and implicit goals are related to preparing young Saudi women for competitive higher-education placements within the country and abroad, and for highly skilled and responsible jobs. One example of such a college is Effat College, the first private non-profit college for women in the Kingdom of Saudi Arabia, established in 1999. The college recruits from all over the world (currently representing 20 different nationalities) and its aim is to create an international campus culture with a lower student to faculty ratio (currently 5:1). The signature points of Effat College are high-technology classrooms and special emphasis on technology and other areas (e.g., architecture and electrical and computer engineering) that were traditionally unavailable to women. It is also important to note that the college is located on the premises of Dar Al-Hanan School, which was established by Queen Effat as the first school for girls in the kingdom in 1955. Now that all girls in Saudi Arabia are eligible for free primary education, the challenge is to extend the tradition upward and to introduce opportunities and choices in the lives of Saudi young women. Effat College uses the western approach to higher education and employs quite a number of foreign faculty members, including those from Europe and the US.

As for comparative aspects of this system, its literacy rates are still low and are quite variable across different states, but they have changed tremendously since independence. Yet, there is huge gender parity in a number of Arab states, with women disadvantaged at all levels of education. The participation of Arab countries in international comparisons is limited, but countries involved in such comparisons as the Progress in International Reading Literacy Study (PIRLS) and the Programme for International Student Assessment (PISA) (e.g., Tunisia) indicate an average level of performance of students compared with their international peers (Willms, 2006). In general, however, there is a shortage of qualified teachers and researchers and, correspondingly, curricula might not be the most effective, which is captured by a relatively low profile of performance of students from Arab countries compared with their counterparts from the developed world. At this point, Arab universities do not compete with international universities in terms of competitiveness of their graduates on the international labour market.

To summarize, the modern educational system in the Arab world is the one consciously built in the 1950s–1970s around issues of Arab identity, Islam, and Arab culture. The distinct feature of this system is, unlike those of India and Africa, linguistic unity: Arabic is the only language of instruction in the public sector. All foreign languages are taught as such. In those rare cases when a foreign language is used in a private institution as the medium of instruction, Arabic and Arabic studies are compulsory. It should be noted that there is a conscientious effort on behalf of the government of Saudi Arabia to support the development of such institutions and to open the Arab system of education to global influences. Also of note is that, after a substantial, conscientious, and successful attempt to 'Arabinize' the western educational system post-independence, Arab states now are opening themselves to western influences, at least in their public and private education.

Conclusion

In this brief essay, I have discussed a possible way of systematizing different types of interactions between the western approach to education and non-western societies. To illustrate this typology, I briefly reviewed the history of a number of different educational systems around the world, commented on their current status today, and provided some data permitting their comparison. It is important to note that, in this essay, because of the rather scarce nature of the literature on education in developing countries, I used not only scientific but also mass media sources. I also cited my own experiences from travelling and working in India, Saudi Arabia, and a number of African countries.

A few concluding remarks are in order to close this discussion.

The first remark pertains to the observation that, although the western educational system is, no doubt, the dominant one today, there is a huge amount of variability on how this system 'performs' in different cultural, religious, linguistic, and societal circumstances.

The second remark concerns the fact that it is obvious, especially from the Africa example, that the predominant system of public education as it exists in the majority of the world does not necessarily always work. It has been suggested (see, for example, the discussion in Serpell's contribution to this volume) that, in the case of many African countries, a radical change in educational approaches might be needed to bring the continent to a position where it can respond to the demands and opportunities of globalization.

Third, it is of interest to note that educational systems have reputations and appraisals, even when they are not systematically compared with each other within educational comparisons studies (e.g., TIMSS). It is an understatement to say that 'rank tables', produced as a result of these international studies, provide us only with a glimpse into an educational system. Other formal and informal means of evaluations contribute to the collective implicit and explicit appraisals of the standings of a particular educational system. As mentioned above, among these means are demands for graduates of a particular educational system by both higher education and job markets.

The fourth remark relates to the quality and quantity of issues that are important or challenging to particular educational systems. For example, what is common for both India and Africa in their attempts to transform the western educational system in a way that is suitable for their cultural landscapes is the necessity to deal with a variety of vernacular languages spoken by people who are to be educated within this western system. This challenge is a huge one and, to my knowledge, it has not been satisfactorily addressed by any of existing educational systems. Thus, the common challenge of language equality is really central to many countries in Africa and Asia where the western educational approach is dominant. On the contrary, the situation in the Arab world is very different, with Arabic being the common denominator of the Arab cultures. The main challenge there, at least in most traditional Arab societies, such as the Kingdom of Saudi Arabia, is the issue of gender equality. Thus, many issues related to curriculum, educational process, and student and teacher progress monitoring are coloured differently depending on what issues are central to a particular cultural adaptation of the western approach.

Fifth, I want to acknowledge, readily, the descriptive nature of this essay. I do not claim to be deeply analytical in my presentation; my intent was to present the breadth of the impact of the western educational system and contextualize specific deep analyses of various aspects of this impact as exemplified in other contributions to this volume. In fact, this description might not even stand a chance as an independent contribution without the other ones presented in this issue.

Finally, to conclude this discussion, I should like to return to the impressive examples of changes to and modernizations of the western educational system in India and the Arab nations. When adopted smartly and modified appropriately, the western educational approach can function productively in the non-western world. And I believe that there are more examples to come in the future. Since the achievement of independence by former European colonies we have seen a number of remarkable transformations of western approaches to education around the world. Some work better than others, and there are more to come. I am in agreement with Robert Serpell when he says, 'We may hope to see … revolutionary insights emerge from the confrontation of western cultural hegemony in the field of education, as third world intellectuals grapple with inconsistencies in the practices they have been handed down from the center' (Serpell, 2005, p. 220). I look forward to learning about these revolutionary insights from my colleagues from non-western cultures.

Author note

Preparation of this article was supported by Grant 5 R21 TW006764-02 (PI: Grigorenko) from the Fogarty Program, as administered by the National Institutes of Health, Department of Health and Human Services. Grantees undertaking such projects are encouraged to express their professional judgment freely. Therefore, this article does not necessarily reflect the position or policies of the National Institutes of Health, and no official endorsement should be inferred.

Acknowledgement

I am thankful to Ms. Robyn Rissman for her editorial assistance.

Notes

1. **South Africa:** isiZulu, Sepedi, xiTsonga, Setswana, Sesotho, Tshivenda, isiSwati, IsiXhosa, isiNdebele, Nama, Afrikaans, !Xun, and Kwedam; **Botswana:** Setswana; **Namibia:** Oshikwanyama, Rukwangali, Oshindonga, Otjiherero, Rugciriku, Silozi, Thimbukushi, Khoekhoegowab, Ju/'hoansi (a San language); **Zambia:** Icibemba, Silozi, ciNyanja, Chitonga, Kiikaonde, Lunda, Luvale; **Uganda:** Luganda, Alur, Dhopadhola. Runyankole, Runyoro; **Lesotho:** Sesotho; **Ghana:** Eυe, Gonja, Akua Pem, Twi; **Malawi:** Cichewa.
2. The general market income category (or *sector*) wherein certain types of income and the means of their generation are unregulated or only loosely regulated by the institutions of society, in a legal and social environment in which similar activities are regulated. In developing countries up to 60% of the labour force works in the informal sector.
3. Compare that with the population of the US (~300mln), where ~7.5% of GDP is spent on education.
4. For an excellent analysis of primary education in India, see Robin Alexander's book *Culture and Pedagogy* (Alexander, 2000).
5. Note that Hindi is a vernacular language for many Indians; here, however, it is separated into a separate category due to its national status.

6. Competition at the nation's most prestigious engineering schools (the Indian Institute of Technology (IIT) with its multiple campuses spread around the country, e.g., Madras/Chennai, Kharagpur, Mumbai, Kanpur, Delhi, Guwahati, Roorkee) is such that it is estimated that, on average, there are fifty applications for each place.
7. ~20% to 35% of the Indian Institute of Technology's graduates.
8. One of the most distinctive features of the Arab world in general and its system of education in particular is that Classical Arabic co-exists with national vernaculars (e.g., Egyptian, Syrian, Jordanian). Whereas all education in all Arab states is carried out in the former, the latter languages are that of mass media, oral exchanges, and leisure (Haeri, 2000).

Notes on contributor

Elena L. Grigorenko received her Ph.D. in general psychology from Moscow State University, Russia, in 1990, and her Ph.D. in developmental psychology and genetics from Yale University, USA, in 1996. Currently, Dr. Grigorenko is Associate Professor of Child Studies and Psychology at Yale and Associate Professor of Psychology at Moscow State University. Dr. Grigorenko has published more than 200 peer-reviewed articles, book chapters, and books.

References

Akala, W. (2006) Modernization versus cultural resilience in education in East Africa, *Journal of Curriculum Studies,* 38(3), 365–372.

Al Karam, A. & Ashencaen, A. (2006, March/April) Creating international learning clusters in Dubai, *International Educator,* 15, 12–15.

Alexander, R. (2000) *Culture and pedagogy* (Malden, MA, Blackwell Publishing).

Annamalai, E. (2004) Medium of power: the question of English in education in India, in: J. W. Tollefson & A. B. M. Tsui (Eds), *Medium of instruction policies: which agenda? Whose agenda?* (Mahwah, NJ, Lawrence Erlbaum Associates Publishers), 177–194.

Barazangi, N. H. (2004) *Woman's identity and the Qur'an* (Gainesville, FL, University Press of Florida).

Chaise, L. (2005) Disparate markets: language, nation, and education in North India, *American Ethnologist,* 32, 460–478.

Chapman, D. W. & Mählck, L. O. (Eds) (1993). *From data to action: information systems in educational planning* (Paris, UNESCO, International Institute for Educational Planning, and London, Pergamon).

Clarke, M. (2006) Beyond antagonism? The discursive construction of 'new' teachers in the United Arab Emirates, *Teaching Education,* 17(3), 225–237

Chopra, R. & Jeffery, P. (Eds) (2005) *Educational regimes in contemporary India* (Thousand Oaks, Sage Publications).

Cole, M. (2005) Cross-cultural and historical perspectives on the developmental consequences of education, *Human Development,* 48, 195–216.

Daun, H. (2000) Primary education in sub-Saharan Africa—a moral issue, an economic matter, or both?, *Comparative Education,* 36, 37–53.

Davidson, J. & Kanyuka, M. (1992) Girls' participation in basic education in southern Malawi, *Comparative Education Review,* 36, 446–466.

Dhesi, A. (2001) Expectations and post-school choice: some data from India, *Education & Training,* 41(1), 14–24.

Dikotla, M. P. (2006) The Molteno Project: company profile Personal Communication, Recipient: L. Jarvin. Accra, Ghana, 28/09/2006.

Fordham, P. E. (1993) *Informal, non-formal and formal education programmes* (London, YMCA George Williams College).

Garnier, M. & Schafer, M. (2006) Educational model and expansion of enrollments in sub-Saharan Africa, *Sociology of Education*, 79, 153–175.

Goetz, P. W. (Ed.). (1989) *The new encyclopædia Britannica* (15th edn. Vol. 18). (Chicago, Encyclopædia Britannica, Inc.).

Greaney, V. & Kellaghan, T. (2004) *Assessing student learning in Africa* (Washington, DC, World Bank Publication).

Grose, T. K. (2006) A surprising shortage, *ASEE Prism*, 15, 24–27.

Haeri, N. (2000) Form and ideology: Arabic sociolinguistics and beyond, *Annual Review of Anthropology*, 29, 61–87.

Hanushek, E. (1995) Interpreting recent research on schooling in developing countries, *The World Bank Research Observer*, 10, 227–246.

Honawar, V. (2005a) The great obsession, *Education Week*, 30th Nov., 30–34.

Honawar, V. (2005b) Indian middle class makes mission out of sending children to college, *Education Week*, 30th Nov., 10–21.

Honawar, V. (2005c) U.S. Leaders fret over students' math and science weaknesses, *Education Week*, 14th Sept., 1–13.

Honawar, V. (2006a) Industrialized nations behind in payouts to 'Education for All' *Education Week*, 19th April, 10.

Honawar, V. (2006b) Study: U.S.-Asian engineering gap overstated, *Education Week*, 4th Jan., 6.

Jayaram, N. (1993) The language question in higher education: trends and issues, in: S. Chitnis & P. Altbach (Eds) *Higher education reform in India* (New Delhi, Sage) 84–119.

Karmani, S. & Makoni, S. (Eds.) (2005) *Islam and English in the post-9/11 era.* (Mahwah, NJ, Lawrence Erlbaum).

Kigotho, W. (2006) Africa's brain gain, *The Times Higher Education Supplement*, 1735, 24th March, 13.

Klein, A. (2006) Spellings joins passage to India on education, *Education Week*, 19th April, 26.

Levin, H. & Kelly, C. (1994) Can education do it alone?, *Economics of Education Review*, 3, 97–108.

Lindow, M. (2006) Falling through the cracks, *The Chronicle of Higher Education*, 31st March, A44–46.

Lipsett, A. (2006a) Colleges take first steps to go co-ed, *The Times Higher Education Supplement*, 1750, 7th July, 12–13.

Lipsett, A. (2006b) Minister who set up tech institutes out of own pocket urges generosity from state, *The Times Higher Education Supplement*, 1750, 7th July, 12–13.

Lloyd, C. B. & Blanc, A. K. (1996) Children's schooling in sub-Saharan Africa: the role of fathers, mothers, and others, *Population and Development Review*, 22, 265–298.

Logan, B. L. & Beoku-Betts, J. A. (1996) Women and education in Africa: an analysis of economic and socio-cultural factors influencing observed trends, *Journal of Asian and African Studies*, 31, 217–239.

MacGregor, K. (2006) Market with a wealth of talent—but should UK plunder it?, *The Times Higher Education Supplement*, 1745, 2nd June, 18.

Martin, M. O., Mullis, I. V. S., Gonzalez, E. J., Gregory, K. D., Smith, T. A., Chrostowski, S. J., *et al.* (2000) *TIMSS 1999 International Mathematics Report findings from IEA's repeat of the Third International Study at the eighth grade* (Chestnut Hill, MA, Boston College, TIMSS International Study Center).

Minnis, J. R. (2006) Nonformal education and informal economies in sub-Saharan Africa: finding the right match, *Adult Education Quarterly*, 56, 119–133.

Morgan, T. (2005) Arab reforms urged to tackle Islamic extremism, *The Times Educational Supplement*, 4650, 2nd September, 16.

Mullis, I. V. S., Martin, M. O., Gonzalez, E. J., Gregory, K. D., Garden, R. A., O'Connor, K. M., *et al.* (2000) *TIMSS 1999 International Mathematics Report findings from IEA's repeat of the*

Third International Mathematics and Science Study at the eighth grade (Chestnut Hill, MA, Boston College, TIMSS International Study Center).

Neelakantan, S. (2005) Higher education proves no match for India's booming economy, *The Chronicle of Higher Education*, 3rd June, A32–A34.

O'Leary, J. (2006) Developing countries 'cannot reverse brain drain', ACU told, *The Times Higher Education Supplement*, 1739, 21st April, 11.

Owino, F. R. (Ed.) (2002) *Speaking African: African languages for education and development* (Cape Town, CASAS).

Pennycook, A. (2000) Language, ideology, and hindsight, in: T. Ricento (Ed) *Ideology, politics, and language policies: focus on English* (Philadelphia, John Benjamins).

Policy Dialogue and Education: African and Portuguese Experiences (2006, March). *Prospects* (Paris, France) 36, 9–96

Political and economic reform in the Kingdom of Saudi Arabia (2005).

Psacharapoulos, G. (1994) Returns to investment in education: a global update, *World Development*, 22, 67–89.

Ramanathan, V. (2005) Ambiguities about English: ideologies and critical practice in vernacular-medium college classrooms in Gujarat, India, *Journal of Language, Identity, and Education*, 4, 45–65.

Reardon, T. & Crawford, E. (1994) Links between non-farm income and farm investment in African households: adding the capital market, *American Journal of Agricultural Economics*, 76, 1172–1186.

Serpell, R. (2005) Optimizing the developmental consequences of education: reflections on issues raised by Michael Cole, *Human Development*, 48, 217–222.

Serpell, R. & Hatano, G. (1997) Education, schooling, and literacy, in: J. W. Berry, P. R. Dasen & T. S. Saraswathi (Eds) *Handbook of cross-cultural psychology* (2nd edn.), Vol. 2: Basic processes and human development (Needham Heights, MA, Allyn & Bacon), 339–376.

The Molteno Project (2005) *Making a difference.* Available online at: http://www.molteno.co.za/index.asp (accessed on 27 September 2006).

Tiruneh, G. (2006) Regime type and economic growth in Africa: a cross-national analysis, *The Social Science Journal*, 43, 3–18.

Tunis Declaration of sixteenth Arab Summit (2004).

UNESCO (1998) *World education report 1998* (Paris, UNESCO Publishing).

UNESCO (2001) *Dakar framework for action.* Available online at: http://www.unesco.org/education/efa/ed_for_all/framework.shtml (accessed on 27 September 2006).

UNESCO (2002a) *Arab States. Regional report.* (Montreal, UNESCO Institute for Statistics).

UNESCO (2002b) *Education for all: is the world on track?* (Paris, UNESCO Publishing).

UNESCO (2002c) *Literacy statistics.* Available online at: http://www.uis.unesco.org/ev.php?ID=5204_201&ID2=DO_TOPIC (accessed on 27 September 2006).

UNESCO (2005a) *Education trends in perspective. Analysis of the world education indicators* (Montreal, UNESCO Institute for Statistics).

UNESCO (2005b) *EFA global monitoring report. The quality imperative* (Paris, UNESCO).

Valverde, G. A. (2005) Curriculum policy seen through high-stakes examinations: mathematics and biology in a selection of school-leaving examinations from the Middle East and North Africa, *Peabody Journal of Education*, 80, 29–55.

Wikipedia (n.d.) *Western world.* Available online at: http://en.wikipedia.org/wiki/Western_countries (accessed on 27 September 2006).

Willms, J. D. (2006) *Learning divides: ten policy questions about the performance and equity of schools and schooling systems* (Montreal, UNESCO Institute for Statistics).

Wojtas, O. (2006) Women eye up graduate job market, *The Times Higher Education Supplement*, 1750, 7th July, 13.

World Bank (n.d.) *Summary education profile: India* 3. Available online at: http://devdata.worldbank.org/edstats/SummaryEducationProfiles/CountryData/GetShowData.asp?sCtry=IND,India)3 (accessed on 27 September 2006).

Index

achievement gaps 55

Africa 167; adaptation of western university practices 31–5; Anglophone 44; British colonies 168; Kenya 11–13, 14, 114; Kpelle tribe 8; lack of educational research in 171; lack of job opportunities 170; literacy rate 169; Uganda 169; undergraduate curriculum 45; Zambia 14, 17, 28, 35, 40; Zimbabwe 17

African educational orientation; indigenous 36

Africanisation 35

Alaska 13, 15; National Council of Teachers of Mathematics 15; natives of 65

alcohol; in social situations 149–50

Alexander, R. 101

Amazonian Bolivia: Government of 151; Ministry of Education 152; schooling in 137–57; Tsimane' 4

anthropology 146; American cultural 107; cultural 137

Aptekar, L. 37

Arab countries 183; education segregated by gender 179; investments in education 178; women's rights 180

Ardilla, R. 23

Ashford, S. 145

assessment 5–19; of cognitive and educational performance 6–8; cultural meaning of 6; familiar and meaningful 9–11

Auckland University of Technology 42

Australia 24

Authentic Instruction 63

Axia, G. 113–33

Azuma, H. 23–4, 115

Baltimore Early Childhood Project 28

Banach, C. 123

Beijing 71, 72, 78

Beijing Normal University; Department of Psychology 81

Bengal 173

Berlin 31

bilateral aid agency 1

Binet-Simon Intelligence Test 77

Blom, M. 113–33

Bourdieu, P. 27

Boxer Indemnity Fund (BIF) 78

Brazil: poverty-stricken communities 40; street children 10

Brehm, J. 144

British Council 98

British East India Company 172

Brofenbrenner, U. 95, 100–1, 105, 107

Cairo 31

capitalism 105

Carnegie Foundation 98

Carraher, T. 10

Cattell Culture Fair Test 13

Cattell, R. 13

Ceci, S. 6

Chaise, L. 175

Chen, M. 16

chicha 149–50

child development; emotional closeness 129

children: Brazilian street 10–11; developing adaptive skills 11–13; Eskimo 13; health status and academia 14; hierarchy-based treatment of 123; material contributions to welfare 38–9; practical skills unrecognised in

standardised tests 13; resource
characteristics 96
China 2, 71–87; Anti-Japanese War 78;
Cultural Revolution 80, 81, 86;
educational policy 3; educational
testing 71–87; Examinations
Administration Centre of the State
Education Commission 82; Imperial
Examination System (IES) 72–6, 80,
83; introducing western psychological
testing to 77; Ming Dynasty 74, 75;
National College Entrance Exam
(NCEE) 71–2, 73, 80–6, 88; Office of
Sending Students to Study in the US
78; other forms of educational
assessment 86; pedagogy 3;
philosophical conceptions 16; Qing
Dynasty 75, 76; revival of
psychological assessment 81–7;
schooling 10; State Ministry of
Education 82; western influence on
assessment 77–9; Western Zhou
Dynasty 73
Chinese Communist Party (CCP) 79
Chinese educational practices 165;
before the People's Republic 76–7;
during 20th century 72–3; western
influence on 71–89
Chinese Ministry of Education 82, 86;
auspices of 86
Chinese Nationalist Party (CNP) 79
Christian Church 31
classroom practices 59
Cognitive Ability Test for Identifying
Supernormal Children (CATISC) 82
Cognitively Guided Instruction 63
Cole, M. 8
collectivism; ideology of 99
Colombia University 77
communism 2
community: Bolivian Amazon 137–57;
Brazilian 40; maintaining schools 150;
Native American 60; poverty-stricken
40

community agents; advocacy for
changes in behaviour 38
Community-Based Education 44
Comparison of Educational
Assessments **84–5**
Complex Instruction 63
Confucian Classics 74
Confucian philosophy 74
Confucius 16, 73–4
contextualised instruction 35
contextualism 95; historical event for 94
Costa Rica 144
critical thinking 102; in preparation of
democratic citizenship 66
cultural anthropology 137
cultural applicability 24
cultural compatibility; in education
53–67
Cultural Ecology of Young Children
Project 103
cultural universals; in education 53–67
cultural validity 24
cultural-historical-activity theory
(CHAT) 61
culture 5–19; approach to concepts and
problems 8; definition of 5; Hawaiian
55; and 'smart' behaviour 8–9; system
of representation 26; traditional 138
curriculum: formal 132; Indian
development of 174; innovation in
36–41; metaphors for 25;
pedagogically essential elements of
46; socioculturally detached 25; text-
based 25; Tsimane' 157; university
24, 45; in Zambia 36–41

Dalton, S. 2, 53–67
Dar Al-Hannan School 181
Declaration of Education for All (EFA)
168
Denver Developmental Screening Test
81
Developmental Expectations
Questionnaire (DEQ) 116

disadaptation 102
Discours de la Méthode (Descartes) 31
Djibouti 179
Doherty, R. 59, 60
Douglass, F. 32

The Ecology of Human Development
    (Brofenbrenner) 95
economic growth; econometric models
    169
education; nonformal 172
education practices: in ancient Greece
    165; in the Middle Ages 165; in the
    Renaissance 165; Roman 165
education system: reinforcing 167;
    western 165–83
Effat College 181
Effective Pedagogy; Five Standards of 2,
    57–66
Egerton, M. 157
El Salvador 144
Elder, G. 97
Elliott, J. 93–108
English Language Learners (ELL) 59
essential-qualities-oriented (EQO)
    Education Project 87
ethnocentrism 1
ethnographic synopsis 149
European academy; social boundaries in
    27
European Enlightenment 31

field experience; connecting with taught
    course 39
Fincher, S. 28, 42
Five Standards of Effective Pedagogy 2,
    57–66; current developmental stage of
    61–3; developmental history of 64;
    evaluation evidence supporting 59–
    60; explaining efficacy of 61;
    feasibility of 65–6; limitations of 64–5;
    place of in educational reform
    programmes 63
Fogel, R. 148

Fordham, P. 172
formism 94
Fortes, M. 35
French academy 27
Froumin, I. 104, 106

Gandhi, M. 32
Gardner, H. 6, 45, 99
Geissler, P. 12
Ghana 168; British Colonial rule of 35
Gibson, J. 26
gifts: and schooling 147, 154; and social
    capital 147
Givvin, K. 54
Gladwin, T. 9
globalisation; of childhood education
    113
Godoy, R. 3
Goetz, P. 166
Goodnow, J. 10
Graduate Management Admission Test
    (GMAT) 87
Graduate Record Examination (GRE)
    87
Greaney, V. 169
Greenfield, P. 26
Grigorenko, E. 4, 17, 82, 165–83
Guatemala 144
Guba, E. 94

Hangzhou University 81
Harkness, S. 3, 113–33
Hawaii 2, 55–6, 58
Helms-Lorenz, M. 8
Henrich, J. 144, 145, 156
Hiebert, J. 53
higher education: adapting western
    practices to Africa 31–5; in African
    sociocultural context 23–46; from
    Latin American perspective 23;
    orthodox western 23–46
higher education practices: in India 176;
    Zambian 167
Hilberg, R. 60

HIV/AIDS 39, 43
Honduras 144
human development; theoretical
    perspective on 25
human welfare; advancement of 30
hypothesis: context-specific 9;
    perceptual-deficit 9

'ideal student': ethnotheories of 113–33;
    qualities **119**; teacher conceptions of
    113–33
ideology: of collectivism 99; of
    democratic pedagogy 101
imperialism; western 76
India 168, 183; Bengal 173; British
    colonisation of 177; development of
    curriculum 174; 'dissemination' of
    education 173; education system
    172–3; higher education system 176;
    languages 173, 174; university
    graduates 176
indigenisation 24
inquiry; nurturing spirit of 31–2
Institute of the Study of English in
    Africa (ISEA) 171
instruction 5–19; authentic 63;
    cognitively guided 63; complex 63
Instructional Congruence 63
Instructional Conversation 56, 59
instrumental variables 152–3;
    regressions with 154; and schooling
    148
instrumentalism; growing 104
integration 24
intellectual development;
    conceptualising 25–6
intelligence 114; analytical 114;
    cross-cultural ideas of 116;
    emotional 133; general factor of 12;
    IQ-based notion of 17; multiple 99;
    social and interpersonal dimensions
    of 115; successful 6; US conceptions
    of 17
internalisation 27

International English Language Testing
    System (IELTS) 87
International Labour Organisation 172
International Reading Association 62
International Study of Parents; Children
    and Schools (ISPCS) 116–17
intervention; and education 94
intuition 102
Inuit peoples 65
Italy; and the 'creative' scientist 120–1

Jamaica 8, 14
Japan 73, 76, 82; higher education 23–4;
    mathematical skills 10; Meiji 73, 76
Jayaram, N. 175
Jennings, J. 150
joint productive activity (JPA) 59

Kamehameha Early Education Program
    (KEEP) 55, 58, 59
Kashiwagi, K. 115
Kaunda, K. 32
Kellaghan, T. 169
Kenya 11–13, 14, 114
knowledge; tacit 11
Korea 73

language: African 168; Arabic 177;
    Chewa 36, 114; development and
    contextualisation of 56; Dholuo 12;
    equality 182; Hindustani 174; Indian
    173, 174; Persian 173; Spanish 148,
    152; Tsimane' 147, 151, 152, 157;
    vernacular 175
Lave, J. 10, 26
Law of Education in the Russian
    Federation (1992) 103
Law School Admission Test (LSAT) 87
learning: decontextualisation of 24;
    democratic 1; experimental 125;
    instruction 14–15; motivation for 120;
    situated 26–7; student project-based
    28–31
Lebanon 178

Lee, S. 115
legitimate peripheral participation 26
Leseman, P. 129
lifelong learner 27
Likhachev, B. 108
Limited English Proficiency (LEP) 62
Lincoln, Y. 94
Lindesmith, A. 57
literacy 113
literacy rate: in Africa 169; low 169; and
    poverty 170
Luria, A. 9

macrosystem 96–7, 107; within society
    102
Mambwe, A. 37
market: economy 149; in small
    communities 150
mechanism 95
metaphor: for curriculum 25;
    root 94
microsystem 96–7, 107; influencing
    macrosystem 99; and proximal
    processes 97
Mill Hill Vocabulary Scale 12, 13
Minnis, J. 171
missionary 151; Christian 173; direct
    oversight over curriculum 152;
    Protestant 157
modernisation 108; societal 107
Moja, T. 27
Moll, I. 34, 35
Molteno Project 171
Morocco 10, 178
Moscardino, U. 113–33
Msolla, P. 33
Munoz, W. 62

Navajo 2, 55–6, 58
Neisser, U. 26
Neo-Confucianism 74
Netherlands: and the 'cheerful
    diplomat' 121–3; classroom practices
    122; teachers 118, 121

New Zealand 24; Auckland University
    of Technology 42
Nicaragua 144
Nisbett, R. 8
Niu, W. 2, 71–89
Nsamenang, B. 36
numeracy 113
nurturing developmental partnerships
    (NDP) 30
NVivo 117

odium; fear of 146
Oliva, A. 113–33
organicism 95
orthodoxy: appropriate existing 1;
    dominant 53–5; in education 53–67;
    underlying transnational 54
Orwell, G. 101
Ottoman Empire 177

Palestinian Autonomous Territories 179
Panama 144
paradigm: contextualist 95; western
    educational 166
parameters; of western education
    model 2
parents: American 116; Asian 18; Dutch
    116; effect on child self-confidence
    129; and experimental education
    programmes 104; Italian 116;
    Latino 18
Parmar, P. 115
participatory appropriation 27–8
Peabody Picture Vocabulary 81
pedagogy: Chinese 3; democratic 101;
    development of alternative system
    55–9; effective 2, 57–66; functional
    value for strengthening teaching 58;
    learner-centred 1; system 62–3;
    traditions of 29
People's Republic of China 76–7;
    scholarly research and development in
    81–2; under Soviet Influence 79–80
Pepper, S. 94

Piaget, J. 94
Poland 117; and the 'social
    entrepreneur' 123–5
political participation; increasing trust in
    society 145
postmodernism 99
Prince, R. 12
probit regressions 155, 156
Process, Person, Context and Time
    (PPCT) 95, 97
Programme for International Student
    Assessment (PISA) 100, 181
Progress in International Reading
    Literacy Study (PIRLS) 181
project course; global dimension of 30
proximal process: changing 103;
    contextualist theory emphasising 102;
    key to theory 96; and microsystems
    97; profoundly influenced by context
    96
psychometric research 6

Rahn, W. 144
Raven Coloured Progressive Matrices
    Test 12
Raven, J. 13
regressions: with instrumental variables
    154; probit 155, 156; Tobit 156
Renzulli, J. 131
Rogoff, B. 12, 27
Rueda, R. 61
Russia 93–108; appropriation of
    physical symbols 98; balance between
    resistance and accommodation 106–
    8; discipline 104; education since
    Soviet Union collapse 3; positive and
    negative effects of change 103–6;
    schooling and society 97–102;
    tradition of authoritarianism 103;
    youth homicide rates 106
Russian education: impact of west on
    93–108; post-Soviet 93–108;
    resistance to change 93–108
Ruzgis, P. 17

St. Petersburg 104
San Jose State University 37
Saudi Arabia 178, 180, 182; and global
    influences 181
Scholastic Aptitude Test (SAT) 82, 83,
    176
Schon, D. 30
school: child's success in 103; dominant
    orthodoxy in 53–5; Koranic 27, 178;
    maintained by community 150;
    Russian 102; safe governing of 86;
    transnational culture of 53–5
schoolchildren; in American cities 28
schooling: in Amazonian Bolivia 137–
    57; Chinese 10; contextualisation of
    56; contribution to social capital 137–
    57; and displays of generosity 146;
    effect on traditional cultures 138;
    effects on earnings 145; endogeneity
    of 145, 156; and gifts 147; increasing
    individual social capital 146; and
    instrumental variables 148;
    mushrooming of selective 106;
    reducing labour help 155; Russian
    97–102; styles of 165–83
Schooling and Social Capital - Review
    139–43
Second World War 168
Sedlak, M. 102
Serpell, R. 9, 182
Shabad, G. 130
Shalem, Y. 34
situated learning 26–7
skills: adaptive 11–13, 13; cognitive 113,
    133
Slominsky, L. 34
social capital: dependent variables for
    147; and gifts 147; proxy variables
    for 138; schooling's contribution to
    137–57
Social Competence 115; Receptive 115
social priming 36
social responsibility; preparation for
    35–6

socialism 105
societal modernisation 107
sociology 107
Soros Foundation 98
sorting: functional 9; hierarchical 9
South Africa 27; post-apartheid 34; society in 34; Vice-Chancellors' Association 33–4
Soviet Bloc; political collapse of 123
Soviet education model 79
Soviet Union 9; collapse of 3, 93, 103; socialisation 100
Spain: collectivistic culture of 130; and the 'sociable academic' 125–7; teachers 118
Spanish: learning as a language 148, 152, 155; schooling and skills in 157
Standards Performance Continuum (SPC) 59, 60
Sternberg, R. 1–2, 5–19, 16, 88
Stevenson, H. 115
student: autonomy in 131; BIF-sponsored 79; Chinese 71; egalitarian mode of discourse 45; Hawaiian 55; independence of 131; international 1; motivation of 127, 131; performance in projects 43; Russian 98; self-confidence of 124, 128; self-regulation of 132; spirit of inquiry 45; traditionally valued qualities in 126; underprepared for university 34; well-balanced 124
student project assignment; evaluating outcomes of 41–5
student project-based learning 28–31
study abroad; standardised tests 86–7
Super, C. 113–33

Tabulawa, R. 1, 98
Tanzania 6; Sokoine Agricultural University 33
taxonomic classification 9
teacher: American 118; conceptions of 'ideal student' 113–33;

democratisation of 107; Dutch 118, 121; humanisation of 107; kindergarten 117, 126; open-minded 43; progressive 124; Spanish 118
teaching: for cognitive complexity 57; in culturally appropriate ways 15–16; developmental 104; idealisation of 18; reciprocal 63
test: ability 7; Cattell Culture Fair 13; Denver Developmental Screening 81; dynamic 7; Raven Coloured Progressive Matrices 12; western standardised 86–7; White Crow 57
Test of English as a Foreign Language (TOFEL) 87
Test of English for International Communication (TOEIC) 87
Testing the Inadequacy of Instrumental Variables **153**
testing procedure; standardised psychometric 2
Tharp, R. 2, 53–67, 55, 56
Timbuktu 31
Tobit regressions 156; results **154**
traditional group cohesion 132
Tsimane' 4; curriculum of 157; language of 147, 151, 152, 157; schooling in 137–57; used in Regression Analysis **148**
Tudge, J. 3, 93–108
Tunisia 178, 181
Twenty Questions Test 6
typology; of western impact of world education 165–83
Typology of Western Educational Systems **167**

Udell, C. 30
Uganda 169
United Arab Emirates 178, 180
United States of America (USA) 3, 24, 73, 82, 105, 176; emphasis on analytical intelligence 114; importance of personal freedom 100;

stressing autonomy and
individualisation 99; teachers 118;
and the 'wild west adventurer' 127–9
United States International Agency 98
universality; of western educational
practices 1–4
universals: cultural 53–67; method on
57
university 23–46; curriculum 45; Ivy
League 79; social problems identified
in 38; types of social intervention 38
University: Bologna 31; Colombia 77;
Lagos 44; Madras 176; Malawi 44;
Mumbai 176; Zimbabwe 44
University of Maryland Baltimore
County (UMBC) 25, 30, 43
University of Zambia (UNZA) 25, 29,
32, 40; Food Science and Technology
42; project work 44; Senate
Examinations Committee 44; Service
Learning Project 36–41, 43; social
history of 42

Vygotsky, L. 2, 7, 55, 94

Wagner, D. 10
Wang, G. 83
Warsaw 123
Waters, J. 45
Wechsler Adult Intelligence Scale 81
Weisner, T. 129

Wells, G. 64
western educational paradigm 166
western educational practices: definition
of 166; impact on post-Soviet Russia
93–108
western higher education 23–46;
decontextualising learning process 24
westerner; middle-class 11
White Crow Test 57
Willms, J. 181
Women's rights; in Arab countries 180
World Bank 98, 170, 172
World Health Organisation 106
Wrigley, H. 28

Yang, S. 16
Yup'ik Scale of Practical Intelligence 13

Zambia 14, 17, 28; Eastern Province
35–6; traditional social practice of
delegation 40; United National
Independence Party 32
Zambia Cognitive Assessment
Instrument (Z-CAI) 15
Zayed University 180
Zimbabwe 17
zone of proximal development (ZPD) 7,
55
Zylicz, P. 113–33